"It has been my privilege to have

years. I have not met anyone else

of the Church and people of Asia. He has experienced missionary life first hand, his research is legendary, and he appreciates the challenges of going to the unreached. Paul has been an invaluable friend, partner, and advisor to AsiaLink since our inception. If you meet Paul, you will know that overriding all of this is his God-given desire to see Asia's billions saved from eternal death."

Colin Dudgeon, AsiaLink, United Kingdom

"We are grateful to Paul Hattaway and Asia Harvest for providing millions of Bibles to the people of China. We cannot find words to express our thanks for the unselfish giving of those who have provided the Word of Life to us."

Brother Chen, senior house church leader, China

"I would like to express our sincere and heartfelt thanks to Paul Hattaway and Asia Harvest for their generous help in providing Bibles to untold thousands of poor Christians throughout India. They also support hundreds of native missionaries who are committed to spreading the Good News to the unreached people groups of India. Multitudes of Indian believers greatly appreciate their love and partnership."

Brother Pankaj, ministry leader, India

"Paul Hattaway is a faithful servant called by the Lord. He is a God-fearing prayer warrior who studies the Bible carefully and walks in the ways of the Lord."

Brother Yun, "The Heavenly Man"

"We are very blessed to have labored for a number of years with Paul Hattaway in providing support to hundreds of faithful and fruitful native missionaries. Paul is one of the great unsung heroes in God's vineyard. His research into unreached peoples across Asia has impacted the work of many mission agencies, including ours. For a missionary who has worked quietly in the shadows, his ardent advocacy for native missionaries has been highly exemplary. We love and esteem our dear brother."

Carl Gordon and Bo Barredo, Co-founders, Advancing Native Missions

"Joining hands with Paul Hattaway and Asia Harvest has dynamically increased the speed by which remote unreached people groups throughout the Himalayas are being reached. Through their loving support, Asia Harvest has accelerated the gospel among those who have never heard of Christ at the top of the world."

Sarwochcha Himal, The Footstool Project, Nepal

"Over the past twelve years we have seen the powerful and lasting impact Paul Hattaway and Asia Harvest have made for Christ Jesus among the Vietnamese people. Paul's driving passion for being about his Father's business, combined with his insight and deep understanding of the spiritual needs of our nation, are a great blessing that has resulted in much fruit for the kingdom of God."

Joshua and Ruth Nguyen, ministry leaders, Vietnam

"Paul Hattaway is a man with a clear focus and passion for the lost. Even after experiencing some health challenges, he has continued to pursue the dream God placed in his heart. This book is the expression of his life calling. I am glad God brought Paul into our lives. Through our partnership, we have planted many churches throughout Indonesia."

Paulus Wiratno, Founder, Mercy Indonesia

"Paul Hattaway and his co-workers have been a tremendous help to our young church planters among unreached people groups in Cambodia. They have aided our workers as they take the Good News of Jesus Christ to villages that have never heard the gospel even once. We thank you with all our hearts!"

Joni Wise, Paraclete Ministries, Cambodia

"Paul Hattaway and his ministry have been a great source of encouragement in empowering church planters among some of the most unreached people groups in the Philippines. Their partnership has been instrumental in major breakthroughs for the kingdom of God. May the Name of Jesus be praised."

Paul Ignacio, HIS1040 Ministries, Philippines

"Our primary goal is to reach the unreached with the gospel of Jesus Christ as we shine God's light to the 150 million people of Bangladesh. Together with Paul and his co-workers we have spread the Good News to the four corners of our country. We deeply appreciate our partnership."

Brother Swapon, Ministry leader, Bangladesh

"The tens of thousands of Bibles that Paul Hattaway and his team have provided for the people of Myanmar are amazing to us and are of the greatest benefit. We have uncountable blessings because of the Scriptures we have received, as only the Bible can transform our country. We are deeply thankful for the blessing Paul has been to our nation for many years."

Brother Joseph, Ministry leader, Myanmar (Burma)

"We are humbled by the support of Paul Hattaway and Asia Harvest to our ministry in Sri Lanka. Literally millions of Scriptures have gone out from here all over the Indian subcontinent because of Paul's vision and heart to extend the kingdom of God."

Daniel Kort, New Life Literature, Sri Lanka

"I first worked with Paul and Asia Harvest in 1992, delivering Bibles to house churches in China. We have increased our partnership together, as we intensify our commitment to providing God's Word."

Gary Russell, Founder, China Harvest Inc

"Paul Hattaway's zeal and dedication for reaching the unreached has highly motivated us. His fervent pursuit of God's call, even in very difficult circumstances, is exemplary. The many years of collaboration with Paul have expanded our vision and helped us see God's big picture. We count it a tremendous privilege and blessing to represent Asia Harvest in Europe."

Jürgen and Ruth Rintz, Stiftung SALZ Germany and Switzerland

"It is our honor to have worked with the author for more than a decade, bringing the love of Christ to unreached people groups in China, India, Nepal, Vietnam, Cambodia, and Myanmar. We cannot find words to express our gratitude to the unselfish giving of Paul and his team, and all who have supported their work."

John Chiang, Founder, Minorities for Christ International

An Asian Harvest

An Autobiography

Paul Hattaway

Monarch
Books

Oxford, UK and Grand Rapids, USA

Published by Monarch Books
an imprint of
Lion Hudson IP Ltd
Wilkinson House, Jordan Hill Road,
Oxford OX2 8DR, England
Email: monarch@lionhudson.com
www.lionhudson.com/monarch

ISBN 978 0 85721 848 3
e-ISBN 978 0 85721 849 0

First edition 2017

Acknowledgments
Scripture quotations taken from NIV (unless otherwise stated), taken from the Holy Bible, New International Version Anglicised. Copyright © 1979, 1984, 2011 Biblica, formerly International Bible Society. Used by permission of Hodder & Stoughton Ltd, an Hachette UK company. All rights reserved. "NIV" is a registered trademark of Biblica. UK trademark number 1448790.
Scripture quotations marked NKJV taken from the New King James Version. Copyright © 1982 by Thomas Nelson, Inc. Used by permission. All right reserved.
Extracts from The Authorized (King James) Version. Rights in the Authorized Version are vested in the Crown. Reproduced by permission of the Crown's patentee, Cambridge University Press.
Scripture quotations marked TLB taken from The Holy Bible, Living Bible Edition, Copyright © Tyndale House Publishers 1971. All rights reserved.

A catalogue record for this book is available from the British Library

Printed and bound in the US, April 2017, LH37

Agent: Piquant. For all enquiries concerning translation rights please contact info@piquant.net

Dedicated to the many Asian Christians I have been privileged to serve.
Thank you for walking the way of the Cross, and for willingly risking your lives so that people may hear about Jesus Christ. Although many have already experienced extraordinary things as the Spirit of God swept millions into His kingdom, the best is yet to come!
"No eye has seen, no ear has heard, and no mind has conceived the things God has prepared for those who love him."

CONTENTS

FOREWORD

A beloved Christian speaker once said that if the Lord's majesty, grace, and power are not being manifested in and through us, He holds us responsible.

Over the years I have come to appreciate that our amazing God, the Creator of heaven and earth, has obviously and graciously chosen Paul Hattaway to be a precious vessel of His majesty, grace, and power.

I first met Paul twenty years ago when I visited his home in Asia. From the start, I saw love, integrity, humility, brokenness, giftedness, and most of all the authenticity of a childlike resoluteness to follow only God's agenda in his life – all the major ingredients for the makings of a champion advocate in the Lord's work.

Paul is indeed a vessel of grace, one that is easily entreated. This is only possible when a heart is permeated with God's love.

The pathway God has laid out for Paul and his family has not been easy. They have shown God's majesty by humbly taking the high road many times when their flesh and natural instincts shouted the opposite.

God has chosen Paul and his precious wife, Joy, to display the might of His power, to impact world missions, and in so doing has sent many of the mighty and the highly credentialed of world ministry scrambling for answers to their own degree of usefulness to the kingdom.

The enemy has never rested in trying to hinder God's plan and to cause Paul and Joy to swerve from their God-given course, but they have faithfully endured through many storms. The fruitfulness of their ministry has grown tremendously as a result of their perseverance and trust in the Lord.

I pray this book brings much glory to God and great encouragement to His people. In this day when many feel discouraged and cynical, may this testimony become a success for His glory.

Bo Barredo, Co-founder, Advancing Native Missions

INTRODUCTION

A few years ago I was asked to share my testimony in a home fellowship meeting. About forty Christians crammed into a large living room, many of them hoping to glean a spiritual secret to propel their lives forward. The pastor began the meeting by giving me a flattering introduction which made me squirm with discomfort. Feeling I needed to bring the atmosphere back down to earth, my first words were, "Good evening. My name is Paul, and I am scum."

Strained smiles and nervous laughter filled the room. The pastor looked concerned, wondering what was about to come. Perhaps he thought my opening statement was a new kind of speaking technique or reverse psychology, but he soon realized I was just telling the truth. After more than twenty-five years serving Jesus Christ among many nations, I was not ashamed to view my life in a similar vein as the Apostle Paul, who wrote, "We have become the scum of the earth, the garbage of the world" (1 Corinthians 4:13).

While I know that in myself I have absolutely nothing to boast about, there is another component to my story that I like to share. A great miracle occurred in my life when I was still a teenager. Totally unexpectedly, I met Someone who completely transformed me from the inside out, giving my life a powerful sense of purpose and direction. His Name is Jesus Christ.

About fifteen years ago, friends who are familiar with my story first encouraged me to write a book so that others might be inspired. I hesitated, not least because my risky work requires me to maintain a low public profile. For years I pushed all thoughts of writing an autobiography to the back of my mind and I concentrated on my work.

In 2013, I realized that twenty-five years had elapsed since I first launched out in Christian service. At the same time, various people wanted to know how our organization had been founded, and asked us what principles had spurred our growth over the years. After receiving a number of these enquiries, I began to seek God more earnestly about whether or not I should share my story. It gradually became clear that the time had come to write my autobiography. I am honored to share it with you, and I hope the Living God will use it to encourage you on your own journey through life.

William Carey, who was dubbed the "Father of Modern Missions," was once asked to share the secret behind his decades of fruitful missionary work in India. Carey replied, "I can plod. I can persevere in any definitive pursuit. To this I owe everything."

Biographies tend to be highlight reels of what has taken decades to unfold in a person's life, and readers may gain a skewed impression that every day has been exciting. The reality, however, is that like William Carey, much of my life and service has consisted of "faithful plodding."

I am greatly honored to have witnessed some marvelous things on my adventure with God, but please don't think for a moment that I am special, or that I have achieved anything meritorious by my own abilities or knowledge. Anything useful that may have sprung from my life has been the direct result of God's grace and mercy to me in Jesus Christ.

May Jesus receive all the glory, for He alone is worthy.

CHAPTER 1

THE MAN WITH HALF A BRAIN

May 2013

I slipped into bed on the night of 29 May 2013. After enjoying a good night's sleep, I awoke the next morning feeling dizzy. When I attempted to get up, I discovered that I was unable to stand or walk. My left hand was as cold as a block of ice and I knew something serious was taking place.

My wife Joy called for an ambulance, and a short time later I was being driven two and a half hours along bumpy and windy roads to the nearest hospital. I could only imagine what Joy and our two young sons, Dalen and Taine, were going through as they followed by car, uncertain what was happening to me in the back of the ambulance.

Upon arrival at the hospital, my bed was wheeled inside and I was given a CT scan. After a while, a doctor with a grim look on his face came to break the news: "Mr Hattaway, you have suffered a massive stroke. I'm sorry to inform you that half your brain has died, and the left side of your body is paralyzed."

My first thought after receiving this grim diagnosis was, "This is not a problem for Jesus! One hundred percent of Lazarus's brain was dead, but the Lord completely healed him and raised him up!" I knew that from a medical viewpoint my situation was dire, but Jesus operates on a supernatural level, and He declared, "What is impossible with man is possible with God" (Luke 18:27).

I have always had an ability to see the funny side of most situations, so with my right index finger I motioned for the doctor to come closer. He leaned forward and I told him, "Don't worry, Doc. If I only have half a brain left, that still gives me an advantage over many people!"

Although I retained my sense of humor, in the following days I had to face my own mortality. Although I had suddenly gained a new appreciation of the fragility of life, most people live as though they will never die, not realizing they are just a heartbeat, a blood clot, or an accident away from standing before the judgment seat of the Almighty God. The Bible says, "Nothing in all creation is hidden from God's sight. Everything is uncovered and laid bare before the eyes of him to whom we must give account" (Hebrews 4:13).

Jesus taught, "If you forgive other people when they sin against you, your heavenly Father will also forgive you. But if you do not forgive others their sins, your Father will not forgive your sins" (Matthew 6:14–15). If it was my time to die, I didn't want to appear before my Maker with any unforgiveness or bitterness in my heart. I made a mental list of people I needed to forgive, and prayed for each one by name.

It was a pivotal time in my life as I lay there in the hospital bed, unable to move the left side of my body. Somehow it was both horrible and glorious at the same time. As I listened to my audio Bible in the still of the night, faith began to rise up in my spirit, and my lips expressed what was bubbling up within. I asked the nurse to close my door as I wanted some privacy. As I poured out my soul to the Living God, I proclaimed the Scriptures out loud: "I am under vows to you, my God; I will present my thank-offerings to you. For you have delivered me from death and my feet from stumbling, that I may walk before God in the light of life" (Psalm 56:12–13).

A deep revelation flooded my soul that it was not my time to die! My work on earth was incomplete and God had much more for me to do. From my bed I declared, "I will not die but live, and will proclaim what the Lord has done" (Psalm 118:17).

In the first few days after the stroke I was only able to concentrate for a few minutes at a time before I needed to rest my brain.

Although the hospital staff would have disapproved if they had known, late one night when all was quiet I managed to pull my laptop out of its bag and painstakingly typed an email message with my right index finger. In it I summarized what had occurred and asked for prayer for me and my family. I pushed the "send" button and it went out to friends around the world. In part, my message said:

> First and foremost, I love Jesus, and I am not ashamed to say I also love serving Him. He has given direction and value to my life. Everything good that has ever come out of me has been the work of Jesus. I'm hoping and praying for a full recovery. I don't believe God has finished with me yet, and I would be incredibly thankful if He would allow this time to pass so that I may once again serve Him. There are still more than 5,000 unreached people groups in Asia waiting to hear about God's plan of salvation. We only have this life to reach them.

Within days, hundreds of supportive messages poured in. The Lord seemed to be raising an army of intercessors from a host of diverse locations. News reached me that numerous church leaders in China and India were fasting and praying for my healing. A missionary friend even informed me that a gathering of 13,000 believers in South Korea paused their conference to cry out in prayer for me. Intercessors in diverse locations like Papua New Guinea, Russia, Ethiopia, and America wrote to say they were storming God's throne of grace on my behalf. As unworthy as I felt of all this love and prayer, I began to experience as never before the inexpressible blessing of being part of the global Body of Christ.

As soon as people began to pray, my spirit was revived and my mobility started to improve. One of my siblings, a non-Christian, called to speak with me. After a brief conversation, he called my wife to express his concern because I "sounded far too happy."

Although my left arm and leg remained numb, God was performing a progressive miracle. Each day I was able to move a little more.

When I first arrived at the hospital they wheeled me around in a bed. After a few days I graduated to a wheelchair. A couple of days after that I was able to shuffle about by myself with the help of a frame. The frame was soon replaced with crutches. The left crutch wasn't much help so it was put under my bed and I made my way around the hospital on a single crutch, making sure I stayed close to the wall so I could lean against it for balance.

Another few days passed and I decided the single crutch was a bit pointless. It was discarded and I began walking around the hospital unaided, much to the amazement of the doctors and nurses!

Perhaps the greatest miracle was that my mind remained almost as sharp as before. At no stage was my speech affected. I was transferred to a rehab facility in another city, where I was taken to see a psychologist. He put me through a series of mathematical and memory tests to see how much brain damage I had suffered. He read a complex story and asked me to repeat as many key parts of the story as possible, in the same sequence. I repeated the entire story flawlessly. He then fired lists of numbers at me which I added and subtracted with ease.

Unaware that dealing with numbers had always been my strong suit, the psychologist struggled to record my accurate answers that flowed almost as quickly as he was able to ask the questions. Finally, he asked me to divide 391 by 17. When I thought about it for a few seconds and told him, "23," a confused look came across his face and he abruptly concluded the session.

One afternoon I attended a group meeting with other patients who had recently suffered strokes and brain injuries. That was when I recognized the extent of the miracle God had performed in response to the fervent prayers of His children around the world. Most of the other patients, including some who were much younger than I was, were in terrible shape. Some didn't have the ability to lift their heads or to speak. Others couldn't remember their names.

I was told I would need to stay in the rehab facility for at least five or six weeks; however, after just fourteen days there, I returned to Joy and the boys, fewer than thirty days since the stroke had occurred. Although there was still a tough path ahead to full recovery, I was overwhelmed with thankfulness for what God had already done, and confident that He would carry it on to completion.

The only explanation the doctors and nurses could find for my dramatic recovery was that I had been "very, very lucky."

I knew that luck had had nothing to do with my rapid improvement. It was all because of the power and grace of Jesus in my life. The Lord once said of those who serve Him,

> "They will be my treasured possession. I will spare them, just as a father has compassion and spares his son who serves him. And you will again see the distinction between the righteous and the wicked, between those who serve God and those who do not."
>
> **Malachi 3:17–18**

The weeks and months following my stroke were very difficult for my dear Joy and our sons. At the time Dalen was aged sixteen and Taine twelve. Although God was restoring my health, it was a humbling experience to go through the rehabilitation process. I had to be retrained in simple things like how to go to the bathroom, how to shave, and how to cut vegetables without slicing my fingers off.

The best purchase we made to aid my stroke recovery was a table tennis table. At first I could hardly make contact with the paddle and the ball, but little by little my hand–eye coordination returned, until I was able to compete in long rallies with the ball flying back and forth across the net at a furious rate. In fact, I became a much better table tennis player after the stroke than I had been before it!

* * *

Several months had passed since the stroke and I felt a strange disconnect in my soul. My heart yearned to be among the people whom God had called me to serve, so at my insistence our family boarded a flight. A few days later we were crammed into a cable car with about twenty other people, heading up the side of a mountain overlooking the Indian Ocean.

Our fellow passengers included two Muslim women from Bangladesh, adorned in traditional attire with silver jewels rimming their brown dresses. Beside them was an Indonesian family from the island of Sumatra – one of the most fascinating places on earth and home to dozens of Muslim and animistic tribes. Other travelers included Chinese, Indian, and Thai tourists, a honeymooning couple from Nepal, and a Tibetan Buddhist monk from the heart of the Himalayas.

No doctor would have recommended the hustle and bustle of Asia as the ideal place to recuperate from a major stroke, but tears welled up in my eyes as I realized my soul was again at peace. Inside the crowded cable car that day my heart overflowed with gratitude to Jesus, the Great Physician. For the first time in months my body, heart, and mind were all in sync. I was home, where I belong, among the people I love.

CHAPTER 2

A WASTE OF OXYGEN

The 1960s was a troubled decade in much of the world. Race riots plagued the United States, and the Vietnam War escalated, with 1968 considered the bloodiest year of the conflict. This occurred against the backdrop of the world holding its collective breath, hoping the Soviet and American superpowers would have enough restraint not to obliterate mankind under a torrent of nuclear mushroom clouds.

Most people living near the bottom of the world in sleepy New Zealand cast little more than a curious glance at world events. Life was simple there, in a country containing just two million inhabitants but upward of forty million sheep. Wool and meat prices were at the forefront of people's minds. After landing there, one Australian pilot loved to announce, "Ladies and gentlemen, we have arrived in New Zealand. Please set your watches back forty years!"

In October 1968, still nine months before man first walked on the moon, Des and Valda Hattaway took a taxi to a hospital in New Zealand's largest city, Auckland. Heavily pregnant with her sixth child, the stubborn Valda waved away offers of a wheelchair at the hospital door, preferring to walk under her own strength. A few hours later she gave birth to her third son, Paul.

I was my parents' last child. Years later my mother, who possessed a keen sense of humor, jokingly told me, "When you were born, we thought about naming you 'Day.'"

I was confused and asked what she meant. She replied, "Well, when you first came out, we declared, 'Let's call it a day!'"

In later years I would read countless Christian biographies. Many authors tell of the godly family heritage they emerged from, with generational blessings bestowing a solid foundation which God used to launch them into ministry.

My story is not one of these.

My mother, from Maori descent and therefore brown-skinned, met and married my father, a fair-skinned European. The Maori are the native Polynesian people of New Zealand. For centuries my ancestors had worshiped idols and lived in deep bondage and violence. When the first Protestant missionaries arrived in New Zealand they were confronted by powerful forces of darkness. In 1865, at a place called Opotiki, the German missionary Carl Völkner was decapitated by the local Maori, who proceeded to pluck out and eat his eyeballs.

After graduating from high school in a rural part of New Zealand's North Island, my mother secured her first job in the capital city of Wellington. Her parents were strict disciplinarians and demanded that she return home for all major holidays. My mother booked a ticket on a train due to depart Wellington on the afternoon of 24 December 1953, scheduled to arrive in her hometown early the next morning, in time for Christmas.

On the evening of the 23rd, however, my mother went out drinking and dancing with her friends. The revelry and subsequent hangover caused her to oversleep and miss the train. Feeling wary of the consequences she would face once her parents discovered she wouldn't be home for Christmas, an extraordinary set of events unfolded that made her worries pale into insignificance.

Just after 10 p.m., as the train my mother had missed surged northward through the central North Island plateau, a volcanic eruption caused the wall of a large crater lake to collapse. The water rushed down the mountainside, destroying a bridge pylon just minutes before the train arrived in the dark of night. The locomotive and the first six carriages plunged from the bridge into a river below, killing 151 passengers. The tragedy came to be known as the Tangiwai Disaster.

It's amazing how the events of our lives and the decisions we make can have a major chain reaction that affects future generations. If my mother hadn't gone out partying the night before, she would probably have died in the disaster. I would not have been born, and none of the events recorded in this book would have taken place.

At the age of thirteen I attended an all boys' high school. Most of my classmates were from Polynesian families low on the socio-economic ladder. The sons of immigrants from Pacific Islands like Samoa, Tonga, and Fiji, many of my classmates were huge boys who towered over the teachers by the age of thirteen or fourteen.

Although at this time I was just beginning my search for truth, I had no doubt that God existed. It was plainly obvious to me. By observing the serenity of a sunset or the majesty of a thunderstorm, I concluded it was preposterous to think we were descended from apes, or that life had begun as a blob of algae on the ocean floor!

One day in class, we were required to write down what we wanted to do with the rest of our lives. Each answer was read out by the teacher. Some students wanted to be scientists, others accountants, and one dreamed of being a drummer in a rock band. When the teacher read my response, a smirk came upon her face and she mockingly announced, "Hattaway says he doesn't care what he does just as long as he's happy!"

My teacher decided to press me further. "Surely you'll agree that being happy results from having a good career and a comfortable standard of living," she challenged.

"No!" I replied. "Happiness doesn't come from material possessions, but from within. I would rather be a happy toilet cleaner than a dismal millionaire."

At the teacher's prompting, the whole class broke into rapturous laughter. In later years there were occasions when my toilet-cleaner theory was put to the test, and I found it to be absolutely true!

My years at high school grew increasingly difficult. It felt like a large prison, and I struggled with most of the subjects. Although I tried hard, my brain often simply couldn't grasp the concept of what was being taught, especially the science subjects. Before long my self-confidence was completely destroyed, and I grew to despise school as each day became a stressful battle.

Most of my teachers didn't believe that I was unable to learn, and assumed that my lack of progress was the result of a poor attitude and that I didn't care about my schoolwork. My English teacher decided I was a lost cause and threw me out of his class for two full terms. Every day I kicked a ball around the field while the rest of my classmates studied.

English was one subject I did understand, however, as I enjoyed the creative process of writing. At the end of the year the national exams were held. Because of my absence from the classroom for two-thirds of the year I hadn't studied any of the topics in preparation for the test. Much to the consternation of my teacher I scored 77 percent in the national exam, coming second in my class.

The challenges I faced at school were hardly surprising considering the dire state of my home life. My father was a hard-working and honest man but, like many of his generation, he was emotionally detached. Not once do I recall my dad telling me or my siblings that he loved us, nor did he give hugs. What I do remember, however, were the frequent severe beatings he delivered with his belt. On many occasions I literally found myself black and blue after a beating.

Our family life had been relatively stable until things dramatically changed around the time I started high school. One of my brothers and one of my sisters experimented with drugs, and a tidal wave of evil swept over them, adversely affecting our whole family. My sister's life spiraled out of control. She was officially diagnosed with paranoid schizophrenia, and spent several years in and out of mental institutions. My parents did the best they could to keep our family together, but they seemed powerless against this demonic onslaught.

From time to time my sister returned to live at home, and, as the saying goes, "all hell broke loose." Her days were characterized by loud, sinister laughter. She told us she often heard the voice of the devil telling her to do things.

One afternoon I stood at the kitchen window looking out on the backyard. My father was kneeling down attending to the garden, with his back to me. My sister emerged from the garage, clutching a small axe we used to chop firewood. As I watched, she quietly snuck up on my father, who was oblivious to her presence. She then suddenly raised the axe and prepared to attack!

Time seemed to stand still, and for a moment I froze in shock at what was about to happen. I opened the kitchen window as fast as I could and screamed, "Dad! Look out!"

Startled by the fervency of my scream, he turned around and saw my sister poised to attack. At that moment she swung the axe at his head. He instinctively raised his arm in self-defense and the axe handle struck his forearm. He leapt to his feet and wrestled my sister to the ground. Seemingly in a demonic trance, she casually walked away as though nothing had happened.

On another occasion my parents went out, and my sister came into my bedroom in a surprisingly friendly and coherent mood. We chatted warmly like we had done in previous years. As I lay on my bed, totally unprepared for danger, she suddenly grabbed two pillows and jumped on top of my chest. Placing the pillows firmly over my face, she held them down with her knees, using her full body weight to suffocate me. I remained pinned down as the breath drained from my lungs, while the room filled with her loud, satanic laughter.

I tried to break free with all my might, but my sister seemed to possess enormous, supernatural strength and I was unable to budge her. It felt as though I was stuck under a bus, unable to move. After about a minute of struggling for breath I knew there was no way to escape, and the life began to drain from my body. Moments before I would have blacked out, an idea entered my mind. I thought that if I completely stopped struggling my sister might think I was unconscious.

I lay as still as I could as another ten seconds passed. Thinking I was dead, she climbed off me and commenced another episode of crazed laughter. Gasping for breath, I staggered to my feet and ran to the bathroom, where I glanced at myself in the mirror. My face had turned purple from the lack of oxygen. After regaining my breath I ran out of the house as fast as my legs could carry me.

For months after this experience I slept with an iron poker beside my bed and with a heavy chest of drawers against my bedroom door to barricade me inside. Frustrated by my defensive wall, on one occasion my sister grabbed a carving knife from the kitchen and attempted to climb through my bedroom window to attack me. Thankfully, she was unable to squeeze through the narrow opening.

The only positive thing to come from these dark experiences is that I had absolutely no desire to try drugs myself. From my early teens I was determined to avoid drugs and alcohol at all costs.

By the time I commenced my third year at high school, my home environment had become intolerable. I longed for the day when I would break free from the chains of both home and school and head out into the world by myself.

One morning in the school hall the Principal announced, "Paul Hattaway, come to my office immediately after assembly." Many of the other students laughed, sensing the fate that was about to befall me.

After making me wait a long time, the stern-faced Principal confidently strode into his office, like a lion stalking its prey. He looked me up and down before finally speaking. "Your attitude is dire, Hattaway, and all the teachers constantly complain about you. It's time for you to move on. We don't want you here any longer!"

Despite my lack of academic progress, my expulsion from school still came as a shock. After calming down from the excitement of his announcement, the cold-hearted man added, "Your life will never amount to anything. You are a waste of oxygen!"

With that, my school days came to an abrupt end. I had recently turned sixteen.

CHAPTER 3

ON GOD'S HOOK

New Zealand was a blessed nation when I grew up there in the 1970s and early 1980s. With beautiful scenery, fresh air, and friendly, easy-going people, there were few problems. At one stage, a study found that New Zealand was sending out more foreign missionaries per capita than any other country in the world. If my homeland was a hub of revival in my formative years, those blessings sadly managed to bypass our household.

My parents proudly claimed to be people of the world, and they wanted nothing to do with spiritual things. As a result, the Hattaway children were not exposed to Christianity. We never attended Sunday school, went on church camps, or had any exposure to religious instruction.

The first time I entered a church building was to do mischief. A boy from the neighborhood convinced me to join him in a raid on the local Baptist church. We agreed to meet at midnight and to wear dark clothing to avoid detection. After entering the church building through a back window, we proceeded to cause mayhem by letting off fire extinguishers, spraying white foam over the walls and pews, and by throwing Bibles and hymn books into the empty baptismal pool. After twenty minutes we decided enough damage had been done. We left the same way we had entered, leaving a huge mess for someone else to clean up.

For several nights, despite my godless upbringing, my conscience was so deeply affected that I couldn't sleep a wink. I stayed wide awake, half-expecting the Almighty to strike me dead for the wicked acts I had committed in His house of worship. My life was quickly heading toward a dead end.

My first job after leaving school was at a local bank, counting the bags of coins brought in by local businesses each day. I picked up other odd jobs, but none of them satisfied my hunger to experience the world. In 1985 I decided to leave Auckland, where I had lived for all of my sixteen years. There were too many bad memories there, and my sister's ongoing problems made me want to travel as far away as possible.

I scrounged together enough money for a one-way ticket to the South Island. I traveled to the small town of Nelson, where days of searching for a job passed without the slightest glimmer of hope. One shop owner told me I should be in school. There may have been work available, but not for a high school dropout. I became acutely aware that the world didn't owe me a living.

An embarrassing incident occurred during my job hunt after I noticed an ad in the newspaper which said, "Salesperson needed. No previous experience necessary."

I called the number and a surprised woman asked if I knew anything about their company. I assured her that regardless of their area of business, I was willing to learn and work hard. Seemingly impressed by my eager attitude, the woman agreed to let me try out by knocking on a few doors to present the company's products to people. I was provided with a small box containing a selection of items and a price sheet.

The woman drove me to a well-to-do part of town. On the way, I noticed that for some reason she couldn't stop smiling. With her encouragement, I walked up to the door of a lovely home and rang the bell.

A middle-aged lady opened the door and asked what I wanted. I stumbled around, trying to find the printed card I'd been given. I finally located it in the side of the box and began to read from it. "Good afternoon. I trust you are well. My name is Paul and I am your local Avon representative. Would you allow me to show you some of our latest products today?"

An incredulous look came upon the lady's face and she burst into laughter. I returned to the car to find the saleswoman also in a fit of laughter. My brief career as an Avon lady was officially over!

A short time later I obtained a job at a warehouse. I was now earning an income and living independently, but my soul remained empty and restless. There was a big world out there, waiting to be discovered.

After working at the warehouse for nine months, I set out on a grueling bicycle journey the entire length of New Zealand's South Island, a distance of approximately 600 miles. On one of the final days of my expedition I visited Milford Sound, with its mile-high snow-capped cliffs rising vertically from the ocean floor, and huge waterfalls tumbling down into bays inhabited by seals and dolphins. My senses could scarcely contain the majesty of my surroundings. That evening, still overcome with awe at God's creation, I lifted my arms to the heavens and said, "Praise you, Lord!"

My bicycle journey convinced me of God's existence more than if I had listened to a thousand sermons. I had experienced the Creator's sermon. At the time, I wasn't sure if it was possible for a human being to personally communicate with God, but some years later I wholeheartedly agreed with the truth of these words I read in the Bible: "Since the creation of the world God's invisible qualities – his eternal power and divine nature – have been clearly seen, being understood from what has been made, so that people are without excuse" (Romans 1:20).

New Zealand's economy struggled throughout the 1980s, and hordes of people migrated across the Tasman Sea to Australia. I joined the exodus, touching down in the huge city of Sydney in October 1986, the day after my eighteenth birthday.

Despite having no contacts or prospects in Australia, I had regained my self-confidence. I believed I could do anything I put my mind to, and that somehow life would always work out well for me. My self-belief was soon shaken, however, when I was unable to secure any stable work. For months I survived by doing casual labor that provided daily pay but no promise of additional work. Sydney was a dog-eat-dog society, and I found myself in competition with millions of other people all trying to get by.

For six months I picked up odd jobs wherever I could find them. They included selling paintings door to door, loading kegs of beer onto trucks, picking watermelons on a farm, stocking shelves in supermarkets, and working as a kitchen-hand in a restaurant.

The lowest point came in mid-1987. My strenuous search for regular work had failed to yield any results and my meager funds had completely dried up. I found myself in a desperate position with no job or money, and nowhere to stay. Being a foreigner, I was unable to obtain any government assistance. Faced with no alternative, I walked to a small public park. I sat down under a tree as the sun went down and a bitterly cold wind swept in from the ocean. As darkness closed in, I searched for the best place to sleep that night. A small block of public toilets was located nearby, and after walking around it a few times I realized I could climb onto the roof by hoisting myself up on pipes and a window ledge. With a final push I hauled myself onto the roof and found a spot in the corner that was out of view to people at ground level. That public toilet block in the park was to be my home for the foreseeable future.

The freezing wind made each passing minute seem like an hour. I huddled against the elements in a fetal position, wearing all the clothing I possessed in the world. Every few hours, when it felt as if I might pass out from the cold, I climbed down from the roof and warmed my numb hands beneath the hand drier in the men's restroom.

Each passing night caused me to be wracked with anxiety, and my belligerent self-confidence shattered into a thousand pieces. I felt like a complete failure, trapped in a foreign country with my back literally up against the wall. I had to find a way to survive, or I was doomed. The words of my high school Principal seemed to be true. Perhaps I was a waste of oxygen after all.

***

Almost a year after arriving in Australia, things could hardly have been worse for me. I was homeless, hungry, and lonely. The cold caused me to endure a number of sleepless nights on the roof in the park, and when the weather warmed up I was forced to swat off huge flying cockroaches that constantly harassed me.

When I had first arrived in Sydney I thought I would easily secure a job and make enough money to further my travels. Now I found myself under terrible mental and emotional strain from my harsh experiences. I was a homeless teenager, unable to see any point to life. I was enveloped by a suffocating web that threatened to entangle me forever. At the age of just eighteen I felt run down and battered. In many ways I was already becoming an old man.

Loneliness was perhaps my most difficult struggle at this time. I was desperately empty inside. I believed in a Creator, but I didn't think He could be approached or known. He was a God who preferred to remain hidden from view, disengaged from the affairs of mankind.

At my lowest point, I tried talking to God. "Oh Lord," I stammered, "It's me, Paul. Can You please help me? I'm not doing too well and I don't know what to do. I really need a job but nothing ever seems to work out. If You are there, can You please help me? Thank You."

The next morning I climbed down from the roof. As I wiped the tears and sleep from my eyes, a local man noticed my rough countenance and kindly gave me a bag of potato chips, which I quickly consumed. He engaged me in conversation, and after hearing of my total failure to find work, he offered me some advice: "Mate, if you want to find a job you need to go to where the work is. You won't find much around here in the central city. Head out to the western suburbs. There are plenty of factories out there and you might get lucky."

Seeing how clueless I was and that I didn't even know how to get there, the man had compassion and gave me instructions along with a ten-dollar bill. I walked to the nearest train station and bought a ticket to Sydney's western suburbs.

For more than an hour the train passed through a number of stations. I disembarked at a place called Blacktown and walked around the streets for hours, not knowing where to go or what to do. I entered the doors of dozens of businesses and enquired if there was any work available, but each time I received an unsympathetic rebuttal.

A heavy downpour occurred, drenching me to the bone. My bag and its few contents became soaked, and my shoes were waterlogged. To appease my hunger, I used the remainder of the $10 the man had given me to buy a pie and a can of soft drink, even though it meant I didn't have enough cash to buy another ticket back to central Sydney. I no longer had the energy or determination to care. My spirit had been completely beaten down and crushed.

As I walked along a street, I came to a canvas factory. As it was late in the afternoon I decided to make one final attempt to ask for work. As I walked down the driveway to the office, a tattooed man in his twenties hurried past me. He was cursing and appeared deeply upset.

I entered the office, my waterlogged sneakers squelching with every step, and asked if I could speak to the manager as I was seeking a job. The secretary told me to fill out an application form. As I did so, the manager emerged from his room and asked, "Are you looking for work? Come in here for a minute."

When he asked what kind of work experience I had, I assured him that although I was young, if he gave me an opportunity I wouldn't let him down and would always work hard.

"You're in luck," he said. "I just fired a guy five minutes ago. Perhaps you passed him in the driveway. You can have his job if you like. Can you start tomorrow?"

"Yes, sir, I would be glad to," I replied.

The kind manager looked at my application form and noticed I hadn't listed an address or phone number. "Where are you staying?" he asked. When he found out I had nowhere to lay my head, he gave me an advance from my first pay check and drove me to a budget hostel a short distance away.

That night I enjoyed a hot shower and slept soundly for the first time in weeks. I was amazed at the dramatic change in my circumstances, but failed to appreciate the connection between my sudden turnaround and my prayer to God the previous night.

Most of the young men at the factory were cold-hearted individuals who spent much time boasting of their alcohol-fueled antics and pursuit of women. I didn't fit into that crowd at all. I was just happy to have a job and a bed to sleep in.

One young man at the factory stood out from the others. He was a skinny blonde kid named Darren, about my age. I noticed that for some reason the other workers seemed to hate Darren. He worked in a different section of the factory, so I had little opportunity to interact with him.

One Friday afternoon I was instructed to wheel a large roll of canvas over to Darren's part of the factory. I pushed my trolley through the doors and located him. Strangely, he was standing still at his machine with his eyes closed. I thought it was a bit weird, but decided to wait until he noticed me before I said anything.

Finally, after a few moments, Darren opened his eyes and found me standing directly in front of him.

"Hi, I was told to bring this roll over to you," I said. He thanked me, but his mind seemed preoccupied with other matters.

A short time later in the locker room as we prepared to leave for the weekend, Darren struck up a conversation with me. I had been in Australia for more than a year, but he was the first person to show a genuine interest in being my friend. After chatting for almost an hour, Darren suddenly asked me a totally unexpected question: "Do you believe in God?"

For a moment I was lost for words, but replied, "I suppose so."

He then asked, "Do you think that if you died today you would go to heaven?"

I proudly responded, "Of course! I'm basically a good person."

When Darren told me that Jesus was the only way to heaven I scoffed and told him it couldn't be so, and that surely Buddhism, Islam, and other religions were equally valid pathways to God, just with different names. I considered it the height of arrogance for any one religion to claim to know the truth when they were all trying to serve the same God.

Darren asked me if I would like to come to his church that Sunday evening. My impression was that only old ladies and weaklings attended churches. On the other hand, my life was so devoid of human contact that I appreciated Darren's attempt to reach out to me, so I arrogantly replied, "I will come along to have a laugh!"

Before I had time to change my mind, Darren wrote down my address and said, "Great! I'll pick you up at six o'clock this Sunday evening."

Darren later told me the rest of the story behind the events at the factory that Friday afternoon. The previous Sunday his pastor had challenged the congregation to step out and invite an unbeliever to attend church with them the following weekend. Darren was a shy young man, but he went forward for prayer. The pastor asked God to give him boldness and to reveal the person he should invite.

Friday afternoon arrived, but Darren had yet to invite anyone to his church. He decided to pause from his work duties for a moment. He closed his eyes and prayed, "Lord, the week is almost over and I'm sorry I haven't asked anyone to come to church with me. Please show me who I should talk to."

That moment he opened his eyes and found me standing in front of him!

My life was about to dramatically change. I had been like a fish on God's hook, and now He began to reel me in.

CHAPTER 4

ALL THINGS BECOME NEW

18 October 1987

Sunday afternoon came around quickly, and I glanced nervously at my watch as the time approached for Darren to pick me up. For some reason I felt terribly ill inside, as though my stomach was being churned in a washing machine. I couldn't believe I had agreed to go to a church meeting. I wondered what was wrong with me!

A cold sweat broke out on my forehead as six o'clock neared. I lived just across the street from a small park, and I decided to walk there to clear my mind. A huge battle was raging in my soul and my thoughts were in turmoil. On the one hand I wanted to stay at the park so that when Darren knocked on my door I wouldn't be at home. On the other hand I had promised to go to church with him, and I wanted to keep my word.

I walked back across the street to my room and had a drink of water as more seconds ticked by. It was now just a few minutes before six o'clock. It felt as if I was suffocating under the pressure. As waves of anxiety and dread swept over me I made up my mind. I could not go to a church meeting! The very thought of it terrified me.

I decided to return to the park, obscure myself behind a tree, and watch Darren come and go. I began to think of a good excuse I could give him at work the next day to explain my absence. As I locked my door behind me and walked out to the street, Darren's yellow van pulled up right in front of me. He wound down his window and called out, "Hi Paul, thanks for waiting. Please jump in!" I climbed into the back seat. For better or worse, I was heading to church that Sunday evening.

I was still a bundle of nerves as we pulled up in front of the church. The first thing I noticed was that it looked like no church building I had ever seen. These Christians met inside a rented warehouse that had been converted into a meeting place. There were no steeples or crosses on any walls.

I stepped out of the vehicle and found myself among a throng of people, mostly teens and young adults, all heading into the building. Just inside the front door a man extended his hand as Darren told him, "This is Paul, my friend from work."

The stranger bellowed, "Welcome, Paul! My name is Mike and I'm one of the pastors here. It's a great privilege to have you as our guest this evening. I hope you enjoy the experience, and you're welcome to come back any time."

I couldn't recall anyone ever being so nice to me before. Although I was still a teenager, I had met a lot of different people in my life and considered myself a good judge of character. Mike seemed to be the most genuine, kind-hearted person I had ever met.

Darren and I sat near the back, and I curiously observed the people around me as we waited for the service to commence. I was dumbfounded as I watched hundreds of people filling the auditorium. They didn't seem normal at all. Normal for me was living in a dog-eat-dog society, where people treated each other with mockery and disdain and used one another to their own advantage.

These people were totally different, and I knew they weren't acting. They treated one another like close friends or family members. I was astounded as I observed them. I didn't dare say it out loud, but I knew immediately what the difference was between these people and everyone else I had known in my life up to that point.

These Christians obviously liked each other, but the difference was much more than that. The difference was that they seemed to genuinely *love* one another! I had never seen such a thing before. Love had been missing from my family, from my harsh experiences at school, and during the years since I had ventured out into the world by myself. I later understood the veracity of what Jesus told His disciples: "A new command I give you: love one another. As I have loved you, so you must love one another. By this everyone will know that you are my disciples, if you love one another" (John 13:34–35).

The meeting began, and another strange thing occurred when a Christian drama group performed a skit. I don't remember what the skit was about, because I was transfixed on the performers themselves. All the men and women on the stage appeared to have faces beaming with light. I found it both baffling and attractive at the same time. I rubbed my eyes in an attempt to come back to my senses. I looked again, and my eyes hadn't deceived me. It almost appeared as if the members of the group had flashlights inside their heads, and shafts of soft light were shining out through their eyes.

Whatever was happening, I knew that the hundreds of Christians surrounding me possessed something that I didn't have. They had a quality in their lives that I had only dreamed of, and didn't think was attainable.

The elderly preacher stood up and commenced his message. I listened attentively to every word. He spoke about what society would be like at the end of the world, how God was setting up His kingdom on the earth, and something about how Jesus would one day return to rule and reign over the nations.

I was deeply affected when he spoke about the need of every person to be a friend of God, and not to be found on the side of His enemies. He taught that by default we are all born as enemies to God because of our sin, and that we desperately need to be transformed from the inside out.

I found myself nodding in agreement with his message. At times I thought my friend Darren must have tipped off the preacher about me, because there was no other explanation for how he could so precisely point out the sins and failures that beset my life. When he read the following passage from the Bible, deep conviction gripped my heart. I identified myself with all of these traits:

> But mark this: there will be terrible times in the last days. People will be lovers of themselves, lovers of money, boastful, proud, abusive, disobedient to their parents, ungrateful, unholy, without love, unforgiving, slanderous, without self-control, brutal, not lovers of the good, treacherous, rash, conceited, lovers of pleasure rather than lovers of God.
>
> **2 Timothy 3:1–4**

At the end of his testimony, the preacher invited those who wanted to put their faith in Jesus Christ to come to the front and pray with him. He claimed that only Jesus could repair a person's broken life. Darren asked if I would like to go forward. Part of me did, but I was shy and didn't want to be embarrassed by walking out in front of hundreds of people. As if he could read my thoughts, Darren offered, "I will walk down to the front with you if you like. There's no need to be embarrassed. I did it myself, and I know it's something you'll never regret."

After a brief moment, I looked at Darren, nodded, and said, "Okay, let's do it."

I could sense every pair of eyes in the church fixed on the back of my neck as I walked up the aisle. The preacher welcomed me with a firm handshake, and I bowed my head and prayed, as did the entire congregation.

I didn't understand every word that I said, but I did know two things. Firstly, my life was a mess, and I was a sinner. I had tried to live my way, and it was a disastrous failure. I wanted to do things God's way from now on. I needed His forgiveness, and I was willing to reach out in faith and put my hand in His. Secondly, I knew that I needed to possess the same kind of qualities as the Christians in that meeting. Whatever beauty they had discovered, I longed and hungered to partake of it.

The prayer concluded, and with my head bowed and tears in my eyes I said a hearty "Amen!"

Then something extraordinary happened.

At the very moment I said "Amen!" my entire world changed. It wasn't merely a psychological or emotional change. My whole body felt dramatically different, as if a ton of bricks had been lifted off my shoulders and thrown to the floor.

Despite my youth, I had become very dark and cynical. My life had already been a brutal battle for survival. At that moment, an inexpressible joy entered my heart and soul. It was incredible.

The service ended with a song, then I was led to a church office where a lady gave me a New Testament and wrote down my contact details. I smiled from ear to ear and could scarcely contain the joy I felt bubbling up within me.

I tried to maintain a calm demeanor out of respect for the counselor, but after a while I simply couldn't contain the joy I felt inside, and it overflowed. I laughed out loud with a sense of profound amazement at God's love and goodness. I knew that I had found the truth – or rather, He had found me. My great joy was like the relief of a man who had just been released from the shackles that bound him his whole life.

I had arrogantly told Darren I would come to his church to have a laugh. I never imagined my prediction would come true in the way it did!

Against all odds, I had experienced the impossible. I had met my Creator, and He was infinitely better and more wonderful than I had ever imagined. I had met the Almighty God, and He had invaded my very being by moving into my heart, mind, and soul!

That night I struggled to get to sleep as I tried to make sense of what had happened to me. One thing I knew for sure was that

I would never be the same again. The cloud of depression I had lived under for years was dispelled, and although my journey ahead would include some harsh experiences, I never again fell into the kind of continual slump of darkness and depression that had been my constant companion before that glorious day.

CHAPTER 5

MY NEW FATHER

If Jesus Christ be God and died for me, then no sacrifice can be too great for me to make for Him.

C. T. Studd

The first few days of my Christian life were remarkable. Now that I had been inwardly transformed, I began to view the world from a completely different perspective. It may sound corny, but flowers suddenly seemed more beautiful, I heard birds chirping happy tunes, and my future seemed full of limitless possibilities.

It literally felt as though my dirty, rebellious heart had been surgically removed from my body and replaced with a brand new model. I experienced the reality of God's promise to change people from the inside out:

"I will sprinkle clean water on you, and you will be clean; I will cleanse you from all your impurities and from all your idols. I will give you a new heart and put a new spirit in you; I will remove from you your heart of stone and give you a heart of flesh. And I will put my Spirit in you and move you to follow my decrees and be careful to keep my laws."

Ezekiel 36:25–27

I was so absorbed by my life-changing experience that world events meant little to me. Years later I discovered that on 19 October 1987 – the day after I met Jesus Christ – the stock markets of the world crashed in an event known as Black Monday. If I did watch the news that day, I didn't pay attention. I had become a new person when I met Jesus, and my life had taken on a completely new orientation and purpose.

My friend Darren took me to a Christian bookstore, where I made two purchases – my first ever Bible, and a book entitled *Operation World*, which provided a snapshot of all the countries in the world and the state of Christianity within them. The Bible became my closest companion and inspiration. I continued to work at the canvas factory, and every spare moment was spent devouring God's Word. I was amazed at each page and couldn't get enough. I was like a starving man at a sumptuous banquet.

One Saturday morning I woke early and read the Bible on my bed. The words captivated me as I read chapter after chapter. I occasionally paused for a drink of water, and only stopped reading that day when I became aware it had become difficult to see the words. The sun had already set, and I had been absorbed in the Word of God for twelve hours straight.

Growing up, I had tried to read the Bible on a few occasions, but I found the words dry and confusing. My father had once read the Bible from cover to cover, but was none the wiser about God at the end of his endeavor than he had been at the start. He was spiritually dead when he started reading the Bible, and remained spiritually dead when he finished. People can study the Scriptures until they are blue in the face, but if they don't read through eyes of faith with their lives surrendered to Jesus Christ, the words won't benefit them. The Bible says, "the message they heard was of no value to them, because they did not share the faith of those who obeyed" (Hebrews 4:2).

Now that I had repented of my sins and invited the Holy Spirit to control my life, the Bible became vital nourishment that I couldn't live without. Before I met Jesus, my eyes and heart were shrouded in darkness. I groped my way through life like a blind man, only occasionally making sense of my surroundings. I had now received my sight, and everything was crystal clear! The Bible describes the difference this way: "The person without the Spirit does not accept the things that come from the Spirit of God but considers them foolishness, and cannot understand them because they are discerned only through the Spirit" (1 Corinthians 2:14).

The church encouraged me to attend a home Bible study with other young Christians. The first time I attended I was shy and nervous, but the warm welcome I received soon melted away my insecurities. The home meetings were a tremendous help to my early Christian development. Every person was invited to contribute, and nobody's opinion was considered less important than another's. The Bible studies were scheduled to finish at about nine o'clock in the evening, but it was quite usual to find people still chatting about Jesus and praying for one another at 1:00 a.m.

Over the following weeks I gradually came to understand that not only had my heart been dramatically transformed, but I was now also grafted into a completely new family. I was still the biological son of my earthly father in New Zealand, but I also had a new heavenly Father, who had a specific plan and purpose for my life.

As I got to know my new Father, I realized I wasn't an accident, and I certainly wasn't a "waste of oxygen". On the contrary, my awesome God knew the exact number of hairs on my head, and He viewed me as His precious child. These words from Psalm 139:13–16 washed over me like a river of cleansing water, giving me a deep sense of my value in the sight of the Lord:

> For you created my inmost being;
> you knit me together in my mother's womb.
> I praise you because I am fearfully and wonderfully made;
> your works are wonderful,
> I know that full well.

> My frame was not hidden from you
> when I was made in the secret place,
> when I was woven together in the depths of the earth.
> Your eyes saw my unformed body;
> all the days ordained for me were written in your book
> before one of them came to be.

Before the Living God revealed His love and acceptance to me through Jesus Christ, my basic religious worldview was polytheism. It seemed logical to me that in mankind's search for God, different cultures had invented various names and methods to find the same Creator. I was convinced that Jesus, Buddha, Mohammed, Hare Krishna, and others were equally valid pathways to the same Supreme Being.

Now that the Spirit of Truth dwelt within me, I understood that Jesus is not one of multiple pathways to heaven, but God declared Jesus to be the *only* way for mankind to come to Him. Countless passages in the Bible reveal the exclusivity of Jesus Christ. He is not merely a good moral teacher, but He affirmed His incomparable position by declaring, "I am the way and the truth and the life. No one comes to the Father except through me" (John 14:6). I started reading the Acts of the Apostles, and before long I was again confronted by the unmistakable uniqueness of Jesus: "Salvation is found in no one else, for there is no other name under heaven given to mankind by which we must be saved" (Acts 4:12).

As I continued to saturate my life with God's Word, some parts of the Bible caused me discomfort. I discovered that Jesus spoke frequently and specifically about hell as a real, literal place of torment. I couldn't pick and choose which parts of the Bible I wanted to accept and which parts I didn't. I realized that I had to accept either all of it, or none of it.

If Jesus was telling the truth, as He surely was, and only those who trust in His salvation can be reconciled to the God of heaven, then the implications were vast and terrible. It meant that billions of Muslims, Hindus, Buddhists, New Age adherents, atheists, and secularists – all who do not trust in Jesus Christ and call on His Name – are lost and headed for an eternity separated from God. It also meant that millions of people who try to lead "good moral lives" but who have not trusted their entire existence into the hands of Jesus are lost, and their good works will amount to nothing on Judgment Day.

A deep responsibility began to dawn on me. It was as if I had just discovered the cure for cancer, and I wanted to tell everyone as quickly as possible so they could experience God in the same way I had. I knew that my Lord Jesus was not *an* answer to people's empty and desperate lives, but He was just as He claimed – *the* answer.

Wanting to tell everyone I could about Jesus, I knelt down and prayed, "Heavenly Father, thank You for what You have done in my life. I have nothing to give You, but dear Lord, if it pleases You, take my life and do whatever You want with it. I belong to You."

* * *

Before the next stage of my journey commenced, I came face to face with another reality. Like most people, I had been raised to think that Satan and demons were myths that helped people explain the existence of evil in the world. I never thought that Satan was a real being who was engaged in a constant and fierce battle with people, especially the children of God.

I was assigned to work the night shift at the canvas factory, which required me to buy my first car, an old banged-up Ford station wagon. A few days later, something felt wrong as I reversed out of the car park at the end of my shift. I got out and discovered a massive hole in one of my tires. It was not a normal puncture, but someone had ripped it open with a lacerated knife.

The next day I replaced the tire, and I finished my shift at two o'clock in the morning. Feeling exhausted, I drove home along

Parramatta Road, one of the main transportation arteries of west Sydney. The streets were nearly deserted at that hour, and my heart was full of gratitude as I worshiped God and basked in His boundless love for me. As I approached a set of traffic lights, a clear and chilling warning suddenly jolted my entire being: "Look out! Satan is about to try to kill you!"

I didn't hear those words audibly, but they couldn't have been any clearer if a man sitting beside me had shouted them in my ear.

I was so stunned by the loud and precise warning that my eyes instantly became wide awake and the hair stood up on the back of my neck. I slowed down and looked around, wondering how the devil might try to kill me. As I approached the intersection, I saw no cars coming toward me, and my rear-view mirror revealed a clear roadway behind.

I had considered every potential danger on the road, but the warning was so real that I knew something was about to happen. The atmosphere seemed charged with electricity. I approached the green traffic light and cautiously made my way through the empty intersection.

All of a sudden I caught a glimpse of an object flying toward me at great speed. A large muscle car came tearing through the intersection from the side road. The car had no lights on, and came straight through a red light. In an instant I realized it was about to smash into me. There was no way to avoid it.

I shut my eyes tightly and screamed out a single word: "Jesus!" There was no time to add "Please help me!" to my sentence. As the car barreled straight at me I grimly braced for the impact, but it never came. Somehow, the car went past me and continued across the intersection at the same breakneck speed. It passed so close to me that my vehicle shook from side to side from the wind created as it went by.

To this day, I'm not exactly sure how God preserved my life that night, but if I had entered the intersection a split second earlier, the paramedics would have been scraping my body parts off the road.

I was so emotionally spent by the experience that I drove home in complete silence.

That night I learned some valuable lessons from my brush with death. I recognized that Satan is a real foe who wants me dead, but I also learned that my heavenly Father is more than capable of getting my attention if He needs to, and He is able to deliver me from trouble. In addition, I discovered the literal truth of God's promise that "everyone who calls on the name of the Lord will be saved" (Acts 2:21).

From that moment until today, whenever my family and I start out on a drive of any significant length, we first bow our heads and ask the Lord to protect us from harm and from every insidious plan of the Evil One.

CHAPTER 6

POWER FROM ON HIGH

> It is extraordinary power from God, not talent, that wins the day. It is extraordinary spiritual unction, not mental power, that we need. Mental power may gather a large congregation, but only spiritual power will save souls.
>
> **Charles Spurgeon**

A couple of months had passed since the glorious evening when I first met Jesus Christ. By His grace and mercy I had commenced a vibrant personal relationship with God. When I learned that Jesus had given His life for me, I knew that the least I could do was to give my life back to Him in return. I was desperate for others to hear about Jesus so they could experience Him for themselves. As I read through the Gospels, I was struck by the words Jesus spoke to a man who had just been delivered from demonic possession. He instructed the man, "Go home to your own people and tell them how much the Lord has done for you, and how he has had mercy on you" (Mark 5:19).

This Bible verse spoke to me in a very personal way, and I knew I needed to share what the Lord had done for me with my family members in New Zealand. I planned to return to my homeland for six weeks, and used most of my savings to purchase a ticket. I had enjoyed my time working at the canvas factory, but they wouldn't allow me that much time off work so I was forced to resign. I didn't know what plans the Lord had in store for me once I returned to Australia, but I was certain that I first had to declare my faith to my family.

My trip home was not only about witnessing to my family. I realized that God also wanted to heal me from some of my bad childhood experiences. I had to tell my father something that had never before come out of my mouth: I needed to tell my dad that I loved him.

Before taking this step, however, God had something vital for me to experience. Although I was a believer in Jesus Christ and was growing in grace and knowledge, I didn't have the kind of power to witness for the Lord that I read about every time I opened the New Testament. I had tried to share my faith with an elderly lady named Dot who worked as a machinist at the factory. Every Monday she asked me what I had done on the weekend. I would tell her I had gone to church and worshiped God, and I did my best to explain what had happened in my life since I had met Jesus. Invariably, Dot would look the other way and sigh. Finally, after several weeks, she stopped asking about my weekends and categorized me as a religious fanatic.

One Sunday evening, shortly before my departure for New Zealand, I was baptized in water. It was a wonderful occasion as my old life was lowered into the water as an enemy of the gospel, only to be raised up to new life as a beloved child of God.

In Western Christianity, the power and importance of baptism has largely been lost. In other parts of the world, however, baptism remains the most vital and dangerous action a believer can take. Fanatical Muslims, Hindus, and Communists may not particularly care when someone claims to be a Christian or even if they attend church meetings, but when they are baptized all hell breaks loose. Thousands of believers are murdered each year following their baptisms. It is a clear-cut declaration to the spiritual realm and to the world that an individual has crossed the line from death to life.

Many Christians say baptism is merely a symbolic act of obedience, but for me it was much more. Something powerful and life-changing occurred when I was baptized. I could identify with the words of Peter, who described baptism as "the pledge of a clear conscience towards God. It saves you by the resurrection of Jesus Christ, who has gone into heaven and is at God's right hand – with angels, authorities and powers in submission to him" (1 Peter 3:21–22).

The following morning I went to work and saw Dot at her cutting machine."How are you, young Paul?" she enquired.

I replied, "Very well thanks, Dot. Last night something really important happened in my life."

As I shared about my baptism and what it meant to me, the Holy Spirit came powerfully upon Dot. This dear old lady, who had previously shown no interest in the gospel, began to shake, and tears welled up in her eyes as God convicted her of her sins.

On numerous other occasions after my baptism, people were deeply touched by the Spirit of God when I spoke with them. On almost every occasion when an unbeliever allowed me to pray for them, they could sense the presence of the Lord Jesus and would cry.

Before I was baptized, sharing the Good News with people was like trying to roll a heavy boulder up a hill. Now, instead of me trying to bring people to Jesus, the Holy Spirit inside of me drew them to Himself. My heavenly Father knew that I needed His power to effectively reach others for Him. I was now ready to return to my homeland and face my family as an ambassador of Jesus Christ.

I spent several weeks in New Zealand visiting family members and friends. At each place I shared how Jesus had changed my life. Some people weren't interested, while others broke down in tears and had many questions for me.

I spent time with my sister, who was still tormented by demons. I asked if I could pray for her, and I bound the forces that had taken control of her life, commanding them to depart in the Name of Jesus. I learned an important lesson. Even though my sister allowed me to pray with her, she wasn't prepared to make Jesus the Master of her life. God never forces anyone to follow Him. He makes the offer, but if they refuse, He doesn't beg them to change their mind.

It was to be many years until I saw my sister again. When I did, she told me how the "magic prayer" I had prayed that day had helped her greatly, and that the worst of her demonic torment had stopped from that moment on. I continue to pray that she will fully surrender her life to the Living God.

Before returning to New Zealand I had told my parents I had become a Christian. By the time I arrived, they had erected defensive barriers around their hearts. I nevertheless shared as much as I could with them in a loving and respectful manner. My mother thought she was already a Christian because she had been baptized as an infant. On several occasions she allowed me to pray with her and was unable to hold back her tears, but she was not willing to make Jesus the Boss of her life.

One evening I was home alone with my father. I told him how much I regretted being a rebellious son and the grief I had brought him. He told me not to worry about it. I looked him in the eyes and added, "I need to tell you something else."

With a lump in my throat, I said, "Dad, I just wanted to let you know that I love you."

He looked away, deeply embarrassed, and didn't say a word in response. My job had been to tell him, and I left the results up to God. I felt a great release in my heart when I said those words, and the years of harsh beatings and abuse began to melt away. I no longer viewed my father as an enemy, but as someone who himself was a victim of sin and dysfunction.

My time in New Zealand was quickly coming to an end, and the savings from my job in Australia had almost been used up. I was down to my last five dollars, had no job or prospects, and absolutely no idea what God wanted me to do. I just knew that Jesus was alive, and I wanted His will to be accomplished in my life.

One of the great blessings of my trip was meeting with Uncle Stan, my father's older brother. A strongly built man with huge hands and forearms like tree trunks, he had never married, but had spent decades traveling the world as a sailor in the navy. Uncle Stan was always full of life and laughter, and my siblings and I had always eagerly looked forward to his visits.

When Uncle Stan heard I was in town he came over to see me. He told me that during his years in the navy he had become ensnared by many vices. One day in desperation he cried out for God's mercy. He had met Jesus, and for many years had remained a committed believer and a faithful member of the local Salvation Army. When I shared the details of my salvation experience, my uncle was overjoyed.

I couldn't believe that during all my years growing up I had been unaware of my uncle's faith in Christ. He explained, "Your parents sat me down many years ago and issued a stern warning. They forbade me to ever share my faith with their kids, and if I betrayed their request I would be barred from seeing any of you again." Heartbroken, but seeing no alternative but to obey my parents' demand, Uncle Stan prayed for us regularly, asking God to reach us in a time and manner of His choosing. He was my only Christian relative. Nobody else shared our faith.

Without a job, money, or transportation, the only church within easy walking distance of my parents' home was a Baptist church – the same fellowship whose building I had vandalized as a youth. I attended two meetings there that proved to be pivotal to my future life.

On 28 February 1988 I walked to the church, unaware that a Chinese preacher named Harry Lee would be sharing his testimony that evening. He had spent eleven years in prison in China because of his faith in Jesus. I sat on the front row with my eyes and ears wide open. During his message, Lee unbuttoned part of his shirt to reveal scars on his chest where he had been cruelly tortured for Christ. He was the first person I had ever met who could say, "Let no one cause me trouble, for I bear on my body the marks of Jesus" (Galatians 6:17).

I had never seen or heard anyone like Harry Lee before. For someone who had spent so long in prison, it struck me that he didn't appear to be downcast at all. In fact, he was full of life and vitality. The presence of the Holy Spirit had caused Lee to overcome the worst that people could do to him. With tears running down his cheeks, he summarized his years of torture and deprivation as "my honeymoon with Jesus."

This dear Chinese saint concluded his testimony by quoting this Scripture:

> Who shall separate us from the love of Christ? Shall trouble or hardship or persecution or famine or nakedness or danger or sword? As it is written: "For your sake we face death all day long; we are considered as sheep to be slaughtered." No, in all these things we are more than conquerors through him who loved us.
>
> **Romans 8:35–37**

That night I walked home in a daze. Prior to that meeting I knew almost nothing about China. Harry Lee had introduced revolutionary concepts about Christianity that would take weeks to process. Before I was able to make sense of the message, however, God had another blessing in store for me. Two weeks later I was amazed to find that a second Chinese man who had spent many years in prison was to speak at the church!

The testimony of George Chen impacted me even more deeply than that of Harry Lee. Chen, who had been incarcerated more than twenty years for his faith, had spent longer behind bars because of his love for Jesus than I had been alive at that time.

A gifted evangelist, Chen had established a small group of house churches in his home province. When the number of church members grew to around 300, the Communist authorities arrested Chen and sentenced him to two decades in prison.

This precious man had learned to appreciate the small blessings of life. Initially he had struggled with the lack of privacy in prison.

There was no chance to pray, sing to the Lord, or have a moment of peaceful reflection. His life was one of exhaustion and hardship, forced to perform hard labor sixteen hours per day, seven days per week.

Feeling as though he was about to lose his mind, Chen discovered that there was one place in the prison where he could be assured of complete privacy. It was the place the other inmates and guards avoided at all times. The toilets in each cell block flowed into an open sewer, full of disease and vile stench. Knowing it would provide an opportunity to spend time with Jesus, Chen volunteered to climb into the waist-high human excrement with a shovel and clean it out daily. He said, "I spent my days standing in human waste, shoveling to make compost. The guards thought I would be miserable, but I was overjoyed. It smelled so bad that no one would come near me, so I could pray and sing aloud all day."

George Chen was finally released from prison in 1978. For years he had assumed the churches he started had been closed down. When he returned home, however, he was shocked to discover, after two decades behind bars, that the original 300 Christians had grown to 5,000!

The precious testimonies of Harry Lee and George Chen were the highlights of my time in New Zealand. They taught me that the kingdom of God cannot be defeated by evil men or governments. Whatever terrible things Satan and the world can throw at Jesus' disciples, His purposes will not be thwarted.

A deep revelation of my heavenly Father's invincibility filled my heart with faith and purpose. There was no reason for me to be afraid. Wherever God would take me, His plans would be fulfilled one way or another. I was now part of an unconquerable army!

CHAPTER 7

A HOLY NIGHT

13 March 1988

If God calls you to be a missionary, don't stoop to be a king.

Jordan Grooms

I sat in awe of God as George Chen concluded his testimony. God's blessings to me that day were far from over, however. The Lord Jesus was about to hurl my life in a radically different direction.

When Chen had finished speaking, the New Zealand mission leader who had brought him to the church stood to share some final thoughts before closing the meeting in prayer. His words changed the course of my life.

"Brothers and sisters," he declared, "George has shared a wonderful testimony of God's faithfulness tonight, but what about you? Don't assume the Lord only wants to use believers in faraway lands. He also wants to use *you*. Will you surrender your life to the service of Jesus Christ?"

About eighty people remained in the meeting, but the mission leader seemed to be speaking directly to me. Everything else surrounding me faded and my whole being focused on his words, like a beam of light illuminating a dark place. He continued with this challenge: "China needs donkeys for Jesus! There is a famine of God's Word and millions of Christians are crying out to the Lord for Bibles. We need able-bodied men and women to come to Hong Kong and carry bags of Bibles across the border into China. Will you be a donkey for Jesus?"

It's difficult for mere words to describe what happened to me next. Like a jolt from heaven, my heart, mind, and spirit knew – without a shadow of doubt – that God wanted *me* to be a donkey for Jesus. I didn't have a job or any money, I was a high school dropout, and I didn't know how to preach. But there was one thing I could do: I was able to use my strong body to haul suitcases and bags of Bibles across the border from Hong Kong to China!

Surging with excitement, I made my way to the mission table at the back of the church to meet the two speakers. "Hello brother," the mission leader said. "What can I do for you?"

"God has called me to be a donkey for Jesus!" I excitedly exclaimed. "Please let me know what I need to do to work with your organization."

He wrote my name down on a sheet of paper as he engaged me in conversation. When he discovered I had only come to faith in Christ four months earlier, the man's countenance changed.

"God has called me to help!" I reiterated. "I'm ready to go, and I have no job or commitments holding me back."

The mission leader was a lovely Christian man, but he was unsure what to do with me. After a few minutes he handed me a piece of paper with the name and phone number of a different organization in Hong Kong. "Try these folks," he told me. "You may not be a good fit with us, but perhaps this other group will have an opening for you."

I thanked the two men and followed them out of the church door into the night. I could scarcely believe it! Jesus had shown me something important that I could do for Him. I was going to be a donkey to China!

As I walked home, my heart was so full of joy it felt as if I was floating on air. I decided to run the rest of the way as I was anxious to share the amazing news with my parents. I burst through the front door, waving my piece of paper with the Hong Kong contact details. My mother was watching television while my father thumbed his way through the Sunday newspaper.

"God has spoken to me!" I proclaimed.

My mother continued watching her show while my father kept gazing at his paper, completely unmoved by my announcement.

"Did you hear me?" I asked incredulously. "God spoke to me tonight!"

My mother turned the volume down on the TV and sighed, "What did God say to you then?"

"He told me to go to China! I'm going to be a donkey for Jesus by carrying Bibles into China!"

My dad ruffled his paper and dryly asked, "When are you going to look for a job?"

They knew I had no money and no job waiting for me back in Australia. I found their complete lack of enthusiasm for my life-changing announcement strange, so I tried again. "You don't understand! God has called me to go to China. It's amazing!"

After a pause of several seconds, my mother calmly asked, "So when do you expect to go to China, then?"

Her simple question stopped me in my tracks. I had been so swept up by the events of the evening that I hadn't yet thought of the timing. Before I had a chance to think it through, I replied, "I don't know… in a couple of weeks?"

Thinking I may have lost my mind, my mother turned the television volume up again and my dad resumed giving his full attention to the day's news. My parents' reaction had been underwhelming to say the least, but I wasn't deterred. The power of the Holy Spirit continued to surge within me and I *knew* that my heavenly Father had instructed me to haul Bibles across the border from Hong Kong to Communist China.

* * *

I retired to my bedroom for the night and opened the Bible. My mind was still flooded with excitement, and it was going to take a while for the adrenaline to settle down. After midnight I began a conversation with the Living God. "Lord Jesus, thank You for calling me to serve You in China. I love You so much. It seems impossible for me to go to Hong Kong, and I only have five dollars left in the whole world. There are many things I don't understand, but I'm sure You have called me, and I trust You to take care of the details."

I was far too energized to sleep, so for the next six hours I communed with the Creator of the universe. It was one of the holiest nights of my life. As I write these words almost thirty years later, the memory of the power and sweetness of God's presence that night still brings tears to my eyes.

I loved the Bible, but I was not yet familiar with all the details or how the various books fit together. I just knew that it was the inspired Word of God and not merely the words of human beings. As I thumbed my way through different pages of the Bible, the Holy Spirit grabbed my attention and brought His Word to life. Certain verses and passages seemed to leap from the pages and lodge themselves deep within my heart and soul.

Tragically, many people think the Bible is a dead book full of outdated ideas. For those who have yet to submit their lives to Jesus that may seem true, but for a Christian with the Holy Spirit dwelling within them, "the Word of God is alive and active. Sharper than any double-edged sword, it penetrates even to dividing soul and spirit, joints and marrow; it judges the thoughts and attitudes of the heart" (Hebrews 4:12).

For hours, the Lord walked me through the Scriptures. Each passage that leapt into my spirit was a life-changing directive from God to me. I remember them all to this day. His solemn instructions became the foundation for my many years of service in the kingdom of God that followed.

To begin with, the Lord directed me to these words: "Do you not know that your bodies are temples of the Holy Spirit, who is in you, whom you have received from God? You are not your own; you were bought at a price. Therefore honor God with your bodies" (1 Corinthians 6:19–20).

In response, I knelt beside my bed and prayed, "I surrender myself to You, Lord Jesus. I belong to You. Do with me whatever You wish. You own me now. You paid a dear price and I am Yours."

When I pointed out to my Savior that I didn't know anyone in the whole of Asia, this wonderful promise provided all the assurance I needed: "The Lord your God goes with you; he will never leave you nor forsake you" (Deuteronomy 31:6).

After I thanked Jesus for this assurance, my attention was directed to this verse: "One who has unreliable friends soon comes to ruin, but there is a friend who sticks closer than a brother" (Proverbs 18:24). Tears streamed down my face when the truth of these words sunk in. I didn't know a soul in Asia, but I would never be alone! Jesus was going with me, and He would stick closer to me than a brother.

After a while, my prayers and petitions focused in on practical matters. I reminded the Lord that I had no job, just a few dollars in my pocket, and no career or skills to earn an income that would help get me to Hong Kong and to sustain me after I landed.

Once again the Spirit of God directed me to a string of Scriptures which became personal promises and a light to my path. When I mentioned my financial needs to the Lord, He responded,

> "Do not worry, saying, 'What shall we eat?' or 'What shall we drink?' or 'What shall we wear?' For the pagans run after all these things, and your heavenly Father knows that you need them. But seek first his kingdom and his righteousness, and all these things will be given to you as well. Therefore do not worry about tomorrow, for tomorrow will worry about itself. Each day has enough trouble of its own."
>
> **Matthew 6:31–34**

The truth of God's Word saturated my heart. I began to understand that not only had the Lord called me to China, but He would also take care of my needs. What a great deal! He would provide everything I needed, as long as I put His kingdom and righteousness above my own needs and desires.

The Holy Spirit impressed on me that I must never ask any person or organization for money, nor was I allowed to drop hints to people about my personal needs in the hope that they might meet them. My job was to focus on the kingdom of God and not be a burden to people I met along the way. I was to pay for what I needed, and ensure that I paid my bills on time. When I read, "Owe no one anything except to love one another" (Romans 13:8, NKJV), I realized the Lord never wanted me to go into financial debt.

Quite simply, my role was to seek the Lord and to make my requests known to Him and not to people. If I looked to people to provide my needs I would not be putting His kingdom first, and my lack of faith would be a sin. I felt this was a clear, non-negotiable instruction from God to me. There would be stark consequences depending on whether I decided to trust Christ alone, or if I chose to trust in man. In Jeremiah 17:5–8 I read:

> "Cursed is the one who trusts in man,
> who draws strength from mere flesh
> and whose heart turns away from the Lord.
> That person will be like a bush in the wastelands;
> they will not see prosperity when it comes.
> They will dwell in the parched places of the desert,
> in a salt land where no one lives.
> But blessed is the one who trusts in the Lord,
> whose confidence is in him.
> They will be like a tree planted by the water
> that sends out its roots by the stream.
> It does not fear when heat comes;

> its leaves are always green.
> It has no worries in a year of drought
> and never fails to bear fruit."

Many other passages of Scripture were illuminated to me that night, preparing me for the battle ahead. I read, "We must go through many hardships to enter the kingdom of God" (Acts 14:22), and, "Everyone who wants to live a godly life in Christ Jesus will be persecuted" (2 Timothy 3:12).

It was a holy and solemn night. The Almighty God dealt with me directly, setting before me choices that would govern the rest of my life. It felt as though the Lord Jesus Christ was making a contract with me – dare I say a *covenant* – and the results would be determined by my obedience or disobedience to His commands.

One final verse brought my conversation with my heavenly Father to a conclusion. He presented me with a clear choice:

> This day I call the heavens and the earth as witnesses against you that I have set before you life and death, blessings and curses. Now choose life, so that you and your children may live and that you may love the Lord your God, listen to his voice, and hold fast to him.
>
> **Deuteronomy 30:19–20**

As a new day dawned over Auckland I finally fell asleep, exhausted but enveloped by the love and peace of God.

CHAPTER 8

THE ADVENTURE BEGINS

Throughout the Bible, God never operates in a frenetic manner. When He does decide to act, though, events can unfold quickly, like a hurricane sweeping in from the ocean.

I planned to sleep in as long as possible after being up all night communing with the Living God, but He had other ideas. My parents had risen early and gone to work, leaving me home alone. At eight o'clock in the morning my deep slumber was shattered by my Uncle Stan's booming voice. "Wake up, wake up, sleepy head!" he roared as he burst through the front door and into my bedroom.

He grabbed me by the ankles and literally dragged me out of bed. "Get up! I have something to tell you," he bellowed as he left my bedroom. Rubbing the sleep from my eyes, I made my way to the kitchen where my uncle was waiting.

A white envelope had been placed in the middle of the table. I didn't know what to say, so he took the initiative. "Listen, young fella. This morning as I was speaking with the Lord, the Holy Spirit told me you need this more than I do." He nodded at the envelope. "Go ahead and open it," he insisted.

I cautiously opened the envelope and was amazed to find it full of cash, $700 in all! My uncle had a meager income and was living on a government pension. He didn't own a car, and he had taken a series of buses across the city to come and see me that morning.

I was shaking, having never been given anything like this before in my life. Sensing my hesitancy, Uncle Stan reiterated that he was simply obeying the Holy Spirit and that I should thank God for His provision. He didn't know what I needed the money for, but was absolutely convinced the Lord had instructed him to give it to me.

I began to share about the two persecuted Chinese pastors who had spoken at the local church, and how the previous evening I had volunteered to go to Hong Kong and be a donkey for Jesus.

"Hallelujah! God told me you need it," he repeated.

I spent the next few hours with my beloved uncle. He prayed for me and encouraged me in the adventure I was about to begin with Jesus. He read parts of the Bible to me, but when he read that "the steps of a good man are ordered by the Lord" (Psalm 37:23, NKJV), I thought, "Oh no, I have a problem, because I'm not a good man. I'm weak and flawed in various ways."

My uncle helped me understand that it wasn't my responsibility to find the perfect path for my life. Jesus once said, "No one is good – except God alone" (Mark 10:18). I was relieved to discover that Jesus is the good man whose steps are ordered by the Lord! My job was simply to remain connected to Him and follow in His footsteps. By doing so, I would automatically find myself aligned with God's will.

Uncle Stan departed, and later that day my parents arrived home from work. I asked my father if he had spoken with his brother about my plans to go to China. "Why would I do that?" he gruffly objected. My dad was embarrassed by my newfound faith and my future plans. The Lord Jesus Christ really was the One who had instructed my uncle to give the money to me. This boosted my faith and assured me that I was obeying God's will, and that the idea of carrying Bibles into China was not a figment of my imagination.

The powerful promises that had leapt from the pages of the Bible the previous night were already coming true. I hadn't mentioned my needs to anyone but God, and He had already started to show His ability to supernaturally supply my needs.

The next day I called a travel agent to book a flight. I would return to Australia for a few weeks before continuing on to Hong

Kong. The $700 my uncle had given me was just enough for a round-trip ticket.

My Cathay Pacific flight was scheduled to leave Sydney for Hong Kong on 5 April 1988. I had to nominate a return date, but I didn't have any idea how long I would be in Asia. The travel agent explained that it would be cheaper to buy a ticket with a six-week return date, but that kind of ticket came with two conditions: it was non-refundable and non-transferable, meaning I couldn't change the ticket once it was purchased. If I didn't board my flight on the designated return date my ticket would be voided.

In Sydney I stayed with John, who was one of the youth leaders of the church. I excitedly shared all the details of what the Lord Jesus had done in my home country. He listened attentively, and rejoiced at how God had miraculously provided for my ticket to Asia.

As my departure date neared, John asked if I was planning to let the pastor know about my trip so the church could pray for me.

"That's a great idea!" I replied. "I would appreciate all the prayer support I can get."

John explained that Christians normally seek permission from their church leaders before embarking on such a major journey. I thought he was joking, so I repeated my experiences, hoping to convince him that God really had called me to carry Bibles to China.

"I know, I know," he assured me, "but it's still a good idea to go and see the pastor and get his permission."

"Permission?" I replied. "Why do I need permission from my earthly brother when my heavenly Father has already told me to go?"

I was to encounter an unexpected response when I informed my pastor about the dramatic new direction in which God was leading me.

The following afternoon I went to the church and made a beeline for the pastor's office. His secretary intercepted me and asked if I had an appointment.

"No, sorry, I didn't know I needed one," I replied.

She said the pastor was very busy and had another meeting scheduled.

"That's okay," I assured her. "I will only take a minute of his time."

When I was told I could enter his office, I opened the door and said, "Hi, pastor. I'm sorry to interrupt. I just wanted to let you know some exciting news! God has called me to China!"

I reached into my pocket and pulled out my airline ticket, waving it triumphantly as proof of God's providence. I wanted to share all the details of what had happened to me, but I knew the pastor was busy so I tried to summarize it in a few sentences. "The Lord has called me to carry Bibles into China and I'm leaving next Tuesday! He miraculously provided the money I need, so I'm off!"

As I waved my ticket again, a look of deep concern came upon the pastor's face. He obviously didn't share my enthusiasm.

The following Sunday was my last one at the church. So much had happened in the five-and-a-half months since Jesus Christ had first revealed Himself to me. I was glad to be at church, but was even more excited about the adventure that was awaiting me in Asia.

The worship part of the service concluded, and the pastor stood up to preach. After five minutes, he did something that those who had been attending the church for years said he had never done previously. He suddenly stopped speaking and looked for me in the crowd. When his eyes met mine, he told me to stand up and move out into the aisle.

It felt like high school all over again! Every eye in the building was focused on me, and people were wondering what I had done wrong.

The pastor issued a public warning to me: "Don't try to run before you have learned to walk," he said. "Stay where you have been planted and don't presume to have heard from the Lord. You need to prove yourself in this country first before heading off to the other side of the world."

After the meeting, a group of believers surrounded me. "Well, I guess you won't be going to China now?" they questioned.

"What are you talking about?" I replied. "God told me to go to China, and He miraculously provided a ticket. Of course I'm still going. I must follow Jesus!"

As a new believer, I was ignorant of church rules and traditions. I didn't know there was a pattern laid out in the Bible for believers to submit to before they went to the mission field. All I knew was that the Lord Jesus Christ had powerfully met with me and had called me to carry Bibles to China.

* * *

Looking back, I later realized how odd it was that two persecuted Chinese house church leaders should happen to speak at the small Baptist church near my parents' home at the exact time I was seeking God's will for the rest of my life. I am probably the last person on earth anyone would choose to be a Christian missionary, but by His wondrous grace, the Lord Jesus called me to serve Him, in the very same church building I had vandalized in my youth!

God's ways are totally the opposite of the world's ways. When He needed a spokesman to deliver Israel from more than 400 years of slavery, the Lord chose a stuttering murderer named Moses. When God had heard enough of Goliath's blasphemies, instead of sending a regiment of trained soldiers to take out the giant, He chose a skinny teenage boy, armed only with a slingshot and a steadfast faith. After Israel had waited centuries for a mighty warrior to wipe their enemies from the face of the earth, God chose to frustrate their expectations by sending a helpless baby, born to an unmarried mother. Can you fathom God's incredible wisdom and matchless humility? His beloved Son left heaven to be born in the open air, surrounded by the stench of camel and donkey excrement. No wonder the Jews failed to recognize Him.

Throughout history the Lord has chosen no-hopers just like me. Religious people are often offended by God's choices, and they sometimes need to overcome feelings of resentment and envy when they see the Spirit of God call people who are less qualified and talented than themselves.

Why does the King of kings and Lord of lords often choose such lowly people to serve Him, going against the grain of everything the world considers valuable – such as upbringing, education, and social standing?

Perhaps part of the answer is simply because God loves to shock those who think they have Him all figured out. The Bible explains it this way:

> God chose the foolish things of the world to shame the wise;
> God chose the weak things of the world to shame the strong.
> God chose the lowly things of this world and the despised things – and the things that are not – to nullify the things that are, so that no one may boast before him.
>
> **1 Corinthians 1:27–29**

CHAPTER 9
A DONKEY FOR JESUS

> If by excessive labor we die before reaching the average age of man, worn out in the Master's service, then glory be to God. We shall have so much less of earth and so much more of heaven. It is our duty and our privilege to exhaust our lives for Jesus. We are not to be living specimens of men in fine preservation, but living sacrifices, whose lot is to be consumed.
>
> **Charles Spurgeon**

On 5 April 1988, I boarded the long flight from Sydney to Hong Kong – my first ever trip to Asia. All my worldly possessions fitted into my backpack. I commenced my missionary career with my Bible, my camera, a few spare clothes, and $50 cash.

After landing, I stepped out into the suffocating heat and humidity of Hong Kong and hailed a taxi to the headquarters of the ministry whose details I had been given in New Zealand. As the red taxi wound its way through the overcrowded streets of Kowloon – crammed with trucks, taxis, bicycles, and pedestrians – a deep sense of peace and belonging overwhelmed my heart. I couldn't speak a word of Chinese, yet somehow the sights, sounds, and smells all gave me a feeling of contentment. I immediately felt at home in Asia. The same feelings remain nearly three decades later.

I had arrived in one of the most expensive cities in the world with very little money, no church support, and just an address and phone number scribbled on a piece of paper. I was not afraid, however, because Jesus was with me and had promised to never leave me nor forsake me.

I located the Bible ministry office and a worker helped me catch a train to the place where I would be staying, in an outer area of Hong Kong near the Chinese border. There, several guest houses were used both as places to pack bags of Bibles and also as dormitories for couriers to sleep. Long-term workers could rent a bed for US$100 per month. I didn't have $100, but I wasn't anxious as I remembered how the Lord had promised to provide for all my needs as I put His kingdom first.

After a good night's sleep, I was glad to discover free packets of instant noodles in the kitchen. Though not the healthiest or most nutritious food, I was thankful for the noodles and Chinese tea that was to provide my nourishment as I hauled heavy suitcases and bags of Bibles across the border into China.

The ministry instructed me to go downtown and apply for a three-month multiple-entry Chinese visa. It would allow me to make as many trips as possible into China over the six-week period I was scheduled to be in Hong Kong.

I soon encountered a problem at the visa office. That special visa was only available to businessmen, and I didn't look the part. I was a nineteen-year-old dressed in my best T-shirt, casual trousers and trusty old sneakers – the only pair of shoes I owned. The official looked at me with disdain and told me to come back the following day.

That night I was deeply troubled. I felt sure my visa application would be rejected and I wouldn't be able to go to China after all. I fell to my knees and prayed fervently, pouring out my heart to the Lord and reminding Him that I just wanted to be a donkey for Jesus. My fears were replaced with faith when I read this Scripture: "I am the Lord, the God of all mankind. Is anything too hard for me?" (Jeremiah 32:27). The Holy Spirit gently assured me, "Don't worry. You will be here much longer than you expect."

The next day I made my way downtown again to learn the result of my visa application. While I waited, the official went to a back room to collect my passport. After a few minutes he approached the front desk, holding my passport open and shaking his head. As the official motioned me to come forward, he said, "I'm very sorry!" My heart sank, but before I had a chance to respond, he added, "You applied for a three-month visa but we gave you a six-month visa by mistake!"

The workers at the Bible ministry were amazed when I showed them my passport. They had never seen a Chinese six-month multiple-entry visa before. That kind of visa was issued in later years, but apparently in 1988 it didn't yet exist!

This incident caused my faith to grow, and I realized I had been anxious for no reason. God was in complete control, and clearly nothing was too hard for Him.

For my first ever trip to China, I was included on a small team of Bible couriers who caught a hover-ferry from Hong Kong to the port city of Shekou in Communist China. It wasn't a long journey, but each minute was nerve-wracking as we skimmed across the South China Sea. I had packed two heavy bags with fifty Chinese Bibles in each, while my team members had adopted a much more conservative approach, carrying just ten to fifteen Bibles each. I figured that if I had come all the way from the bottom of the world to Asia, and the Chinese Christians were so desperate for God's Word, then I should try to carry as many Bibles as possible.

My heart raced as our vessel pulled into the dock and I took my first steps inside the world's most populated country. I filled out a customs form, took a deep breath, and walked undetected past the X-ray scanner with my load of contraband Bibles. I was overcome with relief and exhilaration!

We made our way to a local "safe house," where the Bibles were repacked before being transported deeper into the country to hungry Christians who were crying out for God to fill them with the Bread of Life.

Mainland China was a wonderful place to be in the 1980s. After decades of being cut off from the rest of the world, both old and young alike possessed an unspoilt innocence that I had not seen before, and which was starkly different from the materialistic hardness of people just a short distance away in Hong Kong.

***

Strangely, in some parts of the Body of Christ today, "work" has become a dirty four-letter word. Men and women in the Bible knew what it meant to work hard for Jesus. Paul wrote, "I strenuously contend with all the energy Christ so powerfully works in me" (Colossians 1:29). In the letter to the Romans, three women are mentioned who "worked very hard in the Lord" (Romans 16:12). The Greek word used in that verse implies that they toiled to the point of exhaustion.

One evening at the Bible courier guest house I met a long-term missionary who encouraged me to work hard as I followed the Lord. A plumber by trade, he shared how strange he had found it when he had first arrived in Asia. Many missionaries labored hard for the Lord, but others treated the mission field like an extended holiday, shopping and sightseeing as much as possible and serving God when it suited them.

I will never forget the missionary's words of wisdom to me: "Paul, people in the world work hard at least forty hours per week. Those of us privileged to serve in the kingdom of God should do at least that much work for Jesus. We need balance and rest, but the world is going to hell! Don't sit around watching. Get busy in His harvest field, for the Bible says, 'He who gathers crops in summer is a prudent son, but he who sleeps during harvest is a disgraceful son' (Proverbs 10:5)."

After my first successful trip to China, I was eager to cross the border as often as possible. My motive for working hard wasn't to try to *earn* salvation. Jesus had already taken care of that. Rather, my desire to serve God flowed *from* His salvation. I longed for as many people to know my awesome Savior as possible.

I reminded the ministry leaders that the Lord had given me a multiple-entry visa that nobody else had, so I wanted to make the most of my time and carry as many Bibles as possible. They gave me permission to go to China as frequently as I wanted, except on Sundays. The ministry also paid for the cost of the Bibles and all my travel expenses into China and back. Without their extraordinary generosity, I would have only been able to make one or two trips before my resources ran out.

Six days per week I made trips from Hong Kong into China, using a variety of border crossings. Each time I was loaded down with a large number of Bibles. I met many wonderful believers who had also come to be donkeys for Jesus, and I learned much from their faith and way of life. A godly Asian brother named Richard told me I should pray over the Bibles as I packed them, rather than just operating in my own strength. He explained how the Lord wanted to be involved with every part of our work, and that without the blessing of the Holy Spirit all our labor was in vain. After that, I always bowed my head and prayed while loading up for the day. One of my main prayers was, "Heavenly Father, please blind the eyes of the border guards as we carry Your Word into China today. Please allow us to pass through undetected."

On countless occasions we experienced miraculous answers to prayer as we approached the Chinese X-ray scanners. Border guards who were staring intently at their monitors often became distracted at the precise moment our luggage went through. Once, the guard nodded off to sleep as my bags passed him, and when he awoke a few seconds later I was already on my way out the door! On another occasion, an insect pestered a guard as my bags – packed so tightly with Bibles that they looked like rectangular blocks of concrete – passed through the scanner. As the man wildly waved his arms trying to shoo the insect away, I calmly collected my bags and made my way out of the building and into the streets of China.

These were wonderfully exciting days. I felt as though I had found the reason for my existence. I was privileged to witness the Lord Jesus act powerfully on behalf of His hungry children in China. Seeing Him at work caused my faith to grow and helped me to appreciate what an awesome God I served.

Christians from around the world were constantly arriving in Hong Kong to join the Bible smuggling efforts. Some came for just a few days while others stayed for weeks or months. All were united in our desire to provide God's Word to the house churches of China. After a few weeks of being a part of teams crossing the border, the ministry decided I had gained enough experience to become a team leader.

Apart from the frequent border crossings, my favorite times were when I was able to listen to stories from long-term workers who had traveled deep into China's interior, where they had witnessed the great revival that was sweeping thousands of people into the kingdom of God every day. I sat spellbound as I listened to one report from the mountains of southwest China. A Chinese missionary had visited a remote valley where there was rumored to be a small number of churches. After two days of hiking through the mountains, he came across a distraught man on the trail. The man looked as if he hadn't slept for days and was mumbling to himself. Alarmed, the missionary asked the man what was wrong and if he could help. The deeply agitated man said, "I recently became a Christian, but I am lost and going to hell. I have not heard the audible voice of Jesus, and today is the third day since I became a Christian. I am on my way to throw myself off a cliff at the top of the mountain."

The missionary calmed the man down and asked to be taken to his village so he could hopefully get to the root of the problem. After meeting the rest of the Christians in that valley, the missionary discovered that none of them had ever seen a complete Bible. Instead, they had somehow obtained a single page of the Scriptures, which was all they had on which to base their faith. That one page was from the Book of Acts, when Saul was thrown to the ground and heard the audible voice of Jesus ask him, "Saul, Saul, why do you persecute me?" (Acts 9:4). Because they only knew this tiny slither of God's Word, the villagers assumed that all true Christians must have the same experience as Saul. The missionary remained in the valley and taught the believers for several days. Complete Bibles were later carried in to help them gain a more rounded knowledge of the faith.

This story and others like it added fuel to the flame burning brightly in my heart. I understood the vital urgency of getting Bibles to the millions of Chinese Christians deprived of God's Word.

There was no guarantee that the window of opportunity for providing Bibles would remain open for long, so I was determined to help as much as possible. I developed a daily routine. I would lead a team across the Chinese border in the morning, then return to Hong Kong to reload and make another trip with Bibles in the afternoon. I would then eat my dinner of instant noodles and whatever other food was available at the guest house, and if I had any energy left I would let the other couriers know I was heading into China one more time before the border closed for the night. I told my colleagues not to wait up for me, but if they were to notice that I wasn't in bed by midnight then something had probably gone wrong.

I used my strong frame to haul a lot of Bibles into China. My typical load consisted of a large suitcase packed with more than 100 Bibles, and two canvas bags stuffed with another fifty or sixty Bibles each, which were fastened to a small metal trolley by several bungee cords. In total, I carried around 200 Bibles each time I went to China, weighing approximately 100 kg (220 pounds).

It was hard work, especially during the day when the intense heat and stifling humidity meant that sweat poured off me like water from a tap. I looked forward to returning to the Hong Kong guest house after each trip, where I would peel off my saturated, sweat-stained clothing and enjoy a refreshing cold shower.

On a number of occasions the metal trolleys I used to haul my bags collapsed under the weight of the Bibles. The frames would be bent out of shape and the wheels would fall apart. On one of my evening trips into China the trolley gave out, as did the tiny plastic wheels on my suitcase. I found myself stuck at the border with more than 200 Bibles and no way to haul them into China except by sheer determination. I strapped one of the bags around my left shoulder, another around my right shoulder, and I dragged the massive suitcase along the train platform into the customs building.

I strained with every muscle in my body. If one more Bible had been added to my load I would probably have collapsed on the ground. The straps from the bags around my shoulders dug in deeply as I inched my way forward, hoping to get across the border before it closed for the night. The pain was excruciating, but the Christians in China needed God's Word, so I struggled forward with every ounce of energy I could muster. I saw that the guards were closing down for the night and had already turned off their X-ray machines! Thankfully, I hobbled through with my full load of more than 200 Bibles. When I got outside the building into the night air I let out a muffled, "Hallelujah!"

After delivering my Bibles to the safe house I made my way back to Hong Kong. I had pushed myself too hard, and my right knee had buckled from the heavy load. I staggered onto the train in severe pain, and a short time later was back in the Bible courier guest house, where the lights had been turned off and everyone was asleep.

I peeled off my drenched clothes and hurled them into the overused washing machine. As I showered, I glanced into the bathroom mirror and saw that the bag straps had dug in so deeply that the blood vessels in my shoulders had ruptured. All these years later the scars from that night are still visible.

The next morning I was scarcely able to sit up in my bunk bed because of my injured knee. I don't know if I had shredded my ligaments, cartilage, or what, but my knee was completely wrecked and unable to support my body weight.

I called out for help, and one of the long-term couriers, a young Texan named Mark, asked what the problem was. I explained that I had injured my knee the previous night. Mark asked if he could pray for me. "Dear Lord," he said, "thank You for Your healing power. Please touch Paul's body so that he can continue to serve and bring glory to You. In Jesus' mighty Name, Amen!"

The moment Mark laid his hand on my knee it felt as if a jolt of electricity entered my body. A supernatural power surged through me. After a few minutes, Mark encouraged me to stand up and test my knee. I did so, and experienced no discomfort at all. I walked around the house and even jumped up and down. I was completely pain free!

I resumed my trips into China the following day, but I used a little more wisdom and was careful not to push my body beyond what it could bear. I still worked hard, but recognized that if I was more balanced I would be able to last longer and be a more effective weapon in the hand of God. I often prayed these words of Moses: "Teach us to number our days, that we may gain a heart of wisdom" (Psalm 90:12).

CHAPTER 10

MANNA FROM HEAVEN

God's work, done God's way, will never lack God's supply.

J. Hudson Taylor

For teams to successfully carry thousands of Bibles into China, constant supernatural intervention was required, and the Lord performed many miracles. As a relatively new believer, these precious experiences created a tremendous environment for my faith to grow, and they established a foundation for serving Jesus Christ for many years to come.

On one occasion I led a Bible team to the border, and most of my team members made it through successfully. One lady, on her first ever trip to China, was in line ahead of me and I looked on as she had run into trouble. The X-ray scanner had detected her Bibles and the guard was confiscating them. This sister had traveled all the way from the other side of the world to carry God's Word to the Chinese believers, so she was heartbroken at being caught. Sobbing uncontrollably, she begged the customs officer to let her through. "Please sir, God loves China. Your people need this book. Please let me take them in," she pleaded with tear-filled eyes.

The officer was so touched by her heartfelt request that he took her aside to a small booth, out of view of the other customs officials. He quietly told her to put the Bibles back into her bag and to carry on without telling anyone.

I was next in line with another heavy load of Bibles. The officer ordered me to carry my bag to the same booth that the sister had been in just moments before. "I know you have Bibles," he said. He then leaned forward and whispered, "Your friend said that God loves China and we need this book. I want to know why she cares so much that it made her cry hard when I took them away. Can I please have a book for my personal use? I want to take one home and study it for myself." I gladly handed the man a Bible and told him I would pray for God to reveal His truth to him.

Smuggling Bibles into China was a serious and intense task, but there were also plenty of times for laughter. There was a large box full of used clothing and other travel items at the ministry guest house where we packed our bags. Couriers were encouraged to place the old clothing, towels, shoes, and other items around the corners of the Bibles, to give the bags a more natural, rounded appearance rather than the "square libraries" someone told me my bags looked like.

I was running late one day. My team had already packed their Bibles and were waiting for me outside. After solidly filling two bags almost to capacity with Bibles, I quickly reached into the box and grabbed some of the used clothing to pad my bags.

When I reached the X-ray scanner at the Chinese border, the officer's eyes bulged when the outlines of more than 100 tightly packed Bibles appeared on his monitor. "You have Bibles!" he scowled. "Put your bags on this table."

He unzipped the first of my two bags and a confused look appeared on his face. In my haste to pack that morning, I had inadvertently stuffed my bags with a collection of women's underwear and clothing! The man reached inside my bag and pulled out a bra and other items. In my second bag he discovered more women's items, including a pair of high heeled shoes! With a look of disgust, the officer closed my bags and motioned for me to leave. I continued into China with all 100 of the Bibles. In the following weeks I received many requests to retell the story to other Bible couriers. Some laughed so hard that their sides ached!

I had arrived in Hong Kong with only $50 spending money, and no source of income, church support, or newsletter list. My funds soon dried up and I was penniless. The Bible ministry charged $100 per month for long-term couriers to stay at their guest house, and my first rent payment was fast approaching. I cried out to God. If He didn't help me, I would be in trouble.

Leading the teams into China each day was a great blessing, but I found one thing extremely difficult. After delivering the Bibles, the teams invariably wanted to eat a large meal together to celebrate their success. They always invited me, unaware that I had no money to pay my share. I didn't want to look like a beggar or display an attitude that would spoil their enjoyment, so I often told them I was skipping a meal that day. They assumed I was fasting and went on to the restaurant without me. I did feel a little envious when they caught up with me later and told me of the huge pizzas or Chinese feast they had enjoyed. I bit my lip and kept the fact that I was financially destitute a secret between the Lord Jesus and me, and remembered how God's Word promised that if I sought first His kingdom and righteousness, He would take care of my needs.

Before leaving Australia I had given a Hong Kong postal address to several friends at the church. My address was care of the central post office on Hong Kong Island, a short ferry trip across the harbor from Kowloon where the Bible ministry was located.

One afternoon I went to the post office and was thrilled to discover three letters waiting for me. I took them to the side and opened them. Two were encouraging letters from people saying they were praying for me. The third was a card from a Palestinian lady who had become a Christian at the same time as I had. We had attended a class for new believers together. Her card was folded and sealed with tape, and when I opened it, a crisp $50 bill fell out. I felt like shouting for joy! It was the first donation I ever received on the mission field. Incredibly, as I write this almost thirty years later, she is still a regular supporter of our work.

The money was a great blessing, and enabled me to supplement my normal diet of instant noodles and tea with some fruit and vegetables from the local market.

A short time later that money ran out and I only had two Hong Kong dollars (worth about twenty-five US cents) left in the world. Encouraged that my previous trip to the post office had yielded three letters and $50, I made my way to the ferry terminal again, confident that God would have moved in the hearts of other people to help me. I used one of my two remaining dollars for the ferry trip across the harbor and confidently strode into the post office. I gave my name to the clerk and asked for my mail. She checked a box marked "H" and said, "I'm sorry, there's nothing for you."

I was bewildered. "Excuse me, are you sure?" I enquired. "Perhaps you misunderstood how to spell my family name. It's H-A-T-T…"

"Sorry, nothing for you!" she snapped back.

I walked away from the post office feeling devastated. Had God forgotten me? I remembered the Scripture that said He would never leave me nor forsake me, but I was down to my last Hong Kong dollar, and I had to use it to get the ferry back across the harbor. To make matters worse, my rent was due and I had to pay US$100 to the Bible ministry the following day.

For a few minutes I stood near the entrance of the post office, feeling stunned and confused. Living by faith was turning out to be a lot more difficult than I had expected. I boarded the crowded ferry, and minutes later the gangplank was lowered on the Kowloon side of the harbor and I disembarked. I couldn't believe my journey to the post office had failed to yield even a single letter.

Stupefied with anxiety, I began to question everything that had happened in the previous month. Perhaps God hadn't called me to carry Bibles to China after all? Maybe the whole trip had just been an idea in my head and I should have heeded the pastor's advice and not tried to run before I could walk. I felt stupid and embarrassed. Why did I think the Living God would want to send *me* to do His work, when there were millions of Christians in the world much better equipped?

Feeling down in the dumps, I made my way on foot to the bustling Nathan Road. While I waited for the traffic signal to change so I could cross the intersection, I noticed a man motioning to me from the other side of the road. He appeared to be from the Indian subcontinent, but I didn't know him or why he was trying to get my attention.

The light changed and I made my way across. The man walked straight up to me and put his hand out to shake mine.

"Do I know you?" I asked.

"I want to give you this," he replied, and he slipped a piece of paper into my open hand. I looked down to discover he had given me US$100 cash!

I couldn't believe it! As a throng of people rushed by, I tried to get more information about my mystery benefactor. "Where are you from?" I called out.

"Bangladesh," he replied, as he walked away like a man content to have successfully carried out a task.

The day had been an emotional roller coaster. Now as I made my way home I felt over the moon. How silly I had been to doubt the Lord Jesus Christ. He was patiently teaching me to trust and obey. Seeing that I was a spiritual infant and vexed with worries, the Lord took me by the hand and lovingly showed that He was in total control and would never let me down.

I would experience countless instances of God's miraculous provision in later years, but few were as dramatic as the day He moved in the heart of a man from Bangladesh – a Muslim country and one of the poorest nations on earth. If my heavenly Father could provide for me in such a way, then truly nothing was too difficult for Him. I came to understand, deep in my heart, that Jesus would never fail me. Thankfully, serving God wasn't dependent on my ability to figure things out. Indeed, the Bible says, "If we are faithless, he remains faithful, for he cannot disown himself" (2 Timothy 2:13).

The next day I paid my rent on time, and over the following weeks I received more gifts in the mail at just the right time to meet my obligations. The Lord rarely provided my needs early, but He was never late.

Six weeks soon passed after my arrival in Asia, and my ticket back to Australia was about to expire. I didn't know whether I should stay or leave, so I spoke with some of the long-term missionaries, explaining my predicament that if I failed to return to Australia on the specified date my ticket would be voided and I would be stuck in Hong Kong with no way out. After praying with me, they believed that God had more work for me to do and wanted me to remain in Asia, so I let my ticket expire.

Meanwhile, I heard that I was causing a stir among the church leadership back in Australia. My friend Darren, who had led me to the Lord, wrote to inform me that when I first went to Asia the pastor had used me as a sermon illustration. He told the congregation, "It's a shame when Christians chase fantasies like that young man Paul who just went off to China by himself."

A few months passed, and the pastor heard good reports of how God was using me to lead numerous teams into China with Bibles, and that I was experiencing God's supernatural provision. Darren said the pastor again used me as a sermon illustration, but this time he told the church, "We need to trust the Lord and step out in faith like that young man Paul who went to serve God in China!"

I laughed out loud and thanked the Lord Jesus when I read Darren's letter. Although my home church never financially supported me, it encouraged me to learn that the pastor now recognized that I had a legitimate call to the mission field. Because of my personal experiences, I decided I would never stand in the way of any Christian who stepped out in faith to obey God's call on their life. I believe the Lord would rather His children attempt things for Him and fail than to never take a risk for His kingdom.

CHAPTER 11
DETOUR

As the weeks passed, I was invited to join teams that moved large quantities of Bibles from the border regions to deep inside China. There, for years or even decades, millions of house church Christians had been praying and waiting to receive God's Word. At the time, many fellowships had just one or two old tattered Bibles among 100 or more believers. Many Christians had never even seen a Bible.

I was privileged to be part of a team of ten people that transported forty heavy bags of Bibles by train all the way to Kunming in southwest China – a journey of fifty-four hours in "hard sleeper" class. In total, the forty bags weighed almost a ton. Sweat poured off us as we passed each bag through the train windows and stacked them along the overhead baggage racks in our carriage.

The local house church leaders in Kunming were expecting us, but they had no idea of the large number of Bibles we had brought. They came to our hotel on bicycles, expecting to collect a few bags. They were shocked and amazed when they saw the forty heavy bags stacked against the wall in our room. They dropped to their knees and raised their hands toward heaven. With tears streaming down their cheeks, they gave thanks to the Lord Jesus for every Bible, and for every person involved with donating, printing, and transporting the precious cargo.

Two of the church leaders were so overcome with emotion they spread themselves out over the bags and wept uncontrollably. They cried out, "Dear Lord, thank You! You did not forget us! Many times we felt abandoned, but today we know You have not forgotten Your children in China! May each Bible reach the hands of Your servant who needs it the most, and may each one reap a great harvest throughout our province!"

After all the Bibles had been safely passed on, our team had some spare time, so we visited the Stone Forest – a famous tourist attraction and the center of the Sani tribe. The Sani were the very first ethnic minority group I ever encountered in China, and I was fascinated by their culture and colorful clothing. Before that day, I had presumed China to be full of typical Han Chinese people, and it never crossed my mind that it was also home to numerous distinct people groups with their own history, customs, and languages. This initial experience with the Sani proved to be the start of a long, personal journey of discovering and reaching Asia's ethnic groups – a journey that continues to this day.

A short time later we commenced another marathon fifty-four-hour train journey back to Hong Kong. Our mission had been completed successfully, and our hearts were overwhelmed with love and joy, both for God and for our persecuted brothers and sisters.

After a short rest I joined a similar team to deliver a huge load of Bibles to the capital city of Beijing, which at the time was a forty-hour train journey from south China.

The Apostle Paul said about the churches in Macedonia, "In the midst of a very severe trial, their overflowing joy and their extreme poverty welled up in rich generosity" (2 Corinthians 8:2). Likewise, many of the Chinese believers I met had spent years being arrested, tortured, and imprisoned, yet their faces shone with unbridled joy. They possessed little, yet they were willing to give everything they had to God. In some house church meetings, when large rice sacks were sent around the congregation to collect the offering, some believers were upset that they had no money to give to God's work. Instead, when the sack reached them they stepped inside it, literally offering their whole lives to Jesus.

I knew it was a great privilege to fellowship with house church leaders on those long trips. Many Bible couriers from around the world had sacrificed much to carry God's Word into China, but few ever had the opportunity to meet the recipients of their efforts. I learned that the intensity of the Chinese revival was directly linked to the level of persecution the Church was experiencing. This has always been the case with the people of God. When the Israelites were enslaved in Egypt, the Bible tells us, "The more they were oppressed, the more they multiplied and spread; so the Egyptians came to dread the Israelites" (Exodus 1:12).

Looking back, I believe the need for Bibles in China was so acute in the 1980s that if the Body of Christ had failed to unite to provide God's Word, the state of Christianity in China would be markedly different from what it is today. Each Bible was like placing a log on the revival fires blazing throughout the country. When the final page of Church history is written, the forty-year revival in China may go down as numerically the greatest revival in history.

I didn't realize it at the time, but these glorious experiences in 1988 were just the beginning of my long participation in providing Bibles to the house churches of China – an involvement which started by simply being a "donkey for Jesus," but which grew to a level I never imagined possible.

Each trip into the interior of China gave me a deeper love and respect for the Church in the world's most populated country. I was also blessed to work with many wonderful Christians from around the world who came to carry Bibles. I learned much from them, and grew to appreciate the rich diversity in the Body of Christ. I collected the names and addresses of those who wanted to stay in touch, and before long I had compiled a small list of people who requested to receive news from me so they could pray. This led me to write my first ever newsletter, which was produced on a typewriter and photocopied on a single page. Some of the recipients sensed the Holy Spirit prompting them to send a donation, and a ministry was born.

***

I originally arrived in Asia with just $50 in my pocket and a six-week return ticket, but God had sustained me by a series of providential miracles. He somehow stretched my initial $50 so that so far I had made fifty-two separate trips into China and helped to move thousands of Bibles to many provinces throughout the country.

I so loved serving God in China that once when a team member asked how long I planned to remain in Asia, I quipped, "I plan to stay here for the rest of my life, and then for a thousand years during the Millennium!" My heavenly Father had other plans, however, and after six extraordinary months in Hong Kong and China, the pillar of God's fire began to move on in my life. Although I loved the Bible and read it every day, it was becoming apparent both to me and to other missionaries that a season of intensive study of God's Word would greatly benefit me and prepare my life for future service.

One day an American woman was discussing the Bible with me when she asked, "Do you know the story of the valley of dry bones in Ezekiel 37?"

When I replied, "I'm sorry, I haven't read that book yet," a look of horror and disgust came over her face. She couldn't believe that someone on the mission field was unfamiliar with an entire book of the Bible. I explained how God had called me to China as a new believer just a few months old in the faith, but she was unimpressed and encouraged me to find a Bible School so I could better understand God's Word. I was initially reluctant to accept her advice. After all, I wanted to spend the rest of my life in Asia, and I felt it was where I belonged.

As I wrestled with finding God's will for my life, I read, "My thoughts are not your thoughts, neither are your ways my ways … As the heavens are higher than the earth, so are my ways higher than your ways and my thoughts than your thoughts" (Isaiah 55:8–9). Deep down I knew that if Jesus was truly my Lord, then I had to submit to His guidance and not just do what I wanted to do. I rededicated myself to my heavenly Father and told Him I would go wherever He directed me.

The initial six months I spent on the mission field was a special time in my life. I saw the miraculous hand of God in many different situations, and I witnessed Christianity up close at its very best – the Chinese underground Church in the midst of a powerful, heaven-sent revival.

I later realized that the unconventional way I began my Christian service was a precious blessing from God, but He never intended it to be a template for others to follow. Now, my loving Father wanted me to spend time sitting at His feet to be strengthened by His Word. It felt as if I had reached the limit of my usefulness in Asia at that time. I had much zeal for God, but I didn't want to lack the character and integrity God requires of His children, lest I bring shame to the Name of Jesus by being the kind of person described in the Scriptures: "It is not good to have zeal without knowledge, nor to be hasty and miss the way" (Proverbs 19:2, NIV 1984).

I was informed that my church in Australia had just established a small Bible School and offered one- and two-year courses. I decided to apply in time for the new school year which would commence a few months later. I was now confident that God wanted me to return to Australia, but I had a major problem. I was stuck in Hong Kong without a valid return ticket. My original Cathay Pacific ticket had expired several months earlier, and I clearly remembered the "non-refundable and non-transferable" conditions attached to it.

I did some research and was shocked to discover that the cost of a one-way fare from Hong Kong to Australia was actually higher than a round-trip ticket. Just to get back to Australia was going to cost around $1,000. To my mind, this was an insurmountable amount. My faith wasn't yet strong enough to believe God for such a huge need. He had provided every time I needed funds, but I never had a surplus of more than about $50. Now, I was stuck halfway around the world with neither a valid ticket home nor the money to purchase one.

One morning I found myself alone in the Bible courier guest house. Feeling overwhelmed and perplexed about what to do, I took my problem to the Lord. I knelt down on the living room floor and prayed, "Dear Lord Jesus, I believe You are leading me to attend Bible School in Australia. I'm willing to go back, but as You know, I don't have a ticket and it costs a lot of money to buy one. You told me not to mention my needs to anyone except You, so if You want me to leave Asia, I'm going to need a great miracle. I entrust myself into Your loving hands."

For the next ten minutes I sat down and contemplated what to do next. I still had the expired ticket I had used to travel to Hong Kong, so with no better idea in mind, I got the ticket out and phoned the Cathay Pacific head office in Hong Kong. A lady asked how she could help, and I replied, "My name is Paul Hattaway, and I would like to confirm my return flight from Hong Kong to Sydney, please."

She asked me to spell my name, but couldn't locate my booking in the system. She requested my ticket number, and after a few minutes she said, "I'm sorry, sir, but the ticket you purchased is non-refundable and non-transferable. It has expired and you can no longer use it. Please throw it away. If you wish to travel with our airline you will need to buy a new ticket."

I slumped down on the couch. I had tried my last option but it had predictably failed. Feeling defeated, I began to pray again, crying out to the Living God and asking Him to grant His favor and to help my desperate situation. Then something strange occurred, which I struggle to adequately describe in words.

All of a sudden, like a bolt of lightning, I *knew* God had answered my prayer. I can't properly describe the overwhelming sense I had. My whole being was energized, and I was absolutely certain – without a shadow of doubt – that something powerful had just taken place in the spiritual realm. It was a supernatural grace quite apart from me. I wonder if I had experienced what the Bible calls the gift of faith (1 Corinthians 12:9).

I fumbled nervously as I again dialed the Cathay Pacific office. A different assistant answered and I said, "Hello, my name is Paul Hattaway. I would like to confirm my return flight from Hong Kong to Sydney, please."

A minute or two passed and I could hear the sound of the lady tapping on her keyboard. Then she said, "Mr Hattaway, thank you for waiting. Your flight is confirmed for next Tuesday."

Once again I was awestruck by the greatness of my heavenly Father. He had just provided a free flight for me back to Australia.

I couldn't wait to tell my missionary friends what had happened when they returned later that day. I excitedly shared how the Lord had provided a free ticket to Australia for me, but some of them thought I was making it up. One lady who had worked as a travel agent asked to inspect my ticket. She confirmed to the others that I had a "dead ticket" which had already expired and could not be renewed under any circumstances.

Some of the missionaries were certain I wouldn't be allowed to board the plane. Their doubts rubbed off on me, and on the departure day I asked a friend to accompany me to the airport just in case they refused to let me board. The check-in was hassle free, however, and I was soon leaning back in my seat as the plane ascended above the South China Sea on the start of my nine-hour flight to Sydney.

Perhaps because of the skepticism of the other missionaries when I told them the story, I bottled up this testimony and have only shared it on a few occasions in all the years since. Somehow, God had provided a free international flight for me! I don't understand exactly how He did it, but what I do know is that the next morning my plane touched down in Sydney and I was back on Australian soil, ready to begin the next stage of my journey with Jesus.

CHAPTER 12
TADPOLES

No one has the right to hear the gospel twice, while there remains someone who has not heard it once.

Oswald J. Smith

My friend Darren picked me up from Sydney Airport in his trusty van. Although during the following weeks I faithfully attended church meetings, I felt like a fish out of water. The six months I had spent in China seemed like a lifetime to me. While I had been radically transformed and each day had been an exciting adventure with Jesus, not much had changed in Australia during that time. I felt that I no longer fitted into the local church culture.

When I was asked to share my China experiences with the youth group, it was as if I was speaking a foreign language. My exciting stories of Bible smuggling, miracles, persecution, and revival were met with yawns and sighs. I realized there was little point sharing my testimonies with people who couldn't appreciate them, so I drew back and decided that my wonderful experiences with the Lord Jesus during my fifty-two trips to China would have to remain a special memory between me and Him.

A woman in the church who had served on the mission field wisely assured me that my struggles were common among returning missionaries. She helped me to understand that Christians from different cultures are at various stages of development, and I shouldn't expect believers in easy-going Australia to appreciate the spiritual dynamics of the Chinese Church after decades of persecution. Her advice helped me greatly, and I asked the Lord to enable me to see the Australian Church through His eyes of grace and love.

I was informed about a room for rent in an old farmhouse occupied by three Christian guys in a rural area outside Sydney. It was to be my home for the foreseeable future. Two of my three housemates were also enrolled to study at the Bible College with me.

I needed to find a job quickly, as my funds were once again exhausted and rent was due. There was no public transportation in the area, so I also needed a vehicle in order to find work. I reckoned that if Jesus was truly Lord of all, then He was just as capable of performing miracles in the Western world as anywhere else. I prayed, "Heavenly Father, I really need a job soon, but first I need a car. I don't have any money left, and You told me not to ask anyone but You to meet my needs. I therefore request Your help. I humbly ask, if it's Your will, please give me a car for free."

One of my housemates was an intelligent man in his late thirties named Peter, who later became a brain surgeon. When he arrived home that evening he asked how my job search had gone. When I told him I had asked God to provide me a car for free, Peter delivered a stinging rebuke. "Get off your backside, you lazy bum!" he scolded. "God doesn't work like that! Go and find a job and work hard, and after a while you'll have enough money saved up to buy a car."

I tried to explain how I had used all my money serving God in Asia, and that I first needed a vehicle in order to secure a job. Peter didn't want to hear it, and was disgusted by what he considered to be my misguided faith.

The next Sunday morning I caught a ride to church. After the service, while I was standing at the back of the auditorium wondering what to do with the rest of my day, a young man I had never met came up and spoke with me. He introduced himself and asked what my plans were for that afternoon. When I told him I didn't have any plans, he thrust a motorcycle helmet into my hand and said, "Listen, bro. I need you to do something for me. Can you take this helmet to a friend of mine? His name is Tim and he lives a couple of miles from here. I'd really appreciate it if you could do that for me." He scribbled Tim's address and a hand-drawn map on a piece of paper and left.

I didn't know what to think of this strange request. It was an extremely hot day, and I didn't particularly feel like walking a few miles in the heat to give a helmet to someone I'd never met. With no alternative plans, however, I started the long walk to the mysterious Tim's house, with the helmet in my hand. Sweat poured off me as I walked in the blazing sun, and I finally reached the correct street. As I approached the property, I saw a tall, skinny young man working on his blue Renault car. "Hi, is your name Tim?" I asked.

"Yeah, that's me. What do you want?"

I explained how a guy had asked me to drop off the helmet.

"Oh, thanks mate!" he said. "I really appreciate it."

Tim asked me where I was going. I told him, "To be honest, I don't know. I just wanted to bring the helmet to you."

He continued working on his car.

"Mechanical problems?" I asked.

"Yeah, I'm sick of this thing," he responded. He then glanced up from beneath the raised hood and asked, "Do you want it? It's all yours if you're interested."

We went inside Tim's home and, after signing the appropriate forms, he handed me the keys. "All the best," Tim called out as I drove away. "And thanks for bringing my helmet!"

I drove my blue Renault into the farmhouse driveway and gave a blast on the horn as I pulled up. Peter came out to see what the commotion was.

"I just wanted to show you my new car," I calmly stated. "Isn't God wonderful? A guy just gave it to me for nothing."

Peter's complexion changed suddenly, as if all the blood had just drained from his face. To his credit, he humbled himself and apologized for his harsh rebuke the previous night. For weeks, each time I came home in my car, Peter shook his head in disbelief and muttered, "Amazing. Absolutely amazing."

The Lord Jesus had once again shown His wonderful power to me. His provision and grace weren't limited to believers in countries like China. He would take care of me and provide the resources I needed to follow Him, even in Australia.

I picked up a succession of temporary jobs that summer. I worked as a handyman, laid turf outside a new housing complex, labored long hours manufacturing pre-baked pizzas, picked fruit, and drove a forklift.

Before long, the new school year arrived and I turned up for my first day at Bible College. I enrolled to do the one-year course, along with a diverse group of thirty students. The months went by quickly, and as Charles Dickens once famously wrote, "It was the best of times; it was the worst of times."

On the one hand I greatly benefited from having a concentrated time set aside to study the Bible, and I gained a greater knowledge of God's Word. Up to that point I had treated the Scriptures like a man at a sumptuous multicourse banquet who nibbles on a few tasty entrées before heading to the dessert table for a bowl of ice cream. I had a surface knowledge of the Scriptures and had learned certain verses and passages that encouraged me, but I was becoming a spiritually malnourished Christian. I needed to feast on the meat of God's Word, for the Bible says, "Solid food is for the mature, who by constant use have trained themselves to distinguish good from evil" (Hebrews 5:14).

Unfortunately, as the homework mounted, most of the students struggled with their spiritual lives. The amount of information going into our heads was far greater than our ability to process it. The British theologian John Stott once warned of the dangers of Christian tadpoles in the Church. Tadpoles, he explained, have huge heads but little else. I learned that while multitudes of Christians attend Bible Colleges and seminaries to better understand the Word of God, many forget that they must also cultivate an experiential relationship with the God of the Word. If we focus solely on gathering knowledge, our heads will expand while our hearts shrink.

My China experiences made me a misfit in the class. My entire focus was on being equipped so I could serve God in Asia, but worldwide missions barely rated a mention from the numerous lecturers. Instead, their overwhelming emphasis appeared to be to convince students that the highest attainable goal was to become a pastor in Australia. Everyone except me was sure God was going to bring a great end-time revival to Australia, so the students considered it folly to look any further afield than their own backyard.

I found many classes difficult to endure, as I knew the unreached peoples of the world were at the very center of God's heart and plans. In Australia, most Christians were sitting around waiting for the Second Coming of Christ, but my focus was on the billions of people in unreached nations still waiting to hear about His first coming.

In the classroom, much energy was spent debating which translation of the English Bible is best, but my heart was burdened for the countless millions of Asian Christians who had never seen a single page of the Bible.

* * *

To pay my bills, I obtained work as a gardener at a nearby Baptist School. Each afternoon I would park in the same spot near the school, then would stroll a short distance to a shed where my work supplies were stored. One of the houses I walked past was the home of a large, elderly man named Ed, who could usually be seen listening to the radio while reclining in a comfortable chair on his porch. We always exchanged friendly greetings as I walked past his house.

One day I thought I should get to know Ed better, in case he hadn't yet heard the gospel. When I saw him again the following day, I felt strongly compelled to speak with him about the Lord. I was running late for work, however, and decided I would have to postpone getting to know him until the next day.

I prayed when I got home that evening, asking the Holy Spirit to give me an opportunity to share Jesus Christ with Ed. I prayed that his heart would be receptive, and that he might believe the message of eternal life.

The following day was a Friday, and when Bible College finished I drove to work and parked in my customary spot. I was ready to share the gospel with Ed. I walked past his home, but that day he wasn't sitting in his chair as normal. I decided that when I saw him the following Monday I would definitely share my faith with him.

Ed wasn't home again that Monday, nor the next few days. I didn't know what to do, and just carried on with my work duties. At the end of the week I noticed a woman mowing the lawn outside Ed's home. I asked if she knew when he would return, as I had something I needed to share with him.

"Oh, I'm so sorry," she replied. "Ed passed away last week and we had his funeral yesterday. I'm just tidying up the property."

My heart was overwhelmed with grief. My opportunity to share Jesus Christ with this dear man was gone forever. On my drive home and throughout that night I wept bitterly. I recognized that I too had become like a tadpole. My head was full of Bible knowledge but my heart had grown sick. The Lord had placed the desire in my heart to share the gospel with Ed, but I was too wrapped up in my own needs to obey.

For days, all I could think about was God's warning to Ezekiel:

> "When I say to a wicked person, 'You will surely die,' and you do not warn them or speak out to dissuade them from their evil ways in order to save their life, that wicked person will die for their sin, and I will hold you accountable for their blood. But if you do warn the wicked person and they do not turn from their wickedness or from their evil ways, they will die for their sin; but you will have saved yourself."
>
> **Ezekiel 3:18–19**

Feeling condemned for my lack of obedience, I knelt beside my bed, confessed my sins, and cried out for God's mercy. Thanks to the precious blood of Jesus, I rose from my knees forgiven and cleansed, and determined to never again neglect a clear-cut opportunity to share the gospel with anyone the Holy Spirit has laid on my heart.

CHAPTER 13

CHANGING TRACK

> The principal danger of the 20th century will be: a religion without the Holy Spirit, Christians without Christ, forgiveness without repentance, salvation without regeneration, politics without God and a heaven without hell.
>
> **William Booth, 1899**

During my year at Bible College I was invited to speak at churches around Sydney and the State of New South Wales. The Lord made it clear that I was to fearlessly deliver whatever He told me to share, and not to tickle the ears of my audience by telling them what they wanted to hear. I often sensed the Holy Spirit flowing through me as I preached, filling my mind with the Scriptures and directing my words. The occasions when I was really in tune with the Lord always elicited a response from the congregation. People would be touched, challenged, or sometimes even angered by what I shared, but there was always a response.

One weekend I spoke at a church of about 150 believers in a rural town in the Australian outback, several hundred miles from Sydney. The long drive there afforded me an opportunity to pray fervently, and the Lord laid a challenging message on my heart for the Christians of that town. My text on Sunday morning was taken from Paul's letter to the Ephesians:

> For it is by grace you have been saved, through faith – and this is not from yourselves, it is the gift of God – not by works, so that no one can boast. For we are God's handiwork, created in Christ Jesus to do good works, which God prepared in advance for us to do.
>
> **Ephesians 2:8–10**

I taught that every follower of Jesus is called to do a good work for God, and that we must be careful not to miss our specific call. Our job as believers is to find our God-given purpose and to walk in it. I exhorted the congregation, "Please don't think God will transfer your work to someone else if you disobey Him. He has gifted each of you so uniquely that nobody else is able to do quite the same thing that He has prepared for you. Please respond to the call the Lord Jesus has placed on your life, 'for God's gifts and his call are irrevocable' (Romans 11:29)."

I sensed the Holy Spirit speaking through me as I ministered, and it produced a variety of reactions. Some believers had their heads bowed as they wiped tears from their eyes, while others looked back at me with dark looks of condemnation and resentment.

A woman in her late thirties began to sob gently as the Spirit of God convicted her of an issue in her life. After a few minutes she began to shake and weep uncontrollably. Obviously in deep distress, she walked down the aisle and threw herself onto the floor right in front of the pulpit. By that time she was wailing loudly.

Being relatively new to preaching, I was at a complete loss as to what I should do, so I just ignored her and carried on! Finally, some of the other women came forward and put their arms around her. They led her to a side room, where she continued to wail.

After the service, the pastor and his wife invited me to a local restaurant. As we waited for our meals to arrive, the lady who had been so anguished in the meeting joined us, and sat down directly across the table from me. I enquired if she was alright, and she replied, "I'm so embarrassed. Please forgive me. I have never acted that way in a church service before."

I assured her I wasn't offended, and that it was obvious the Holy Spirit was dealing with her deeply. She shared her story:

> I have been a Christian since I was a young girl, and Jesus has been the Rock of my life. I love Him dearly. When I was a teenager, God called me to be a missionary in India. It was clear and unmistakable. I consulted my parents and church leaders, and after much prayer they confirmed my call. I began looking into the appropriate training required to pursue this great vision.
>
> A short time later, a handsome young man named Greg began attending our church. He was a strong believer, and he had a good reputation with everyone who knew him. I told Greg that God had called me to India. He assured me he would pray daily as I figured out the next stage of my journey toward becoming a missionary.
>
> Over time, Greg and I fell in love. We married, and I was soon pregnant with the first of our three children. Greg has been a wonderful husband and father. He loves the Lord, and God has clearly blessed us over the years. All our children are strong and healthy. Greg owns a successful business, and we enjoy being involved with the church.
>
> When you shared that I was God's handiwork and that He has prepared a specific work for me to do, the Holy Spirit convicted me of disobedience. I have never been to India, and despite His blessings in my life, I know that I have missed the very best God had for me. I was unable to contain the deep guilt I've been carrying around for the past twenty years."

I subsequently met many other Christians who had similarly missed God's plans for their lives. Satan is very cunning. He loves to distract believers from obeying the purpose for which they were saved.

Usually, he doesn't try to sidetrack us by sending a temptation that is obviously wrong. More often, the enemy is content to tempt us with a situation that's second best, as long as we miss the main calling of God on our lives.

This lady's testimony caused me to re-examine my own call to Asia. I remembered the remarkable way God had first called me to be a donkey for Jesus, and the miracles He had performed when I stepped out in faith. My heart yearned to return to Asia. I hadn't lost my focus, but the Lord desired to build a more solid foundation in my life before He would release me to go back.

* * *

As the year at Bible College rolled on, it became increasingly noticeable that the spiritual lives and enthusiasm of most of the students had markedly dimmed. By the middle of the year it felt as though my own heart was hanging on to God by a thread. Of course, I still believed in Jesus – I would have been crazy not to after all the extraordinary ways He had revealed Himself to me – but those experiences seemed to be fading away.

I found myself in the same position as countless other Christians down through the ages. My initial "honeymoon period" with Jesus had ended, and I had reached a crossroad in my walk with the Lord. My heavenly Father didn't want me to base my faith on inconsistent feelings and experiences, but to be established firmly in the truth of His Word, "for we live by faith, not by sight" (2 Corinthians 5:7). God wanted me to know that even if my hold on Him was shaky at times, He had my life securely in the palm of His hand and would never let me go. I was privileged to serve a Savior who said of His followers, "My Father, who has given them to me, is greater than all; no one can snatch them out of my Father's hand" (John 10:29).

When I was a young boy growing up in New Zealand, I played rugby on Saturday mornings. One season I was part of a useless team, and by half-time we often trailed our opponents by twenty to twenty-five points. The coach would invariably walk onto the field and shout, "Come on, guys! You can do better. You are down by twenty points but don't give up!" He would never actually instruct us what to do differently to turn the game around, though. The second half would commence, and we would predictably end up losing by forty or fifty points.

It seemed to me that my home church in Australia was a lot like this. The shallow teaching delivered each Sunday from the pulpit didn't come close to providing the meat of God's Word I needed to become a strong Christian. I heard numerous "positive" messages on faith, but what I really needed was to learn how to overcome sinful desires, how to become a God-fearing man with good character, and how to live a life of integrity that brings honor to the Lord Jesus Christ.

In the Parable of the Sower, Jesus spoke about people who fall away from the faith. He said:

> "The seed falling on rocky ground refers to someone who hears the word and at once receives it with joy. But since they have no root, they last only a short time. When trouble or persecution comes because of the word, they quickly fall away."
>
> **Matthew 13:20–21**

I saw myself reflected in Jesus' words, and it caused me to shudder. I had heard the Word and immediately received it with joy. I took off like a shooting star – all the way to China – but my life lacked a solid and healthy root. No matter what it cost, I had to discover how to become the kind of person Jesus next spoke about in the parable:

> "The seed falling on good soil refers to someone who hears the word and understands it. This is the one who produces a crop, yielding a hundred, sixty or thirty times what was sown."
>
> **Matthew 13:23**

Oh, how I wanted my life to produce a crop for Jesus! I didn't want to fall away. The Lord died for me and I loved Him because He first loved me. At the same time, I realized that if my life was ever going to bear the kind of good fruit God required, He would need to reconstruct it from the bottom up.

As the year progressed and my head became increasingly jammed full of Bible knowledge, I became deeply aware that I had a sinful, stubborn heart and that I desired to live for myself. I needed someone to show me how to live by the Spirit and not be controlled by the flesh, for the Bible says, "There is therefore now no condemnation to those who are in Christ Jesus, who do not walk according to the flesh, but according to the Spirit" (Romans 8:1, NKJV).

In desperation I tore off my religious mask and poured out my heart to God. Sharing my deep burdens with Him, I prayed, "Lord Jesus, I'm dying here. I want to love You, but my heart is wicked. Please help me. I need real Christianity! I don't care what it costs, Lord, but please help me to have a real faith, and teach me to fear You! Do whatever it takes to make me holy and to give me integrity. Cause me to know the true Jesus as revealed in the Scriptures, and rescue me from the delusion of creating a false god in my own image. Father, I beg You to take control of my life and transform me into the image of Your Son."

In my spare time I read books by followers of God who had walked in holiness and righteousness – people such as A. W. Tozer, Andrew Murray, E. M. Bounds, and Charles Finney. Through their teaching, I discovered riches in Christ and a power from the Holy Spirit that counterbalanced the superficial teachings I was receiving during the day at the Bible College.

Practical teaching designed to help students live for Jesus Christ and to overcome sin was absent from the Bible College curriculum, and the fruit of this half-baked theology began to show through. Over time it produced deadly consequences. One friend with whom I have remained in contact told me that the majority of the thirty students at our Bible College have fallen away from the faith and no longer follow the Lord. I knew many of my classmates well. They were zealous for the Lord, but because of the watered-down sermons being preached every week and the toxic environment it fostered, they tragically fell into moral depravity and away from the faith they once professed.

I was no better than any of my fellow students. If I had not broken away, I probably wouldn't have lasted very long either. One Sunday morning, about halfway through the school year, I simply couldn't bring myself to attend the church any longer. I felt that my journey with God had gone as far as it could as part of that congregation, and I was desperate to be around real Christians who hungered for truth. I drove to a smaller fellowship in a country town about thirty miles away, and quietly took a seat in the back row. What a great blessing awaited me! The preacher used words that had fallen out of the vocabulary at the other church: words such as "repentance," "holiness," and "sin." The message was like water to my parched soul. I had found a new place to fellowship.

Although I eventually graduated from the Bible College at the end of the year, I never again attended the church where I had met the Lord. In later years it continued to grow in size and influence, but the basic message remained the same. Many believers thought they were experiencing revival there, but I had tasted genuine, heaven-sent revival in China, and its character was fundamentally different from the so-called revival in Australia. The movement of God in China caused people to repent of their sins and humbly cling to Jesus Christ in self-sacrifice and love. The Australian model pandered to people's pride; repentance was never mentioned, and Jesus was seen as merely a means to obtain material blessings.

I will always be thankful to my heavenly Father for revealing His Son to me at that church in October 1987, but my journey had taken a sharp turn and I was now heading in a different direction. I greatly enjoyed attending the small country church. Although no congregation this side of eternity is perfect, I was able to fellowship with genuine believers who desired to grow in Christ. The pastor invested time getting to know me, and when I shared my passion for the unreached nations of Asia, he encouraged me to pursue God's call on my life. My change of direction meant I was now on the right track to accomplish God's call on my life.

CHAPTER 14
RETURN TO THE BATTLE

FEBRUARY 1991

> If you give God the right to yourself, He will make a holy experiment out of you. God's experiments always succeed.
>
> **Oswald Chambers**

I once heard about a businessman who bought a brand new sports car for his son's seventeenth birthday. The excited teenager grabbed the keys and took off down the highway in his powerful new toy. Fifteen minutes later he crashed into a concrete barrier and died.

The Lord Jesus doesn't entrust the keys to His kingdom in such an irresponsible manner. He spends time building godly character into the lives of His children, often through struggles and hardship, to ensure that they are mature enough to handle the tasks He wants them to perform.

After my year at Bible College ended, I was more eager than ever to return to Asia and continue my service for the Lord. God's timing was not my timing, however. There were more things He wanted to teach me. At the dawn of the 1990s I was still in Australia, working as a full-time cleaner in Sydney's northern suburbs. My workdays began in the late afternoon and continued into the early hours of the morning. I saved as much money as I could for an airfare back to Asia, but whenever my bank balance neared the level required to purchase a ticket, a major unexpected expense would reduce my savings back to zero.

I was ready to sacrifice myself if necessary for the kingdom of God in Asia, but the Lord Jesus had more humble plans for my life. He wasn't interested in what I could sacrifice. He wanted to ensure that my heart belonged to Him and that I would be willing to obey whatever He told me to do. Instead of allowing me to return to Asia to fulfill my dreams, God had me cleaning dozens of filthy toilets and urinals every night. I continued in this humiliating work for an entire year.

With each passing day the Holy Spirit gradually broke me and softened my attitude. One night I bent over another smelly toilet and brushed the flecks of human excrement from the sides of the bowl. All of a sudden, I sensed that the Lord Jesus had me exactly where He wanted me!

I had graduated from Bible College with a head full of knowledge, and now the Lord was graciously providing some practical life experiences to help the doctrine trickle down from my head to my heart.

Previously I had cried out to God, "Do whatever it takes to make me holy and to give me integrity. Please cause me to know the true Jesus as revealed in the Scriptures." I felt my current situation was the answer to my prayer, and I rejoiced at the wisdom of God: "Thank You, Lord," I declared. "If You want me to spend the rest of my life cleaning toilets for You, then that's what I'll do. You know what's best and I submit to You. Not my will, but Yours be done."

From that moment on, a fresh peace and joy entered my life. The Apostle Paul taught, "Whether you eat or drink or whatever you do, do it all for the glory of God" (1 Corinthians 10:31). Instead of feeling frustrated and viewing each toilet as a disgusting inconvenience, I now saw each one as an important stepping stone on my journey back to Asia.

My loving heavenly Father was breaking down my pride and rebuilding my life, just as I had requested. My time as a cleaner helped me to love and appreciate Jesus more than ever. I didn't return for a second year of formal Bible training, but I learned many priceless lessons from the Lord during my year as a toilet cleaner. The Bible says, "Believers in humble circumstances ought to take pride in their high position. But the rich should take pride in their humiliation – since they will pass away like a wild flower" (James 1:9–10).

The nearer I drew to Jesus Christ, the more I became aware that it wasn't difficult to live a righteous life. It was impossible! I found I could never live a righteous life for God by my own effort and striving. My job was to surrender daily to the Holy Spirit – to relax and allow His righteousness to live in and through me. I was beginning to learn the secret to the Christian life. Before I could hope to live for Jesus, I had to die to myself so that His life could shine through me. The Apostle Paul wrote, "I have been crucified with Christ and I no longer live, but Christ lives in me. The life I now live in the body, I live by faith in the Son of God, who loved me and gave himself for me" (Galatians 2:20).

My two and a half years in Australia proved to be a crucial, formative time as the Holy Spirit reshaped my life. Finally, He decided I was ready to return to His service in Asia. The Master Potter graciously lifted me off the shelf and sent me back to the mission field to bring glory to the Name of Jesus.

I had gradually become integrated into my new church in Australia. Although the pastors didn't fully understand my vision, they recognized the call of God on my life. In February 1991, a special commissioning service was held in which the leaders of the church prayed over me and sent me back to Asia with their blessings and prayers.

After the service, many well-wishers came up and offered me words of encouragement, but a single sentence spoken by an elderly disabled man named Bruce has remained lodged in my heart to this day. Bruce was a larger-than-life man in his seventies who always sat on the front row at the church with his walking stick in his hand. After most people had left the building, Bruce called me over. He looked me in the eye and said, "Young man, never forget one thing: The greatest *ability* you will ever have is your *availability*."

* * *

Instead of returning to China straight away, I felt that the Lord first wanted me to visit other Asian countries. I decided to use Bangkok, Thailand, as a base to carry Bibles into the Communist countries of Laos and Vietnam. I carefully calculated how much money I would need for my travel, accommodation, visas, and food in order to carry as many Bibles as possible to the persecuted Christians in those two countries. No matter how often I looked at my budget, I concluded I was $180 short of having enough to cover my expenses. I was sure the Lord would move someone to give me the shortfall before I left Australia, but nobody did. After praying for a miracle, I boarded my Singapore Airlines flight without enough money to accomplish what I believed God wanted me to do in the following weeks.

Upon landing in Thailand, I waited patiently for my backpack to emerge on the baggage carousel, but after more than an hour I realized it was missing. I felt devastated! All my clothes except the ones I had on were gone, as was the large pack itself, which I had intended to use to haul the Bibles into Laos and Vietnam. I filled out a missing baggage form and made my way out of the airport to downtown Bangkok, where I stayed at a guest house.

After a difficult night's sleep, the new day dawned and I didn't know what to do next without my pack. I even began to wonder if I had made a mistake in coming to Southeast Asia. Even if my luggage hadn't been lost, I still needed an additional $180 to cover my expenses.

Throwing myself on the Lord's mercy, I dropped to my knees in prayer. This verse came to mind: "Now faith is confidence in what we hope for and assurance about what we do not see" (Hebrews 11:1). I asked God to forgive me for doubting Him. The Lord Jesus had taken care of my needs from the moment I had first committed my life to Him, and He was still firmly in control. When I accepted this fact, the peace of God returned to my heart.

Just moments after I rose from my knees, there was a loud knock on my door. I opened it to find a Singapore Airlines representative with my backpack in his hand. He offered an apology, and asked me to sign a form confirming that my lost bag had been returned to my satisfaction. Before leaving, he said, "Sir, we deeply regret the inconvenience you have experienced, and we would like to compensate you for our mistake." He handed me an envelope. I sat down on my bed and found that the airline had given me exactly $180!

How silly I had been to doubt God. He had my situation firmly under control the whole time, and now I had enough to pay for my trips to Laos and Vietnam.

Buoyed by this development, I joyfully packed eighty Lao Bibles into my backpack. The following evening I caught an overnight train to northeast Thailand, and then boarded a boat across the Mekong River that separates Thailand from Laos. Visiting the forgotten country of Laos in those days was like stepping back in time. There was no customs inspection at all, and I successfully carried my heavy load of Bibles into the capital city of Vientiane.

I was given the name and phone number of an underground church leader who would take the precious cargo from me. For the first two days my calls to the number went unanswered, and I began to feel a little anxious as I waited at my guest house on the outskirts of the city. The guest house was managed by a young man in his early twenties named Noi. He had been given the job because of his ability to speak a little English. One morning as I showered in my room, I sang out praises to the Lord.

Later, Noi approached me at the breakfast table and said, "Mr Paul, I heard you singing. The words were very beautiful and I can tell that you know God. Can you please help me to know God too?"

For the rest of the day I did my best to share the gospel with Noi, and despite the language barrier he seemed to understand the heart of the message. I was scheduled to leave Laos the next day and travel back to Bangkok, but I still hadn't been able to contact the pastor to drop off my load of Bibles. That evening, after dark, Noi helped me hire a Russian-made van, and we made our way to the address of a house church I'd been given as a last resort in case something went wrong.

I was nervous, because I didn't think the Lao believers would appreciate me turning up on their doorstep with a young Lao man who might have been a government agent for all they knew. I decided it was a risk I had to take, otherwise the eighty Bibles would have been wasted. Noi knocked on the door, and an elderly lady opened it and welcomed us inside. About thirty Christians had gathered for a meal and had just sat down to eat together. They invited us to join them, and were overjoyed when I opened my huge pack and revealed the Bibles.

As we enjoyed the sumptuous meal, several of the Lao believers befriended Noi and explained the gospel to him in a much clearer way than I had been able to. He knelt down and asked Jesus Christ to forgive his sins and to accept him as a child of God. Noi became a member of the Body of Christ that night. It was a joyous occasion, both in the little Lao house church and in heaven, for Jesus said, "I tell you, there is rejoicing in the presence of the angels of God over one sinner who repents" (Luke 15:10).

I left Laos the following morning, amazed at the goodness of God and His matchless wisdom. Just a few days earlier I had fretted about losing my luggage. Now, I had safely delivered eighty Bibles to the underground Church in Laos, and a new believer had been left in their care. I haven't seen Noi again since that day, but I believe I can safely assume he is the only person who has ever been attracted to the Lord by my singing!

Several days later I flew into Ho Chi Minh City (formerly Saigon), and successfully delivered another large load of Bibles to the Vietnamese house churches. Once again, I was greatly blessed to enjoy rich fellowship with believers who had suffered much for the gospel.

The church movement I delivered the Bibles to had begun just three years earlier, after a dozen believers were expelled from the government-sanctioned church when they refused to stop preaching the gospel. The Holy Spirit empowered those dozen men and women in a special way, and in just three years there were already more than 1,000 believers in their house churches. The leaders were busy training many new workers and sending them to unreached areas throughout Vietnam.

The senior leader of that church movement was a man named Quang. Few foreigners visited Vietnam in those days, so he took time out from his busy schedule to host me and drive me around the city on the back of his motorcycle. Vietnam was suffering from the effects of the imminent collapse of the Soviet Union. The economy had fallen apart when the Soviets had stopped propping it up. Quang took me to visit the city zoo, but it resembled a slaughterhouse. Food shortages had led the hungry locals to kill and eat many of the animals, including the zoo's only elephant.

On my final night before leaving Vietnam, Quang's wife asked me to pray for them. She explained that her husband was under tremendous pressure from the authorities, and she had packed a bag of clothes and essentials in case the police came and took him away in the middle of the night.

The next day, as my plane took off and I looked out the window at the vast Mekong Delta below, my heart rejoiced in the goodness of God. Not knowing if I would ever return to Vietnam again, I thanked the Lord Jesus for allowing me to serve His Church there. Straight away, the Holy Spirit whispered to my heart, "I will bring you back here many times."

Several weeks later I was staying at a missionary guest house in another country. I picked up a ministry newsletter and read that Quang had been arrested in Vietnam and sentenced to three years in prison. I wondered if the bag of clothes his wife had lovingly prepared was with him in his cell.

I learned many things from Quang and the other persecuted

believers I met in Asia. Many preachers say, "Before someone can die for Jesus, they must first be willing to live for Him."That sounds logical, but I discovered the opposite is equally true. Before we are able to live for Jesus, we must first be willing to die for Him. The Lord taught:

> "Whoever wants to be my disciple must deny themselves and take up their cross daily and follow me. For whoever wants to save their life will lose it, but whoever loses their life for me will save it."
>
> **Luke 9:23–24**

Despite the imprisonment of their leader, that house church network in Vietnam continued to flourish in the face of intense persecution. The thousand Christians at the time of my first visit to Vietnam mushroomed to tens of thousands of believers in more than a thousand congregations, and a vast multitude of Vietnamese people experienced salvation through the blood of Jesus Christ.

CHAPTER 15

AN ASSAULT ON THE SENSES

After my precious time in Laos and Vietnam, I traveled extensively for nine months throughout many other parts of Asia as the Lord directed me. Bangladesh, India, Sri Lanka, Nepal, Thailand, and Indonesia were all part of my journey.

In Indonesia, which is home to more Muslims than any other country, I met many Christians who willingly risked harsh persecution to reach their Muslim neighbors. I also had some interesting culinary experiences there. While visiting the Indonesian island of Sulawesi, a friend and I trekked up a high mountain inhabited by an animistic tribe. The villagers were very hospitable and warmly invited us into their bamboo hut for lunch. Just outside the door I noticed that some nets had been spread with what looked like a sticky substance on them.

When lunch arrived, we discovered the nets had been used to catch large green flies, which were proudly presented as our main course. My friend and I looked at each other, trying to come up with an excuse we could use to miss the meal, but we remembered the Lord's clear instructions to His disciples: "Stay there, eating and drinking whatever they give you" (Luke 10:7).

Recognizing that this dear family had honored us by lovingly preparing their best food, and that we were probably the first representatives of Jesus Christ they had ever met, we bowed our heads, thanked God for the food, and tried our best to appear cheerful as we ate the flies accompanied by a bowl of rice. After getting past the initial crunch of the wings, they didn't taste too bad.

I visited another tribe where the people ate with their hands from large wooden bowls. The food was reasonably tasty, but I felt a little sick after seeing their method of washing the dishes. When we had finished eating, my hosts hung the bowls on a nail attached to a beam, and called their mangy dogs to come inside and lick them clean. The bowls then remained in place, ready for the next meal!

Most of my time was spent in India, where for months I criss-crossed the country by train. It has been said that India is "an assault on the senses." I came to appreciate the truth behind that statement as my sight, hearing, taste, smell, and touch were frequently overwhelmed. I fell ill on a number of occasions.

During a sixty-hour train journey from northeast India to the central city of Hyderabad, my face became infected after I fell asleep face-down on the floor in the area between two carriages. I was in a state of exhaustion, and unbeknown to me, the sink had overflowed and I was sleeping in half an inch of mucus and sewerage from the nearby latrine. By the time I arrived in Hyderabad, the left side of my face had blown up to twice its normal size and I looked like the "elephant man"! I met up with a mission team, who found it difficult to look at me, so I held a small towel over the left side of my face to help ease their discomfort. Later that day I was taken to a medical clinic. A course of antibiotics soon took care of the infection, and my appearance returned to normal.

My fondest memories of India are the times I spent with the Body of Christ. The contrast between unbelievers and Christians there is as stark as anywhere I've been in the world. The overwhelming spiritual darkness in India causes the disciples of Jesus to stand out like beacons of light and hope amid a sea of despair.

I traveled with an Indian ministry to remote villages, where we showed the evangelistic *Jesus* film to hundreds of Hindus and Muslims. The film is entirely based on the Gospel of Luke. Often, when we reached the crucifixion scene, many villagers burst out sobbing, shocked and horrified that the wonderful Jesus, who had displayed nothing but love to people, was brutally put to death on a cross. Five minutes later the same villagers clapped and cheered when they saw Jesus alive again, victorious over death!

At the end of the movie, an Indian evangelist would stand before the people, answering their questions and exhorting them to repent of their sins and place their trust in Christ. In many villages, small congregations were established and placed under the care of trained pastors after a single showing of the *Jesus* film.

The months I spent in India were intensely difficult, but I wouldn't trade them for anything. They made me mentally tough, and taught me how to endure hardship. God was with me, and I learned many important lessons that prepared me for later service. India is a place where Christians must walk in the power of the Holy Spirit if they are to be of use. Powerful demonic forces are present there, and they cannot be overcome by mere human reasoning, for "The kingdom of God is not a matter of talk but of power" (1 Corinthians 4:20).

One afternoon, I visited the Red Fort in New Delhi. I walked around a corner and saw a crowd of about fifty men and women transfixed by someone standing in front of them. I moved closer and saw that they were being entertained by a snake charmer. The man's venomous king cobra was almost vertically upright above a basket, mesmerized by the sound of its master's flute. I immediately discerned that this was not merely a human trick, but was demonic in nature. Standing at the back of the crowd, I whispered, "In the Name of Jesus, I bind all evil forces here." The snake instantly became limp and dropped down into the basket. I thought I would casually slip away, but the snake charmer knew something had caused his performance to fail. He furiously looked around at the gathered crowd, and the moment his eyes met mine he stood up and shouted curses at me. I prayed fervently as I quickly put some distance between myself and the agitated man and his snake!

That day I learned there is great power in the Name of Jesus Christ, even at the whisper of His Name. Satan and his forces are terrified by the power and authority in Jesus' Name, for it is "the name that is above every name, that at the name of Jesus every knee should bow, in heaven and on earth and under the earth, and every tongue acknowledge that Jesus Christ is Lord, to the glory of God the Father" (Philippians 2:9–11).

India is a unique country, and it remains the greatest challenge for the Body of Christ in the world today because of its incredible ethnic and cultural diversity. Remarkably, India is home to more than 2,100 distinct unreached people groups – more than 1,600 groups more than the second highest country in the world (China). In a few years, India will also overtake China as the world's most populated country.

Over the years, I have visited India numerous times, and although it has never ceased to be an "assault on my senses," I have great hope for the salvation of India. The light of the gospel is burning brightly in rural parts of the country today. Millions of people have become Christians in recent years, and a tremendous revival is unfolding.

As the kingdom of God continues to advance throughout India, I believe there will be terrible hardship for many Christians. Satan never stands idly by while God's servants bring in the harvest. Thousands of believers have been killed or severely persecuted in recent years, and they may be just the first fruits of a huge bloodbath. Whatever results, God's kingdom will prevail, and the salvation of Jesus Christ will be made known among millions of families who have never heard His Name.

In the state of Odisha, more than 500 Christian men were buried and burned alive by Hindu fanatics during one diabolical persecution a few years ago. Multitudes of Christian women and children suddenly found themselves widowed and orphaned after all the men were murdered. A local newspaper in Odisha later published a story under the interesting headline "Christian Elephants Attack Persecutors." The article detailed how herds of wild elephants had stormed villages where some of the worst persecutors lived. In one village, a herd emerged from the jungle exactly one year to the day after the homes of thousands of Christians were burned to the ground by angry Hindu mobs. The elephants first attacked an expensive piece of machinery owned by one of the chief persecutors, then destroyed his house and farm. The beasts went on to rampage through the rest of the village, demolishing the homes of the thugs who had participated in the cruel attacks, while leaving Christian homes untouched.

Nobody had ever heard of elephants behaving like this before. Witnesses said they appeared to be on a mission. According to the article, the smaller elephants entered the villages first, before rejoining the herd. The larger elephants soon followed to complete the destruction, and 700 houses in thirty villages were reportedly destroyed. As a result, the fear of God fell on the people of Odisha. Many were convinced that the attacks by the "Christian elephants" were an act of divine retribution for the persecution of God's children.

* * *

One afternoon during my extensive travels throughout India, I sat and watched the hustle and bustle of life on the street outside my window. The Lord touched my heart with compassion, and a fire was lit within my spirit to do all I could to reach the people of that great and needy land. After intently observing one family as they went about their daily tasks, I penned the following poem, entitled "Anger and Pain":

Look at the mother, rushing along,
Forehead marked, baby due;
A slave from cradle to grave.

See the father, manly and calm,
Grizzled face, sweat-stained clothes;
Enslaved to the dusty land.

Look at the little girl, laughing at play,
Innocent until sin knocks,
And she commences the struggle of life.

See the little boy, grubby with zeal,
Acting tough 'til the day he graduates
To the lofty heights of his father.

Look at the grandma, wise as an owl,
Face lined with the history of the world;
Her memory full of meaningless days
Of toils and journeys that never led upward,
Of prayers and petitions to gods with no ears,
Of sorrow and heartache at life's void reward.

See her husband, now passed away,
Called to account before the Almighty's throne,
Unable to answer the God he's not known,
Confused why he never heard His Name.

With terrified rage welling up in his heart,
He's led away past the multitudes, weeping,
Seething with anger, mostly reserved for
Those Christians, standing ashamed to the side,
Who never bothered to share their Good News.

CHAPTER 16

A HEAVENLY VISION

April 1991

> Let my heart be broken with the things that break the heart of God.
>
> **Bob Pierce**

My travels took me to the Himalayan kingdom of Nepal for a few months. Nepal was a tightly controlled country at the time, and Christians were persecuted for their faith. Prayer meetings were often held in secret, with believers pressing pillows or cloth over their mouths to muffle the volume of their prayers, lest their neighbors report the gathering to the police.

A ministry in Kathmandu asked if I would travel to western Nepal to help deliver a load of Bibles to a rural community of new believers. I jumped at the opportunity, and a few days later I joined a Nepali Christian named Ramesh on a seventeen-hour bus ride to the west side of the country. It was the first stage of an arduous journey that almost ended my life.

Our first stop was the town of Nepalgunj near the Indian border. After resting for the night, we caught another bus deeper into the mountains. I was only able to fit fifty Bibles into my backpack, owing to the large size of the Nepali Scriptures. My pack weighed at least 50 kg (110 pounds), and it felt as if I was carrying bars of iron. Instead of sitting inside the bus, Ramesh and I decided to travel in the "air-conditioned" compartment. We climbed onto the roof and sat inside the spare tire that was secured to the roof by ropes.

Typically, bus journeys in Nepal are exciting experiences. This was a particularly hair-raising ride, as our driver navigated the narrow dirt roads at breakneck speed. As he drove around blind corners, with the cliff edge just a few feet away, he would calm his nerves with an occasional swig of whiskey or a puff of marijuana. It didn't help my state of mind when I glanced down from the roof and saw the burned-out shells of wrecked buses and trucks at the bottom of the valley floor, thousands of feet below.

That day we commenced our travels on the plains of southern Nepal, not far above sea level. Eight hours later we were at more than 10,000 feet above sea level, in the midst of the Himalayas. Through the day we had crossed numerous mountain passes and traversed into deep valleys, only to begin climbing again toward the next pass.

After sunset we arrived at a small town and found lodging for the night. The following morning Ramesh woke me before dawn. We had a full day's hiking ahead of us if we were to reach the Christian village by nightfall.

I set out with great determination that morning. What a great joy it was to deliver God's Word to new believers! I looked forward to meeting my Nepali brothers and sisters, with whom I would spend eternity.

After a few hours of difficult hiking, my heavy backpack felt as though it weighed a ton, and the energy began to drain from my limbs. I knew I was holding Ramesh back, but he was my guide and translator and I would have been totally lost in those mountains without him.

For hours I pressed on, one step at a time. I was determined to reach our destination and deliver the Bibles, no matter what. By mid-afternoon, as we climbed yet another steep incline, I sensed

I was in trouble. I was sick from both ends, and my body shook from dehydration and the stress of my endeavor. A few hours later I felt even more disorientated, and was barely able to walk. Feeling frustrated, Ramesh could see I wasn't going to make it to the village, which still lay three hours ahead.

We passed a tiny village of homes constructed from uncut stones and dried mud, before continuing up another hill. We were now in a remote area, far from any road, as the sun began to set. When we reached a clearing at the top of the next hill, I sat down to rest. Feeling too exhausted to unclip my pack, I just lay on my back.

Ramesh was growing increasingly anxious. Being a local, he knew the dangers of spending the night outside in the Himalayas. Wolves, jackals, and other wild animals roamed the hills at night, in addition to some of the world's most venomous snakes and spiders. "Okay, Paul, let's go!" he ordered. "We've got to get moving! We can't stay here any longer – it's too dangerous. We Nepalis say only crazy people sleep out in the open."

By this time I was scarcely able to acknowledge Ramesh. My mind had become clouded and confused. I was so weak that the most I could do was to motion with my index finger, signaling to my guide to go on alone. "Okay, brother," he exclaimed. "I'll go ahead and will try to send someone to help you."

That was the last time I ever saw Ramesh.

I was now alone, and a chill ran through my body as the last rays of sunlight descended behind the mountain peaks. I had never before felt so totally devoid of energy, and my mind seemed to be shutting down.

Ironically, I knew what was happening to me, but I wasn't able to do anything about it. A few days earlier in Kathmandu, I had picked up a magazine at the mission guest house and read an article about altitude sickness. Every year, many trekkers in the Himalayas perish from it. Altitude sickness strikes people who ascend too quickly, before their bodies have time to adjust to the reduced air pressure and lower oxygen levels. Many people die when, in their weakened state, they simply close their eyes and fall asleep. Their lungs fill up with fluid, causing them to suffocate, and they never wake up. The medical term for this fatal condition is pulmonary edema. I already had most of the symptoms and was coughing uncontrollably. A bubbling sound was coming from within my chest as my lungs began to fill with fluid.

Even though I knew what I was suffering, I was completely powerless to overcome it. The only solution for someone suffering from altitude sickness is to quickly head down to a lower altitude, in the hope that their body will adjust to the thicker atmosphere.

Another half-hour passed, and it was now completely dark. The temperature had plummeted, and for the first time I was aware that I was about to die. An overwhelming exhaustion enveloped me. Every cell in my body wanted to rest. My eyes were heavy, and I was on the verge of nodding off to sleep.

A few months earlier I had read *Foxe's Book of Martyrs* – a book full of stirring accounts of Christians who had died heroically for the gospel. I wondered if my church in Australia would ever learn how I had died.

Incredibly, at the point of my greatest weakness, pride rose up within me. I wanted my friends to know I had perished while serving Jesus, so I made a huge effort to pull my personal Bible out of my pack and place it beside me. When my body was discovered, I wanted people to know that I had been reading God's Word to my very last breath!

As I contemplated the end of my life, I suddenly had a dramatic and life-changing experience. Firstly, my heart was overwhelmed with "the peace of God, which transcends all understanding" (Philippians 4:7). I *knew* – without a shadow of doubt – that I was going to heaven. It was a supernatural revelation, not something I conjured up by myself. I didn't merely hope or wish that my eternal destiny was secure. My confidence had nothing to do with me. I had numerous faults and my life was still very much a work in progress. Every particle of my being, however, knew I was saved because of the blood of Jesus Christ. It was His blood that made me acceptable to God, and nothing else. I realized I was saved not because I was good enough, but because Jesus is good enough.

"Lord Jesus," I whispered, as tears welled up in my eyes, "I'm coming to see You soon. Thank You for saving me. Thank You for Your precious blood. I love You."

Now lying on my side, I turned on a small pen light that I kept in my Bible cover. Mustering my last ounce of energy, I opened the pages to near the middle of the book. I looked down to find I had opened my Bible to Psalm 91. When I read to the end of the psalm, these words grabbed my attention:

> "Because he loves me," says the Lord, "I will rescue him;
> I will protect him, for he acknowledges my name.
> He will call on me, and I will answer him;
> I will be with him in trouble,
> I will deliver him and honor him.
> With long life I will satisfy him
> and show him my salvation."
>
> **Psalm 91:14–16**

As I pondered these beautiful words, a heavenly vision suddenly flooded my spirit. It lasted no longer than a few seconds, but it came with such clarity that I will never forget the details. Some people have suggested I may have been hallucinating because of my weakened state. All I know is that this brief encounter altered the course of my life and resulted in me loving the Lord Jesus with a greater passion than ever before. What happened is difficult to adequately explain, but I will attempt to do so.

In the vision I was positioned high up in the air, looking down upon a vast open plain containing countless millions of Asian people, from myriad ethnic groups. Each person was adorned in their traditional tribal clothing. The colorful sea of humanity stretched to the distant horizon, further than my eyes could see. As I gazed upon the vast multitude, a deep, overpowering sense of God's love and compassion flooded my soul. These words about Jesus were impressed on my mind: "He had compassion on them, because they were harassed and helpless, like sheep without a shepherd" (Matthew 9:36).

The vision ended as abruptly as it had begun, and I remained alone in the dark of the Himalayas, lying on the cold ground. For the next ten or fifteen minutes I was awestruck by the vision. My heavenly Father, in a moment of time, had shared His heart with me for the lost peoples of Asia. His amazing love so overwhelmed me that I could scarcely contain it. It felt as if my heart might explode within me.

After the vision, a deep sense enveloped me that I was not going to die that night. God had shared a glimpse of His heart for a reason. He wanted me to invest the rest of my life taking the gospel to as many Asian people groups as possible. I realized my work was far from complete, and Jesus wanted me to live!

Although I felt spiritually uplifted from my heavenly experience, I was still unable to move and I remained completely devoid of energy. As I looked up into the star-filled sky, I began to shiver uncontrollably, and wondered how I was going to survive the night without a sleeping bag or warm coat. As I lay there, I thought I heard a sound way off in the distance. My ears perked up, but all I could hear was the chirping of crickets. A few more minutes passed, and again I thought I heard a tiny sound in the distance. Then it stopped again. The third time I heard the sound, I knew my mind wasn't playing tricks on me. I really was hearing something. It sounded like a faint trickle of water, ebbing and flowing in intensity. Sometimes it was louder, then it would fade away for a few minutes before returning.

As the time went by, it was apparent that the sound was getting closer. It was now just a few hundred yards behind me, and I recognized the sound as the tinkling of a bell. Someone was coming down the trail toward me!

A Nepali man and his donkey emerged into the clearing. The donkey had a small bell around its neck, which tinkled as it walked along. Because of the hills and valleys, the sound waves had reached my ears when the donkey was at the top of a hill, only to disappear when it went down into a hollow.

The man didn't say a word to me. He looked at me lying in the dirt and immediately summed up the situation. He lifted up my pack, and with a great struggle managed to secure it with rope across the back of his donkey. He then helped me to my feet, and although I was unstable, the Lord provided a boost of energy and I was soon staggering back down the trail from where I had come earlier that day.

After about thirty minutes we reached the small village of stone and mud houses that Ramesh and I had passed hours earlier. The man motioned for me to wait while he spoke with a woman who managed the only shop in the village. Beneath the shop was a tiny space with a small opening. I got on my hands and knees and crawled inside. The woman pushed my pack into the opening, said some things in Nepali that I couldn't understand, and left for the night.

Although the Lord had spared my life, I remained extremely ill. For days I lay under the shop, too sick to move. The lady brought me water and some lentil soup, but everything that passed my lips immediately came back up. She gave up trying to provide me with sustenance and brought me an old broken bucket to throw up in.

That Nepali woman was like an angel to me, emptying my bucket every day and trying to cheer me up by bringing children from the village to stare at me. That part of Nepal remains isolated and far from the normal tourist routes. I was almost certainly the first foreigner any of the locals had ever seen.

Finally, after remaining there for a full week, I regained some strength and was able to contemplate my situation. The next day I decided to try to retrace my steps back to the capital city of Kathmandu. I walked all day back to the road and hailed a bus. This time I took a seat inside. From Nepalgunj I bought another ticket for the long journey back to Kathmandu. I was upset because I had failed to deliver the Bibles to the new believers, but had hauled them all the way back to Kathmandu, where I placed them back on the shelf at the mission guest house.

During the week I spent recovering beneath the shop, I expected my friend Ramesh to come back and find me, but he never did. I found out later that he had continued on to the Christian village, hoping I would be able to make my own way back to civilization. I asked the ministry leaders to thank Ramesh for sending the man with his donkey to rescue me. They replied, "Ramesh says he doesn't know what you mean. He didn't send anyone with a donkey."

I weighed myself on a set of scales at the guest house, and was shocked to discover the toll my illness had taken on my body. I had lost 23 kg (50 pounds) during the ten days I was away.

Looking back, I believe the experience in Nepal had two major effects on my life, one negative and the other hugely positive. On the negative side, something was permanently altered in my body from the stress and trauma of the altitude sickness. From that time on, my metabolism functioned in a haywire manner. I could put on weight quickly, and also lose it quickly. This led to great swings in my physical well-being. More importantly, on the positive side, the brief vision God shared with me of His heart for the peoples of Asia revolutionized my life and service for Him.

Although the Lord Jesus had first called me in 1987 and had thrust me onto the mission field while still in my teens, with the benefit of hindsight I believe the ministry of Asia Harvest commenced that night in April 1991 atop the remote Himalayan mountain. My heavenly vision in Nepal was the launching pad for everything that has happened in my life since that day. Over the years, God has unfolded this vision in amazing ways, as the remainder of my story will reveal.

My hope and prayer is that one day, like the Apostle Paul, I may be able to say, "I was not disobedient to the vision from heaven" (Acts 26:19).

CHAPTER 17
THE TEMPTATION

My long and eventful nine-month journey through Asia proved to be a pivotal time in my life. Although I never attended a formal mission school, I received a thorough education from God during my travels. Today, our ministry has a significant and effective work in every one of the countries I first visited in 1991.

I caught a flight from India to Hong Kong, and commenced the next stage of my adventure with Jesus. I was thrilled to rent a small place in a remote area of Hong Kong, just a stone's throw from the Chinese border. My humble abode was a tin shed used for storage and to hang laundry, but it was large enough for me and I was glad to call it home. The rent was just US$100 per month, which was unheard of for any kind of accommodation in one of the world's most expensive cities.

My new home soon gained a legendary reputation among my fellow missionaries. Living there meant becoming part of the food chain! The dwelling was owned by a Hakka Chinese family who operated a poultry farm with 5,000 caged chickens right outside my door. Every morning the chicken excrement was hosed down and swept into a small creek behind the property. At those times the smell was unbearable. One friend who came to visit had to turn back, gagging from the overpowering stench. Colleagues mockingly dubbed my home "the chicken coop."

The chicken waste and newly hatched eggs attracted many rats and mice, against which I waged a constant battle. The rodents, in turn, attracted snakes. One evening, as I was preparing to go to sleep, I heard a rustling noise outside. At first I thought it was the wind, but then I leapt out of bed when a giant python squeezed through the gap beneath the iron gate that served as my front door. I grabbed a tennis racket to defend myself, but the python slithered behind some boxes stacked against the wall. I sprinted outside, probably the most terrified I've ever been. I alerted my landlord, who came with a flashlight to inspect my home, but failed to find the snake. He concluded it had left the same way it had entered, and was angry with me for not capturing it. My cowardice had cost his family a bountiful supply of snake meat and snake-skin soup!

Some may shudder at the description of my living conditions, but I was overjoyed to have a place to call my own, where I could shut the door and spend time alone with God. In later years I lived in more attractive and hygienic dwellings, but I fondly remember those early days as precious times when God taught me to be content regardless of my circumstances. Like the Apostle Paul, I was able to say:

> I know what it is to be in need, and I know what it is to have plenty. I have learned the secret of being content in any and every situation, whether well fed or hungry, whether living in plenty or in want. I can do all this through him who gives me strength.
>
> **Philippians 4:12–13**

I reconnected with the Bible courier ministry I had worked with three years earlier. They asked me to lead teams across the border, but things felt different. The borders were the same and the need for Bibles in China remained great, but something had changed during my absence. I was particularly disturbed by one new trend that had taken place. Most of the Bible ministries now included teaching books inside the bags of Bibles being carried into China. The books often contained the pet doctrines of a particular denomination, which made me feel very uncomfortable. I had met many Chinese church leaders in 1988, and not one of them had ever asked for doctrinal or teaching books. Their constant request was, "Please bring us the Word of God."

* * *

The Lord Jesus continued to lay a solid foundation in my life, but whenever He builds something for His Father's glory, the devil is not far behind, and is busy laying traps to ensnare believers. All of God's servants inevitably arrive at a key moment on their journey, an important crossroad. A wrong turn may mean that their ministry never flourishes as God intended. In the worst cases, their faith may be shipwrecked by unwise choices.

By late 1991 my finances had dried up and I was struggling to survive. My home church in Australia had pledged to support me monthly, but for much of the year I hadn't received anything from them. To make matters worse, church members sometimes sent me notes saying things like, "We were glad to put the extra $100 in the offering for you last Sunday." Not only was the church failing to send what they had promised, but it appeared that they were even pocketing donations that people had designated for me. I didn't want to whine about my missing support. After all, I hadn't asked the church to support me, but they had offered to do so. If they had decided to focus elsewhere, who was I to complain?

At the time I was praying for enough money to buy a laptop. I had never owned a computer before. A new feature called email was just beginning to take off. Before email, if I needed to communicate quickly with someone on the other side of the world, I had to make a costly international phone call or send a fax.

Instead of seeing an increase of funds in response to my prayer, however, my bank balance fell to just a few dollars. I went to the local market and used all of my remaining money to buy a couple of potatoes and onions. As I consumed the last mouthful, I recalled how God had supernaturally provided for me during my first time in Hong Kong, and I prayed He would again come through.

Then, unexpectedly, what appeared to be an amazing blessing from God fell into my lap. At the time, China's economy was just beginning to open up to the outside world, and foreign investors were able to purchase land to build factories. A Chinese Christian named Mark approached me with what seemed like a wonderful opportunity. He worked for a Hong Kong-based company that was buying thousands of acres of farmland in south China. They were looking for a foreigner to represent them, because investment laws at the time meant that deals involving foreigners resulted in more favorable tax breaks.

I immediately told Mark I wasn't a businessman but that I was called to serve God, and I didn't know anything about the kinds of deals he was involved with. "Don't worry, brother!" he replied. "It's not complicated at all, and it won't take up much of your time. You will be a representative of the company, and you'll simply need to grab your passport and go along with them once or twice while they broker a land purchase. It's easy and won't interfere with your service for the Lord."

I told Mark I would take time to think about it. The next evening he turned up at my door. "Sit down, Paul," he said. "You're going to be amazed. I spoke with my boss today, and he said they have a new land acquisition lined up in two weeks. He wants you to accompany him. They will pick you up and cover all your expenses. If you sign as a representative of the company and the purchase goes through, they will pay you HK$100,000 for your help."

One hundred thousand Hong Kong dollars was equivalent to about US$13,000 at the time. I could scarcely believe it! This development, coming at my lowest financial point when I was struggling to survive, was so unexpected that I knew it had to be either a miracle from God or a trap of Satan.

My first instinct was to brush the whole thing off. I told Mark I couldn't be involved because it would be dishonest of me to claim to be an employee of the Hong Kong company. Mark came again the following day. He had just spoken with his boss, who had assured him that the company was willing to hire me legally. An employment contract was being written up for me to sign. I would be an official representative of the company, and they would provide business cards to confirm it. When I again balked at the offer, Mark went outside to make a call. He returned a few minutes later with a big smile on his face. "Okay, brother," he said. "My boss is growing anxious because time's running out on the land deal. He needs you to commit, and will double your pay to HK$200,000 cash! Half will be paid in advance, and half after the deal has been signed."

My thoughts were in a spin. This all seemed too good to be true, but the assurances that I would be a legal employee of the company had removed some of my reservations. I told Mark I would continue to pray about it, and would let him know as soon as I had an answer from the Lord.

For most of that night I remained awake, seeking God's will. If this was a trick from the devil I wanted nothing to do with it, but I also didn't want to turn down the opportunity only to discover later that it had been God's provision for the work He had called me to do. I was confused, and my prayers didn't provide any clarity.

The next day I decided to share my predicament with two American missionaries. I met with them separately and carefully relayed the whole story. I told them what was required of me, and how much compensation I would be paid.

The first missionary declared, "Paul, this is a great blessing from God! He has surely performed a miracle for you. You'll be able to travel throughout China for quite a while with that much money. Go for it!"

The second missionary listened intently before saying just one sentence: "If you go ahead with this, you will enter into a realm of demonic deception that will take years to extract yourself from."

I returned home with my friends' words ringing in my ears. I had hoped for some clarity, but their totally contradictory advice left me even more confused.

For the next several days I continued to seek God's will. I locked myself in my room and cried out to Him, but there was no response. Mark returned every day to ask if I had reached a decision. He grew increasingly frustrated, until finally he told me his boss had issued an ultimatum. I had twenty-four hours to commit, otherwise they would hire another foreigner and compensate them instead.

That night I went for a walk to clear my mind, but a sense of direction from the Lord continued to elude me. It seemed as though God had closed His ears to my prayers and there was no point discussing the matter further. Two clear choices had been presented to me, and heaven was watching to see which fork in the road I would take.

After returning home from my walk I opened the Bible, and for the first time in almost two weeks things became clear to me. The Holy Spirit convicted me and helped me see that the real battle lay within my heart. I read, "Keep your lives free from the love of money and be content with what you have, because God has said, 'Never will I leave you; never will I forsake you'" (Hebrews 13:5).

Next, I read how the Apostle Paul had exhorted Timothy, "Godliness with contentment is great gain. For we brought nothing into the world, and we can take nothing out of it. But if we have food and clothing, we will be content with that" (1 Timothy 6:6–8).

When I read the next two verses of Paul's letter, my decision became crystal clear:

> Those who want to get rich fall into temptation and a trap and into many foolish and harmful desires that plunge people into ruin and destruction. For the love of money is a root of all kinds of evil. Some people, eager for money, have wandered from the faith and pierced themselves with many griefs.
>
> **1 Timothy 6:9–10**

These Scriptures provided the same warning as the second missionary I had consulted. I was now fully convinced of God's will, revealed through His Word. Even though it was after midnight, I walked to the public phone box and called Mark to break the news. After apologizing for waking him, I announced, "I don't want to be involved with this scheme! It's not right. Your boss will have to find someone else. Please don't speak to me about it again. My decision is final."

Mark simply said, "You're crazy!" and hung up.

Once I had made my final decision I was greatly relieved. For the first time in weeks the peace of the Holy Spirit returned to my heart. I ran home and shouted "Hallelujah!" as I walked through the door.

An extraordinary thing happened immediately following this experience. A few days later I went to the post office and discovered that several letters had arrived. The first one contained a $100 donation. It was the largest gift I had received for a long time. Two other letters contained checks of $25 each, and the final letter included $50. I was no longer bankrupt, and was able to pay my rent on time. In the next few weeks others sent donations and shared how the Spirit of God had directed them to support my work. Their assistance enabled me to serve the Lord more freely, without the stress of wondering how I would pay my next bill, or if I would have enough money to eat that day.

Finally, after more than a month since God had helped me resist the financial temptation by the skin of my teeth, a letter arrived from my home church in Australia. The mission pastor apologized profusely, explaining that his secretary had mistakenly filed my monthly support checks inside her desk drawer and had forgotten to send them to me. Six months of misplaced support was combined into one large check. The following day I bought my first ever computer and printer, which proved to be a tremendous help in my service for the Lord.

From the start, I kept meticulous records of each donation received and every Bible delivered. It is a practice that continues to this day. In 1991 I received a total of US$6,329 in donations.

The Lord stretched that money so that not only was I able to live in one of the most expensive cities in the world (albeit in my modest "chicken coop"), but it also allowed me to lead teams around China and other parts of Asia.

The following year saw God double the support I received, to $12,241. It nearly doubled again to $23,895 in 1993. Not once did I ask any person or church for financial support, nor did I make my personal needs known to anyone except the Lord Jesus. I simply got on with His work, and the Lord did as He had promised on the night He first called me to serve Him: "Seek first his kingdom and his righteousness, and all these things will be given to you as well" (Matthew 6:33).

The lessons from my temptation were seared deep into my conscience. Looking back, I believe if I had chosen the wrong path that day, the money would have become a curse in my life, and I would have found myself both inwardly devastated and disqualified from serving the Lord.

God reminded me that it wasn't my job to run my life, nor was I to serve Him however I saw fit. Instead, I needed to serve the Lord only as He directed me. I nearly joined the long list of Christians derailed by Satan because they made critical errors based on human rationale and greed, rather than being obedient to the Scriptures and the leading of the Holy Spirit.

By the mercy and grace of God, a ministry had suddenly sprung up around me in a completely natural, unforced way. By this time I was sending bi-monthly newsletters to several hundred interested people. The newsletter needed a name, so I called it "Asian Minorities Outreach" to reflect the vision God had given me. Later, the name of both the newsletter and the ministry was changed to Asia Harvest.

CHAPTER 18

FOUNDATION STONES

> As you come to him, the living Stone – rejected by humans but chosen by God and precious to him – you also, like living stones, are being built into a spiritual house to be a holy priesthood, offering spiritual sacrifices acceptable to God through Jesus Christ.
>
> **1 Peter 2:4–5**

As God began to shape a ministry around the work He had called me to do, I keenly desired to structure things differently from most other missionary organizations. I didn't want to do something just because tradition dictated it should be done a certain way. On the contrary, I decided to wait upon the Lord and not rely on human wisdom. The desire God placed in my heart was to set up a ministry that would allow Christians around the world to pray for and support the work on the frontlines in Asia. My two main priorities were to provide Bibles to strengthen the persecuted Church, and to help establish the kingdom of Jesus Christ among unreached people groups.

Just as a building is only as strong as its foundation, so a person starting out in Christian ministry needs to ensure that their life is securely anchored to the Word of God and under the control of the Holy Spirit. If left to flourish, small character flaws grow into large defects which can bring about a Christian's demise. For years it may appear that everything is fine, but in due course a person's life will come crashing down if the foundation is faulty. Jesus said these somber words about a man who built his house on the sand: "The rain came down, the streams rose, and the winds blew and beat against that house, and it fell with a great crash" (Matthew 7:27). I couldn't see much point in trying to achieve great things for God if my personal life was broken and brought dishonor to the Name of Jesus Christ.

After consulting a number of experienced missionaries, it was apparent the devil enjoyed much success defeating God's servants in three main areas. If I was going to last in ministry, I needed to surrender control of these areas daily to the Holy Spirit, and allow Him to build a strong foundation in my life. The main areas of temptation can be summarized by three words starting with the letter G – *gold*, *glory*, and *girls*.

The first temptation, *gold*, was the one I had recently almost succumbed to. The allure of money is obviously not confined to those in Christian service, but ministers are in a precarious position because the funds that come through their hands are not their own. They are tasked with the grave responsibility of distributing the offerings people give to God's work. Stealing from people is a terrible sin, but to steal from the Almighty invites His direct wrath. When Eli's wicked sons abused this great privilege, the Bible says, "This sin of the young men was very great in the Lord's sight, for they were treating the Lord's offering with contempt … it was the Lord's will to put them to death" (1 Samuel 2:17, 25).

I read that in the United States at that time, just 4.3 percent of Christian giving went to support foreign mission work; of that, a mere 0.3 percent was used to reach the least evangelized nations of the world. With shocking statistics like those, I was determined to cherish the resources that passed through my hands and to stretch them as far as possible for the kingdom of God. Accordingly, I worked hard to find the best and most economical way to operate, so that the maximum number of people would hear the Good

News of Christ's salvation. From the start, donations were handled with the utmost care and integrity, a practice that continues to the present day. This approach has enabled us to print more Bibles, to support more evangelists, and to get the most out of the activities the Lord has guided us into.

From the start, our ministry has been transparent in the area of finances, and we make our annual financial statements available to anyone who requests them. In latter years we have voluntarily engaged a company to conduct an independent audit of our finances, and have placed their audit report on our website for anyone to inspect.

By taking these extra steps, we hoped to follow Paul's example of how ministers of the gospel should openly walk, when he wrote:

> Rather, we have renounced secret and shameful ways; we do not use deception, nor do we distort the word of God. On the contrary, by setting forth the truth plainly we commend ourselves to everyone's conscience in the sight of God.
>
> **2 Corinthians 4:2**

Another policy many Christians have come to appreciate is our diligence in providing receipts and personal notes to all supporters, regardless of the size of their gift. One elderly couple began supporting Asia Harvest after we sent a receipt and an encouraging note to their nine-year-old granddaughter, who had broken open her piggy bank to send us a $5 donation. By operating in this way, we have formed a bond of trust with people.

In recent years, people have sometimes asked what our annual budget is. This question always causes me to smile, because we have never operated with a budget. A budget implies we have fixed expenses to meet. Our method has been much simpler: if a thousand dollars comes in for Bibles, we print and distribute a thousand dollars' worth of Bibles. If ten dollars comes in, we provide ten dollars' worth of Bibles. This is how our budget has always worked, and consequently we have rarely worried about God's provision.

The second main temptation my heavenly Father required me to overcome was in the area of *glory*. Many Christian ministers over the years have found themselves entangled in a web of lies, false reports, and exaggerations. The Lord impressed on me how critical it is not to inflate numbers. This temptation seems particularly strong among missionaries, who often feel under pressure to provide exciting stories to their supporters back home. One colleague even liked to boast about how his reports were "evang-*elastic*," meaning he felt at liberty to stretch the facts as needed. Predictably, his ministry later became mired in controversy and his reputation was tarnished.

In my travels throughout Asia I visited mission organizations with huge buildings and many staff members. While God clearly calls different ministries to serve Him in various ways, I felt the Lord wanted to do things differently through me and those I would later work with. He wanted Asia Harvest to be as streamlined and as flexible as possible, and this would enable us to send vital resources to the frontlines of the battle in Asia with minimal delay.

To this day, many people assume Asia Harvest must have impressive headquarters with many employees. In reality, much of our administrative work is done by volunteers who share God's vision for the salvation of Asia. They work from various parts of the world, often from a spare room in their home or from a desk in their garage. As a result, we have always desired to be the smallest ministry we can be, with as few staff as possible. God has nevertheless allowed us to have a large influence for His kingdom.

This simple approach has helped us avoid the trap of seeking "glory" for ourselves. We don't care if people hear about Asia Harvest or not. What matters is that people hear about Jesus, for He promised, "And I, when I am lifted up from the earth, will draw all people to myself" (John 12:32).

The third main area of temptation starting with G that the Living God required me to overcome by the power of His Spirit was *girls*. Multitudes of Christian ministers have shipwrecked their lives on the jagged rocks of sexual sin. Early in my Christian life, I recognized that this temptation would be a struggle for me. During my year at Bible College in Australia, most of the students were at an age when our hormones were raging. Aware that sexual sin begins as an emotional connection between two people, I decided to counter the threat by paying little attention to my female classmates. Some of them thought I was a snob, but as a red-blooded young male it was the best way I knew to help me keep my eyes on Jesus and not flirt with temptation.

As the Lord challenged me to surrender this part of my life to His control, I adopted some practical steps that I thought would help me, regardless of whether I remained single or was married. For example, I decided to never counsel or be alone with a woman who was not my wife. It is not enough for me to simply say, "God knows my heart." The Bible instructs me to not only avoid acts of evil, but also to "abstain from all appearance of evil" (1 Thessalonians 5:22, KJV).

These three major temptations of gold, glory, and girls are areas in which I have experienced God's marvelous grace, but that doesn't mean I am strong in any of them or that I can afford to sit back and feel content. I realize the battle for my integrity is a daily struggle which will continue to my last breath. Any time I begin to feel confident in my own ability to resist sin, I'm reminded of the Apostle Paul's exhortation: "If you think you are standing firm, be careful that you don't fall!" (1 Corinthians 10:12).

Decades later, I look back on the structures that the Lord Jesus built into my life, and I'm thankful for His sustaining grace. Despite my many imperfections and weaknesses, God established a foundation in my life that was able to withstand the fierce storms that followed. Without His wisdom and power, I would have collapsed long ago.

***

In the summer of 1992, a team of more than twenty teenagers from a church in Arizona flew to Hong Kong to work with me. For the next two months we carried thousands of Bibles to hungry believers in several countries. Their visit was both a tremendous blessing to the churches in Asia and a life-changing experience for the young Americans.

The team carried almost a ton of Bibles to the Hmong people in a remote part of southwest China. The Hmong had recently experienced a huge revival owing to the shortwave radio preaching of a Hmong evangelist named John Lee. For years, Lee, from his base in California, faithfully broadcast the gospel in his native language. Despite not receiving any feedback from his target audience, he continued to produce daily programs, not knowing whether anyone was listening. God honored John Lee's perseverance in a remarkable way.

One day, an old Hmong man was tuning his radio when he suddenly heard his own language being spoken. He ran outside and gathered his family to listen with him. Together, for the first time in their lives, they heard about a man named Jesus. Although they didn't comprehend the message, the Hmong were excited to hear their own language on the radio. By the following day the old man had notified the entire village, and hundreds of people gathered around their radios to listen to the program.

The old man had plenty of spare time, so over the next few months he walked to eighteen Hmong villages in the valley. In each community, he tuned everyone's radios to the correct frequency so that they too could hear John Lee's broadcasts. Thousands of people were now listening to the gospel every day, and their hearts and minds gradually opened to the truth.

Over time, the radical teaching so gripped their hearts that the Hmong decided they must choose either to accept the gospel or to never listen again. The leaders of all eighteen Hmong villages gathered for a crucial meeting to discuss the problem. After much debate, they decided all of their people should become Christians!

Without any churches, evangelists or pastors to advise them, the new Hmong believers decided to obey whatever the radio preacher instructed them to do. One day the program was about God's hatred of idolatry. In response, the Hmong immediately smashed their idols and tore down the ancestral tablets that had adorned the walls of their homes for centuries. When they heard a teaching about water baptism, in simple faith they dug pits in the ground, filled them with water from a nearby stream, and baptized each other.

This move of God among the Hmong people was anything but superficial. He was moving powerfully in their midst. Drug addicts were delivered from their bondage, broken marriages were repaired, and many wrongs were made right.

At the time, John Lee and his radio ministry were still unaware of these extraordinary events that were taking place. Then one day, Lee taught about the Lamb's Book of Life. Again, the Hmong didn't fully understand the teaching, but they all agreed they needed to be included in this book! Months later, a large package arrived at the radio ministry's California office. The curious staff saw that the package had been mailed from China, and they opened it to discover a bundle of papers with the names and signatures of some 10,000 Hmong people. Attached was a cover letter, saying, "Dear Sir, please include the following people in the Lamb's Book of Life!"

It was a great honor to deliver several thousand Hmong Bibles to these hungry Christians. Almost as soon as the American team returned home, their church saw the positive impact the trip had made in the lives of their young people, and they launched a plan to send another large team the following year. This was the start of a period of hosting numerous short-term mission teams from around the world. Tons of desperately needed Bibles were purchased, hauled across borders, and delivered into the hands of believers in the closed Asian countries of China, Vietnam, Laos, and Myanmar.

After the teams returned home and shared their experiences, I began to receive invitations to speak in many countries. This, in turn, resulted in more support from churches and individuals. God had first established a foundation of integrity in my life, and now He was causing an effective ministry to spring up from the fertile soil.

CHAPTER 19

GOING NATIVE

Foreigners can never successfully direct the propagation of any faith throughout a whole country. If the faith does not become naturalized and expand among the people by its own vital power, it exercises an alarming and hateful influence, and men fear and shun it as something alien.

Roland Allen

I look upon foreign missionaries as the scaffolding around a rising building. The sooner it can be dispensed with, the better; or rather, the sooner it can be transferred to other places, to serve the same temporary use, the better.

J. Hudson Taylor

During my travels in the Muslim country of Bangladesh I stayed at a hostel operated by a traditional European mission. The hosts were kind and welcoming, but I found the experience surreal. Their mission compound was surrounded by a high concrete wall topped with barbed wire and shards of broken glass, to dissuade anyone who might be foolish enough to attempt to scale it. An armed security guard sat in a booth at the only entrance to the property. The mission was like a fortress, completely separating the Christians inside from the masses outside. Although I understood the dangers of working in an Islamic nation, I couldn't imagine how that mission would ever be able to effectively reach the 150 million lost people of Bangladesh. It reminded me of what Mahatma Gandhi, the "father of modern India," once told his missionary friends: "Noble as you are, you have isolated yourselves from the very people you want to serve."

Later, I visited the Yao ethnic group in south China. Few of the two million Yao people have ever believed in Jesus Christ. Over a cup of tea, an American missionary, speaking fluent Chinese, began to share the gospel with a Yao family. Within minutes a crowd gathered to see what was happening. The missionary declared in a loud voice, "Please listen carefully. We bring good tidings to you! This is the most important news you will ever hear in your life. We have come to tell you about the Son of God, who came to earth two thousand years ago…"

As the curious villagers listened intently, an elderly Yao woman came in from the fields and placed her bundle of straw on the ground. My colleague continued his message by repeating, "This is the most important message you will ever hear! God sent His Son two thousand years ago…"

At that, the old woman interjected, "Wait a minute! You claim this is the most important news we'll ever hear. I don't believe you. If what you're saying is true, then why has it taken you two thousand years to come and tell us about it?"

Experiences like this confirmed in my heart that a radically different approach was needed if the Lord Jesus would ever receive His inheritance among all the people groups of Asia. In China, India, and many other Asian countries, Christianity is viewed as a foreign religion, and therefore something to be shunned and treated with deep suspicion. When foreign missionaries conduct frontline evangelism, this misconception of Jesus being a Western deity is often reinforced. To me, it was blatantly obvious that Asian Christians were much better placed to reach their own people. I was convinced that Asians sharing Christ within their own culture was by far the best way for the gospel to flourish throughout Asia.

During my travels I met many courageous Asian men and women who loved Jesus Christ and desired to make Him known among the unreached. However, they often lacked the necessary resources to implement God's call on their lives. Surrounded by millions of lost people, they frequently felt discouraged and overwhelmed. With a little encouragement and practical help, I hoped the Asian Christians would be able to launch out and achieve their call to reach the lost.

The realization that Asian Christians are best placed to reach their own people may seem obvious to many, but I have been amazed to find resistance to this basic concept throughout the Western Church. Many traditional organizations are convinced that the Great Commission will only be accomplished by sending "the West to the Rest," and nothing anyone says will convince them otherwise. Once when I visited the denominational headquarters of a large mission in the United States, the executives asked me to share a brief message with the staff. The room filled with tension the moment I mentioned the necessity of coming alongside the Asian Church to help them get the job done.

A strategy of serving the Church in Asia does not mean that Westerners aren't needed. Most Asian church leaders I meet are not looking for handouts. They tell me with tears in their eyes how eagerly they desire to partner with strong Western believers for the sake of the gospel. The tragic consequence of the traditional mission approach is that many Western missionaries miss out on the joy of serving God with their Asian brothers and sisters. Consequently, the diverse gifts and strengths the Holy Spirit has placed within different parts of the Body of Christ are not utilized as He intends.

I gradually came to understand that my chief role was to create a support structure for the Church in Asia, through which strategic resources could be provided to help them complete the Great Commission. Adopting this approach meant I needed to sit down and ask church leaders to open their hearts and share their God-given hopes and dreams.

It took considerable time and effort to develop the kind of deep mutual trust needed to form healthy partnerships to effectively advance the gospel. The Lord wanted our ministry to have an attitude of serving the Asian Church, not the other way around. When the kind of partnership exists where all sides are content to remain hidden as long as Jesus is exalted, a powerful spiritual dynamic emerges. Paul's ministry was conducted this way. He told one church, "What we preach is not ourselves, but Jesus Christ as Lord, and ourselves as your servants for Jesus' sake" (2 Corinthians 4:5).

To some, adopting a support role might seem like a comfortable position for me and my colleagues to take, but I have noticed that whenever military conflict erupts, the first thing each side attempts to do is to bomb the opposition supply lines. If they can cut off their enemy's access to resources, they will isolate the frontline soldiers, leaving them as easy targets. We have experienced enough spiritual bombardment over the years to know that this principle applies just as much to Christian work as to physical combat.

During the Gulf War in the early 1990s, I read that twenty-six full-time support workers were required to place and sustain each American soldier on the frontlines of the battle. Without the myriad trainers, mechanics, engineers, communication experts, analysts, cooks, and other support personnel, the soldiers would be unable to successfully complete their task. I recognized that the same principle is true in the Body of Christ. Both frontline soldiers and those who provide supplies are crucial in the work of God's kingdom, and both are rewarded by the Lord. King David once declared, "The share of the man who stayed with the supplies is to be the same as that of him who went down to the battle. All shall share alike" (1 Samuel 30:24).

The pervading "West to the Rest" mission philosophy remains widespread today. Many Western churches and organizations simply cannot imagine the Great Commission as anything other than Western Christians taking their message to the rest of the world. Tragically, this narrow mindset is a major reason why half the world is still waiting to hear the gospel two thousand years after Jesus conquered the grave.

* * *

Like many Christians, I had been conditioned to think that God's plan is to reach all the countries on earth. The Lord Jesus said, "This gospel of the kingdom will be preached in the whole world as a testimony to all nations, and then the end will come" (Matthew 24:14). This verse confused me, because there are already disciples of Christ in every geopolitical country on earth, but the Lord has not yet returned.

One day, I discovered that the word translated "nation" in English Bibles comes from the Hebrew word *goy* and the corresponding Greek word *ethnae*, from which we derive the word "ethnic." This realization made me feel that I had found a key to solving a mystery. Armed with this key, the scales fell from my eyes and I was now able to read the Scriptures in a new light. I saw that hundreds of passages in both the Old and the New Testament revealed God's master plan to redeem all ethnic groups. Despite being one of the major themes of the entire Bible, I had failed to recognize it.

God first revealed His wonderful redemption plan to Abraham, whom He told, "I will bless those who bless you, and whoever curses you I will curse; and all peoples on earth will be blessed through you" (Genesis 12:3). Centuries later, Jesus commanded His followers to "go and make disciples of all nations [ethnic groups]" (Matthew 28:19). It is a great encouragement to know that God is accomplishing His plan, and one day there will be "a great multitude that no one could count, from every nation [ethnic group], tribe, people and language, standing before the throne and before the Lamb" (Revelation 7:9).

I learned that of the approximately 7,000 unreached ethnic groups in the world today, a staggering 5,000 are located in Asia. I was in the most strategic place to make a difference for my Lord!

One night I had a vivid dream which deeply impacted my life and altered the course of my work. In the dream, I was walking along a mountain trail that was strewn with rocks of various shapes and sizes. The rocks represented different unreached people groups. Some were huge and others relatively small, but all were deeply entrenched in the soil on the side of the mountain. As I walked along, I tried to push them loose so that they would tumble down into the valley below. I sat down on the ground and used my legs to push against the stubborn boulders with all my might, but they didn't budge from the positions in which they had been entrenched for centuries.

In my dream I grew frustrated by my lack of progress, when all of a sudden groups of Asian men and women approached me on the trail. Seeing what I was trying to do, they immediately began to dig away dirt and pebbles from around the base of a large boulder. Now that many hands were united in the same task, the boulder finally began to move. When it lurched onto its side we let out a great victory shout! We began shoving and kicking it some more, and it finally rolled over again. Before long, the seemingly immovable boulder was careening down the side of the mountain, crushing everything in its path as it gathered momentum.

When I almost died from altitude sickness in Nepal, God showed me a beautiful vision of His loving heart for the lost sheep of Asia. Now, through this vivid dream, He refined my call and revealed what the main focus was to be for the rest of my life.

My role wasn't to personally try to start churches among Asia's unreached peoples, but to dislodge rocks and pebbles by raising prayer and awareness within the Body of Christ. After a while, with God's anointing, Christian fellowships would be established among those groups. As the gospel continued to spread, the communities of believers in each ethnic group would gather their own momentum and would prove impossible for the devil to stop. By helping to bring in the harvest, I hoped to be counted among those who "look forward to the day of God and speed its coming" (2 Peter 3:12).

I soon discovered that Satan and his armies don't react kindly when unreached people groups are being delivered from centuries of spiritual oppression. Each nation liberated by the blood of Jesus Christ means that the devil's final destination in the lake of fire is one step closer. I needed to prepare for unrelenting spiritual warfare. The Bible warns, "Woe to the earth and the sea, because the devil has gone down to you! He is filled with fury, because he knows that his time is short" (Revelation 12:12).

CHAPTER 20

JOY

As I continued to throw myself into my work, for the first time I began to feel very lonely. I knew Jesus was with me and had promised to never leave or forsake me, but my thoughts began to contemplate how wonderful it would be to have the companionship of a wife to share my journey with.

The truth is that although I had a very high opinion of Jesus, I thought very lowly of myself. I couldn't imagine that any woman would be interested in marrying me. If I were to find one who did, she would need to be very special, because I had no money or worldly prospects, and I lived in a small tin shed known as "the chicken coop". All I had to offer a potential wife was my call from God, and I knew the path was likely to become very rocky along the way.

Growing up, I had never had a girlfriend. I had wanted one, but I had attended all-boy schools and had consequently acquired no skills to help me interact with members of the fairer sex. I felt very awkward whenever I was around women. As feelings of loneliness gnawed away within me I began to pray, asking the Lord to perform a miracle if it was His will for me to get married.

During a phone call with the pastor of my home church, he asked how I was doing and whether or not I'd developed any romantic interest. I told him I was feeling quite lonely but it was almost impossible for me to find anyone compatible owing to my call from God and my determination not to swerve from it. He provided some wise advice. "Don't worry," he said. "Whatever you do, don't divert from God's call. Keep doing what He's told you to do, and if the Lord has someone for you, He's more than capable of bringing her across your path at the right time."

A short time later, a large mission team visited Hong Kong to work with a Bible courier ministry I had never interacted with. That ministry was led by an elderly American couple, along with their son and daughter-in-law. They were short-staffed at the time, and asked if I was available to help lead the team into China alongside their two long-term workers: a middle-aged Canadian man, and an attractive twenty-one-year-old American lady named Joy.

Joy came from a small town of a few thousand people in Idaho. I had never previously met anyone from Idaho, but the few opportunities we had to speak with one another were marred by my awkwardness. At the time I spoke with a heavy New Zealand accent, and she struggled to understand much of what I said.

From the first time I met Joy I was stunned by her beauty. She was physically gorgeous, but what attracted me most was her inward beauty. Having been raised in a godly family, Joy had loved the Lord Jesus since she was a little girl. When she was just four years old she begged her mother to allow her to be baptized. When the church leaders discovered that her request was based on her love for God and a conscious desire to obey Him, they didn't see any reason to refuse her request, and she was baptized into the family of God.

On a human level I felt that Joy was out of my league. Although I thought there was little chance I could ever marry her, I decided to discreetly enquire about her status, just in case. "Forget it!" the Canadian missionary tersely informed me. "She has a serious boyfriend back home and they're planning to get married soon."

This news didn't surprise me, and it immediately put to rest any thoughts I had of pursuing the young lady. I didn't realize, however, that the Canadian missionary had just told me a bare-faced lie. Joy was single and had no marriage plans at all. The missionary fancied

Joy for himself, and he didn't want me as a potential competitor.

After that initial contact I went about my work in China, and I didn't see Joy for a few months. One afternoon, I was surprised to receive a call from the son of her ministry leader. He had a small group coming to carry Bibles to a house church in the coastal Chinese city of Xiamen. They needed someone to lead them, and he asked if I could go, as the Canadian missionary had another commitment and nobody else was available.

"Let me pray about it," I replied.

The ministry leader said, "Thanks, Paul. Let me know your answer as soon as possible." He then added, "By the way, I think you have met Joy. She will be traveling with the group too."

To be honest, after receiving this news I found it rather difficult to seek God's will with an undiluted heart! The next day I confirmed my availability to make the journey to Xiamen. Several days later we flew into the bustling seaside city, loaded down with suitcases and bags of Bibles.

In those days it wasn't possible to buy return air tickets for flights inside China. Travelers had to personally go to a city and then purchase a ticket to their next destination. After we had safely handed over all our Bibles, I went down to the airline office and tried to buy tickets back to Hong Kong. I was unaware that the annual Qingming Festival was about to commence, when Chinese families return home to sweep their ancestors' graves. Because of the Festival, all flights out of Xiamen were sold out for the next several days. I attempted to book train or boat tickets, but they too were unavailable.

I was stuck in Xiamen several days longer than expected, with the small team of Bible couriers and the young American lady named Joy! Those few days were wonderful, as our team enjoyed a mini vacation. Joy and I laughed heartily and had a happy time together as we got to know each other in relaxed surroundings.

The Festival finally ended and we flew back to Hong Kong, where I received a hostile reception from the Bible ministry, especially from the Canadian man. They were convinced I had manufactured the delay so I could spend time romancing Joy, and they didn't believe a word of my explanation about the effects of the Qingming Festival on local travel arrangements! I made my way home to my chicken coop on the China border, while Joy returned to her ministry's guest house. We didn't see one another again for weeks, but our special time in Xiamen had resulted in the seeds of a mutual attraction taking root in our hearts.

Over the following few months I prayed hard, asking my heavenly Father to perform a miracle if Joy was the one He wanted to be my life partner. Joy was everything I could hope for. Because she was already pursuing her own call from God, I wouldn't need to persuade her of the validity of my vision for Asia.

Joy had left home at the age of eighteen to attend a Bible College in the state of Tennessee. While she was there, God opened her heart to His work around the world, and she traveled to Hong Kong to help carry Bibles into China. She had already been serving for almost a year when I first met her.

Although our different ministry obligations meant I wasn't able to see Joy regularly, I obtained the phone number of her guest house and called her most evenings. The times we spent chatting on the phone were exhilarating, and each time I couldn't wait for our next conversation.

Unexpectedly, one morning the son of her ministry leader called to ask if I could help him move some furniture in his van. I agreed to help, and was thrilled to discover that he also had plans to pick up Joy and drop her back at their guest house. My heart pounded in my chest when I saw her again!

After completing the tasks that day, the leader dropped me at a train station so I could make my way back home. As I exited the van I turned around and shook Joy's hand. "Nice to see you again," I calmly stated, trying not to betray my nervousness.

"When will I see you next?" she sweetly enquired.

"Oh, I don't know," I replied. "Probably never."

As I closed the van door I glanced at Joy in the back seat, and thought I saw tears welling up in her eyes.

Thinking I had done well by acting so cool under pressure, I consoled myself with the knowledge that I would soon be back home talking with her on the phone. I was also comforted because Joy had given me the number of her home in Idaho. I kept the number in a secure place, wondering if it might come in handy one day.

* * *

My evening conversations with Joy were always the high point of my day, while on those occasions when we were unable to connect I was left feeling empty and sad. One evening I called her at the normal time, and for more than an hour we chatted about the Lord and shared what we'd done that day. As we concluded our call, my heart glowed with admiration for Joy. She had become a close friend, and I was falling deeply in love with her.

Five minutes later my phone rang unexpectedly. It was Joy, but something was obviously wrong. "Paul, I'm so sorry," she stammered. "Please don't call me again. We can't talk anymore."

I was devastated and confused! I wanted to know what had happened in those few minutes, but she was unwilling to share the reasons for her sudden and dramatic change of mind.

Several days of silence followed, until I could hardly stand it anymore. I found the courage to call Joy again, even though she had explicitly asked me not to. She sounded hurt, but still managed to deliver a chilling message: "Please don't contact me again. We are not meant to be together. If it was God's will, things would be different. Don't try to talk with me, see me, or write to me ever again, okay?"

I didn't know how to respond. It felt as if a claw of darkness had descended upon me and ripped out my heart. Our call ended, and I was left alone in my isolated tin shed, with only the sound of clucking chickens to keep me company.

* * *

Joy: From the first time I met Paul, I was attracted to his strong, decisive leadership qualities and his sense of humor. I also admired the genuine call of God I saw on his life. I looked for opportunities to talk with him, but he didn't seem interested in me. We traveled together with a small team to Xiamen and we got along well. I loved every moment I spent with him.

A week or two later, however, I was devastated when he told me that I would probably never see him again. I was confused, but when he called me a few days later I was relieved and very happy.

One evening, the leader of the ministry I worked with tried to call me for more than an hour. When he finally got through, he was enraged to find out I had been talking with Paul. I sobbed as his fierce anger came down the phone line against me. He demanded I break off the relationship immediately, firmly stating that I was not allowed to talk to, see, or write to him ever again.

With quivering lips I called Paul back and asked him not to contact me again. I knew he was heartbroken, and I could hear the deep sadness and confusion in his voice.

CHAPTER 21

INTIMIDATION

> I know enough about Satan to realize that he will have all his weapons ready for determined opposition. Only a simpleton would expect plain sailing in any work of God.
>
> **James O. Fraser**

Several more days passed, and I still had no idea why Joy had cut me off so abruptly. Then I received a call from the elderly leader of Joy's ministry, a man I will call Calvin. He and his wife Rhonda had been away in the United States, so I had never met them before. Calvin said they would appreciate having an opportunity to meet me, and invited me over for dinner at their home. The following afternoon I made my way to their comfortable apartment.

Rhonda welcomed me at the door and showed me to a chair in the living room, where I met Calvin, a small man in his late sixties whose deep wrinkles made him appear even older. The atmosphere was extremely tense, and it was clear that our time together was going to be stressful. It was soon apparent that they hadn't welcomed me into their home to get to know me. They had invited me over to issue a threat.

"We understand you have taken a liking to Joy," they said. "Well, we treat her like she is our own daughter. Joy's parents entrusted her into our care while she's in Asia, and it's our job to protect her. We are letting you know that you won't be seeing Joy again.

We have forbidden her to talk with or see you, and she has agreed it's the best thing to do. It's your choice what course of action you decide to take, but if you cause Joy to break her vow, we won't hesitate to send her back to America. Now, you wouldn't want such a disgraceful thing to happen to her, would you?"

Calvin and Rhonda stared at me over the rims of their glasses, their fiery eyes awaiting my response.

I paused for a moment while my mind raced, thinking about how I should respond. I wanted to say, "Shut up! Who do you think you are? It's none of your concern and I will pursue Joy if I like. Get out of my life and mind your own business!"

Calvin and Rhonda had put me on the spot and backed me into a tight corner. Instead, I looked at them and said, "Alright. I don't want anything bad to happen to Joy, so I will leave her alone."

I made the long journey back home to my chicken coop. A month went by, and I found myself so burdened by what had taken place that for the first time since I had met Jesus Christ, I fell into a deep depression. I locked the door of my home and didn't want to see anyone. I stayed up at night and slept during the day, and was so devoid of energy that I wondered if I had suffered an emotional breakdown. I knew it was going to take me a while to recover.

In my darkest moments of confusion and depression, however, I couldn't shake a thought from my head. Deep within, I still believed that Joy was supposed to be my wife. It had certainly felt that way during the limited times we had spent together, and on every subsequent occasion we had spoken on the phone.

I sensed a real possibility that all of the fierce opposition against Joy and me was originating from Satan. I therefore held on to a flicker of hope that somehow, somewhere, it would all work out between us. If it didn't work out, I couldn't imagine ever being interested in marrying another woman. I believed God had already revealed my wife to me, but she had been cruelly snatched away.

Another month passed without a word from Joy. Then one night a typhoon lashed in from the South China Sea, drenching everything in its path. Despite the foul weather, I felt I needed to get out of my home and connect with the Lord Jesus Christ. One way or another, I was desperate to receive an answer from Him regarding Joy. At one o'clock in the morning, I decided to ride my bicycle to a remote bay in a place called Sha Tau Kok on the Chinese border. The torrential rain and howling wind made it impossible to ride, so I sheltered my bicycle behind a wall and continued on foot, drenched to the bone.

After a while, I came to an intersection where the road branched off into the mountains. Feeling paralyzed with deep sorrow, I desperately needed to hear from the Lord right at that moment. If Joy was supposed to be my wife, then I needed the Living God to do a miracle and make a way for us to reconnect. If it wasn't His will for Joy and me to marry, I needed to surrender my hopes and dreams to the Lord, and try to forget I had ever met her.

At that time of night I had the country road to myself, so I knelt down on the side of the road and poured out my heart to my heavenly Father. With raw emotion I cried out at the top of my voice, "Dear Lord Jesus, please have mercy on me! Please reveal Your will. If Joy and I are not meant to be together, please remove this deep pain from my heart. If You want us to be husband and wife, I beg You to perform a miracle. Please do something, Lord!"

I felt I should humble myself before the Lord Jesus Christ by prostrating myself on the road. Knowing that no vehicles were likely to come because of the dire weather and the time of night, I went into the middle of the isolated road and lay face down in the driving rain for about ten minutes, groaning in agony as I released the situation into God's hands. It was the kind of intense prayer described by the Apostle Paul:

> The Spirit helps us in our weakness. We do not know what we ought to pray for, but the Spirit himself intercedes for us

> through wordless groans. And he who searches our hearts knows the mind of the Spirit, because the Spirit intercedes for God's people in accordance with the will of God.
>
> **Romans 8:26–27**

As I prayed, a deep sense enveloped me that Jesus was in control. Even though I didn't understand what was happening, He knew, and my job was to trust Him with all my heart. I felt humbled by His awesome presence, and after a while I returned home and dried myself off. Before drifting off to sleep, I opened my Bible and read these words of Jesus:

> "Very truly I tell you, unless a grain of wheat falls to the ground and dies, it remains only a single seed. But if it dies, it produces many seeds. Anyone who loves their life will lose it, while anyone who hates their life in this world will keep it for eternal life."
>
> **John 12:24–25**

"Yes, Lord," I sighed. "Now I understand. You haven't called me to love my life, but to give it up to You. I hand Joy back. She's Your daughter, and she belongs to You. Not my will, but Yours be done."

I fell into a deep sleep, emotionally and mentally exhausted.

* * *

The end of 1992 was approaching and I was scheduled to visit North America. Friends had arranged for me to speak in various churches, and one of my first stops was Phoenix, Arizona. My host family could tell I was carrying a deep burden, but I didn't want to share my pain with them, so I kept the story of my relationship with Joy to myself. One afternoon, a friend asked if I would like to attend a prayer meeting being held at someone's home. I really didn't feel like meeting anyone, but before I was able to say no we were on our way to a gathering of about twenty intercessors, none of whom I had ever met.

We parked on the street and walked up the driveway to the house, where the prayer meeting was already in progress. My friend knocked and we were told to come in. As I stepped through the front door, the insect screen snapped shut behind me with a loud bang. I glanced apologetically at the circle of intercessors, who were mostly middle-aged women. One lady looked up, and our eyes met.

I found a place to sit down, and a few minutes later my friend introduced me and I was given a warm welcome. The lady who had noticed me when I first entered the house then suddenly declared, "Young man, we have never met before and I know nothing about you, but I need to tell you that when you first entered this house I looked into your eyes and I saw that a spirit of witchcraft is oppressing you. Can we please pray for you?"

I was taken aback. A spirit of witchcraft? My flesh wanted to cry out in protest, "I'm sorry, but you are badly mistaken! I'm a servant of Jesus Christ, and I'm not involved in any dark arts. I have seen the Lord move in amazing ways…"

Thankfully, before any boastful words came out of my mouth, the lady gently added, "Please allow me to explain what I mean. Witchcraft doesn't only occur when someone actively engages in wickedness. It may also be defined as the ungodly spiritual control and manipulation of one person over another."

Her explanation made me feel more at ease. I shared how I had lost the woman I believed God had chosen to be my wife, and I described how I had been manipulated into agreeing to leave her alone.

The intercessors gathered around, laid hands on me, and prayed up a storm! They encouraged me to renounce the moment I had submitted to the ungodly demands of the elderly couple in Hong Kong. They prayed against all demonic forces that were arrayed against me to prevent God's will from being done in my life.

Only later did I realize that the deep depression I had been under for months had commenced the very moment I had nodded my head and verbally agreed to the demands of Joy's ministry leaders. In effect, by refusing to stand up against Calvin and Rhonda, I had willingly submitted to them. They had been like schoolyard bullies, and I had given in to their insidious demands. My compliance had invited a spiritual darkness into my life which had plunged me into confusion and depression.

That prayer group in the suburbs of Phoenix helped break me free from the power of Satan. When they prayed, it felt as though a heavy burden was released from me. I left the meeting feeling like a new man! The dark cloud lifted, and the remainder of my time in the United States went well. I was able to minister effectively, and many lives were touched in the meetings where I spoke.

I had foolishly agreed to Calvin and Rhonda's demands that I stop pursuing Joy because of fear. I had been afraid of hurting Joy if she were to be sent home in disgrace, and I hadn't wanted to show disrespect to those elderly Christians who had a good reputation in the missions community. My fears had provided a foothold for the enemy to bring spiritual bondage into my life. The Bible says, "Fear of man will prove to be a snare, but whoever trusts in the Lord is kept safe" (Proverbs 29:25).

This experience taught me how easy it is to be lured into the demonic trap of fear and intimidation, but the Word of God and the prayers of other believers can set us free. Intimidation is an awful curse for a Christian to give in to. It is one of Satan's favorite tools; left unchecked, it will ultimately lead to our demise. Even the great prophet Elijah gave in to intimidation. Just hours after he saw fire fall from heaven and experienced a great victory over the false prophets of Baal, the wicked Queen Jezebel vowed to cut off his head. A terrified Elijah fled into the desert, where he "came to a broom bush, sat down under it and prayed that he might die. 'I have had enough, Lord,' he said. 'Take my life; I am no better than my ancestors'" (1 Kings 19:4).

If we give in to intimidation, it's easy to lose a correct sense of perspective, which may ultimately require the Lord to set us aside from His service. After Elijah lost his perspective, God commanded him to appoint Elisha as his replacement. His ministry had come to an end.

I learned an unforgettable lesson that day in Phoenix, and I determined to never again allow anyone to intimidate me. I would refuse to agree to any ungodly demands, and if I ever saw that couple again I would tell them what I wished I had said that night I visited their apartment.

The Lord graciously allowed me to overcome this experience. Today, almost twenty-five years later, God has helped me to never be intimidated like that again, although many have attempted to use that tactic against me. My subsequent journey has contained many rough patches and difficult times, but I have never again experienced the persistent, overpowering depression I did during the dark period before the Lord delivered me from the oppressive spirit of witchcraft.

CHAPTER 22
AMERICA

> Jesus has many who love His kingdom in heaven, but few who bear His cross. He has many who desire comfort, but few who desire suffering. He finds many to share His feast, but few His fasting. All desire to rejoice with Him, but few are willing to suffer for His sake ... Those who love Jesus for His own sake, and not for the sake of comfort for themselves, bless Him in every trial and anguish of heart, no less than in the greatest joy. And were He never willing to bestow comfort on them, they would still always praise Him and give Him thanks.
>
> **Thomas à Kempis (1380–1471)**

I spent much of 1993 serving the Lord throughout Asia, while still feeling inwardly devastated by my shattered relationship with Joy. I did my best to put her out of my mind, but it was difficult. No matter how hard I tried, I couldn't escape the thought that this beautiful young lady was supposed to be my wife, yet she remained under the wicked control of her ministry leaders, who had forced her to agree to never contact me again. I didn't see Joy or hear any news about her for many months. There was absolutely nothing I could do to win her or to alter the situation.

Then one afternoon I unexpectedly saw Joy as she was walking along the bank of a canal in Hong Kong. After a brief exchange of pleasantries, we continued on our separate ways. Although we only talked for a few seconds, the moment our eyes met, the deep love I had for Joy again welled up in my heart. I was still completely smitten by her. Following our brief encounter, I didn't have any more contact with Joy for months.

In October 1993, as I recovered from a grueling trip to southwest China, an Australian missionary popped by to say hello. In the midst of our conversation he casually asked, "Do you remember that American girl, Joy? I heard she's flying back to America soon. Didn't you fancy her for a while?"

It was the first time I had heard Joy's name mentioned for a long time. A full year had passed since our relationship had been cruelly upended by Calvin and his wife. I was saddened to learn that Joy would soon be leaving Asia, and I sensed that my chance to know her had slipped away. If she was leaving permanently, I wanted to at least say goodbye.

A few days later I mustered up the courage to call her. I prayed for God's peace to envelop me as I nervously dialed the number. The last time I called Joy a tsunami of trouble had swept into her life, and I didn't want to cause her any more strife.

I was surprised when she answered straight away. The moment I heard her lovely voice say, "Hi, Paul," my heart again melted. I told her I had heard she was going home. "Yes, I'm leaving next week," she confirmed.

When I asked if I could see her one last time to say goodbye, Joy replied, "No, that's not a good idea. Things have been quite difficult for me recently, and seeing you won't help the situation. I'm sorry it turned out so badly for us. If God was in it, things would have worked out differently."

My hopes were again dashed, but I was glad to have spoken with Joy one last time. Our relationship was truly dead and buried. My emotions had been crushed for so long that I had reached the stage where I just didn't have the energy to fight anymore. I truly gave up on the possibility of marrying her. Nobody on earth could do a thing to change the situation.

To help relieve the burden of my lovesick heart, I composed a poem about Joy, which I kept between myself and God. My poem is entitled "I Give you Back:"

And now I must give you back.
Though my heart aches
And tears well up in my eyes,
I must give you back to Him.

As my soul releases you,
I cast off all my hopes and dreams
And face the future without your smile.

For me the cross of Jesus still waits
To be carried down the narrow path
Where teeming millions perish.

Thank you, sweet lady,
For enriching my life.
There will surely come a perfect Day
When we can renew our friendship
In a place without sorrow or tears.

So now I commend you to Jesus,
To the lover of your soul,
And immediately I know
It's with Him you belong,
And my hurting subsides.

Goodbye, Joy.

* * *

A pattern had emerged that saw me fly to North America at the end of each year, where I traveled extensively to speak in many churches, schools, and home groups.

In the winter of 1993–94 I committed to a heavy schedule of meetings throughout the United States and Canada. At the time, Delta Airlines offered special month-long standby tickets. I took full advantage of the deal, criss-crossing America and visiting many churches. In one thirty-day period I took twenty-three flights and spoke at meetings in nine different states – great value for a ticket that had cost just $400.

That winter I was exposed to a large cross section of American Christianity. I literally preached in the A to Z of churches, as I shared in several Amish congregations, one Zion Church, and dozens of other fellowships in between.

I also experienced a wide variety of American culture. On one occasion I was invited to the palatial home of a world-famous entertainer, and in Texas I spent an afternoon sharing my testimony with the players and staff of the Houston Oilers NFL team just days before a crucial play-off game. Although my experiences with a few famous Americans were interesting, I felt most comfortable around the simple folks of America's heartland.

When my dizzying spell of twenty-three flights in thirty days concluded, I joined up with a friend, Luke Kuepfer, whose father led a conservative Mennonite church in Ontario, Canada. Luke and his dad had arranged a grueling schedule for us. In five weeks we spoke at thirty-three meetings across half a dozen US states and one province of Canada. We had a wonderful time and experienced God's favor. We often spoke twice in a day before driving many miles to the next destination, only to fall into bed before rising early to do it all again the next morning.

Before the trip I knew almost nothing about Amish or Mennonite history and practice. I recognized they were a deeply religious people, and arrogantly thought I might be able to help them enrich their relationship with God. What transpired was quite the opposite. In each new town I met Christians who possessed a purity, humility, and depth of relationship with Christ that was greater than my own. Their homes were harmonious and their children respectful. I learned to love and appreciate this precious part of the Body of Christ.

My lengthy trip that winter proved to be the start of a long and enduring connection between our ministry and the Amish and Mennonite communities of North America. It was a special time of God's favor, and only later did I realize that they rarely open their pulpits to outsiders. To this day, many of the strongest prayer and financial supporters of our work are from the godly Christians in those peaceful farming communities.

I sensed a strong desire among many Amish and Mennonite youth to put their faith into action. At one church I was asked what they could do to help the work in Asia. Without thinking, I blurted out, "Talk to Luke. He's planning to bring a team over – maybe you can be part of it." Luke was shocked. We had never talked about him bringing a team, but enthusiastic young believers began signing up to come!

A team did travel to China with Luke the following year, and over time a new ministry under his leadership was established in Asia, helping young Mennonite believers serve on the mission field. A young lady named Amy came on one of the first teams. Luke and Amy are now happily married, and the ministry they founded continues to serve God throughout Asia.

During my journey I came to appreciate the American people, the nation's diversity and God-given freedoms, and its natural beauty. Without hesitation, I can say that the friendliest people I have met anywhere in the world are found in rural areas of the United States.

I also met many Christians with deeply pessimistic views of their nation. They had written off their country and were waiting for the judgment of God to befall them. Although America clearly has many deep moral problems that threaten its freedoms, I discovered that it is also home to millions of godly, humble disciples of Jesus. They quietly and faithfully follow the Lord, and their lives provide tremendous light and salt to their communities. They are the real heart of America – the kind of people of whom God has said, "'On the day when I act,' says the Lord Almighty, 'they will be my treasured possession. I will spare them, just as a father has compassion and spares his son who serves him.'" (Malachi 3:17).

As my blessed trip drew to a conclusion, I traveled to the state of Indiana, where I stayed for a few days in the home of an elderly Christian lady named Sue. She was a vibrant believer, whose rich faith in the Lord taught me many vital spiritual lessons.

Sue lived alone and was getting on in years, so I presumed she was a widow. At the dinner table, I noticed she was wearing a wedding ring, so I asked her to share her story. About twenty-five years earlier Sue had been happily married and was busy raising a family. Her world suddenly fell apart when her husband ran off with his young secretary, abandoning Sue and the children. She felt devastated and struggled to stay afloat, while she constantly prayed that her husband would come to his senses and return home. He never came back, and he ended up marrying his girlfriend. Sue continued to cling to Jesus.

When I asked her why she still wore her wedding ring after so many painful years, Sue replied without a trace of malice in her voice, "I don't believe I will ever be reconciled with my husband. He made his choice and has moved on. However, one day long ago I stood before the Almighty God and a church full of witnesses. I promised to remain faithful to my husband until death. Some Christians might think I'm crazy, but I decided to continue to wear my wedding ring, not out of regret, but as a sign to the Lord that I have remained faithful to my vows. I have no desire to remarry while my husband remains alive."

I was amazed at Sue's rich faith and trust in Jesus. It stood in stark contrast to many believers today, who measure the value of a relationship by what they can get out of it. Sue was a selfless, broken child of God with a sole desire to remain faithful to the covenant she had made before God. Each day she spent hours in prayer, interceding for the lost and for whoever the Lord laid on her heart.

I didn't plan to share any of my personal struggles with Sue, but she lovingly asked questions in a way that opened up my heart, until my eyes began to moisten from the burden I was carrying within. From the depths of my soul gushed forth a torrent of pain as I recounted the details of my failed courtship with Joy. I told Sue how we had met and described how our relationship had come crashing down, even though I believed Joy was God's choice of wife for me.

When I told Sue how the elderly ministry leader in Hong Kong had made Joy promise to never contact me again, Sue sighed deeply and said, "Don't worry. God can do the impossible. I come from a similar church background to Joy, where speaking negatively against a Christian leader is considered a heinous sin. I understand the intense pressure she was placed under. Now that she has returned to America, Joy is no longer under the authority of that evil man in Hong Kong. I'm going to pray fervently for God's will in this matter."

Before I said goodbye to Sue, she advised me not to end my American trip without attempting to visit Joy.

CHAPTER 23
A LOVE REVIVED

Christmas 1993

> I have now to ask, whether you can consent to part with your daughter early next spring, to see her no more in this world; whether you can consent to her departure, and her subjection to the hardships and sufferings of a missionary life; ... to every kind of want and distress; to degradation, insult, persecution, and perhaps a violent death.
>
> **Adoniram Judson, in a letter to his future wife's father**

My short stay with Sue in Indiana had radically altered my perspective. It had been helpful to talk with an older woman about my experiences with Joy, and I decided it was time to find out, once and for all, if there was any chance of Joy and me being united in marriage.

A few days later I nervously called Joy's home in Idaho. I had retained the invaluable scrap of paper with her number since she had first given it to me more than a year earlier. Joy was surprised to hear my voice on the phone, and she sounded hesitant. When I told her I would like to fly to Idaho to spend some time with her, she said she would need to ask her dad's permission. The next day I called back and was thrilled to hear that her father had granted his approval! I quickly booked a ticket, and a few days later my plane touched down in Pocatello, Idaho.

I hoped Joy and I would quickly fall back into the warm friendship we had enjoyed in Asia. The long time we'd been apart had been emotionally torturous for me, but I was confident that as soon as we were together again we would have no trouble reconnecting. I planned to tell Joy how much I had missed her, and to tell her for the first time that I loved her. If everything went well, I even dreamed of sweeping her off her feet and asking her to marry me!

From the first moment I was reunited with Joy, I sensed something was badly wrong. She was still incredibly beautiful, but part of her seemed to be missing. The spark of life I had found so irresistible appeared to have dimmed. Her eyes no longer sparkled like they used to, and she appeared limp and lifeless compared to the vivacious woman I had known in Asia.

I didn't want to put any pressure on Joy, so we just engaged in small talk, catching up with what had happened in the year since we had last been permitted to see each other. We went out for lunch, but my efforts to break the ice with humor fell flat. It seemed as if she was carrying a heavy internal burden. Finally, as she choked back tears, she said, "Paul, something terrible occurred during the last year of my time in Hong Kong."

She went on to tell me how Calvin, the elderly grandfather and head of the Bible ministry in Hong Kong, had spent months gradually manipulating his way into her life. He would try to get her alone as much as possible in the ministry guest house, or while driving around Hong Kong in his van. On one occasion, Calvin and his wife Rhonda were out in their van with Joy seated in the back, when Calvin pulled over at the entrance to a park. He ordered his wife to get out and catch a taxi home because he wanted to spend time alone with Joy!

The situation reached its lowest point just days before Joy flew back to America. Calvin called Joy late one night and told her to go immediately to the airport because a team was arriving unexpectedly. Joy got out of bed and made her way to the airport, only to discover there was no team. Calvin took Joy to a dark, isolated spot and declared his love for her. He then grabbed her and tried to fondle her, but she pushed him away in disgust. Calvin was in his late sixties and Joy was twenty-two at the time.

After being dropped back at the guest house, Joy was unable to sleep. For her remaining days in Asia she walked around in a daze. After a year of being harassed, threatened, and groomed by a sexual predator, she felt utterly worthless.

As Joy and I drove away from the restaurant, I was angry at the old man for his wicked behavior, but now everything suddenly made sense. I understood why Calvin had hated me so intensely from the first time we met, and why he had done everything possible to block any potential romance between Joy and me. I never imagined that the married grandfather and minister of the gospel had viewed me as a rival for Joy's affections!

I also understood why Joy had lost her spark and looked so burdened. I had submitted to the demonic control of that depraved couple for only a short time, yet it had plunged me into months of deep depression, until the day in Phoenix when I had been delivered. I could scarcely imagine the weight of demonic oppression bearing down on Joy. She had spent a year being stalked by a wolf in sheep's clothing, a sick man who masqueraded as a respected mission leader.

Before traveling to Idaho, I thought I would only be there a few days, just long enough to find out if there was any future hope for Joy and me. Now I realized that I needed to stay longer, to encourage Joy and to pray with her. I booked accommodation nearby, and each afternoon Joy picked me up and drove me back to her family's home in the tiny town of Rupert.

On the first night after learning what had happened to Joy, I filled my pocket with coins and walked down the street to a public phone. I called several key Christian friends, including Sue in Indiana. After summarizing what Joy had shared, I asked them to pray fervently for her.

Over the next few weeks I led Joy through a daily process of denouncing any spiritual oppression that had come upon her through the unholy manipulations of Calvin and Rhonda. In the same way that the Phoenix prayer group had helped me, I laid hands on Joy, bound all evil powers in Jesus' Name, and asked the Holy Spirit to bring wholeness and healing to her life.

After several days, Joy began to look more like her former self. A little smile returned to her face, but she was going to need time to recover from her heavy ordeal. Meanwhile, I got to know Joy's parents. They were a hard-working couple who feared God and loved their three daughters. We got on well from the start, and a warm relationship developed. They had been shocked to learn of Joy's experiences in Hong Kong.

One afternoon, Joy and I drove to a lake. Although the temperature was below freezing, we went for a short walk around the lake's edge before stopping beneath a willow tree. All of a sudden we embraced, hugging one another tightly. We didn't want to let go, and for what seemed like an eternity we continued to cling to each other, as some of the pain and confusion from our long separation drained from our wounded hearts. It was the first hug we had ever shared.

Unexpectedly, I ended up spending Christmas Day with Joy. God gave me the greatest Christmas gift I had ever received. My beautiful Joy was safe in my arms, and I was determined to do whatever was necessary to help and protect her.

I wanted to stay longer in Idaho, but my ninety-day US visa was about to expire, and I had made previous commitments to host teams in Asia. With much reluctance, I told Joy I was unable to stay in the country any longer without overstaying my visa.

As 1994 commenced, Joy and I discussed marriage for the first time. The more I got to know her, the more it became clear that she was God's choice for me. If the rough start to our relationship was anything to go by, we figured that if we were to be united in marriage, our journey together would likely be both exciting and extremely difficult. We talked about how a Christian couple with even a one percent view that divorce is acceptable will likely not last the distance. After years of pressure, that one percent would grow until divorce would become an acceptable option. We agreed that regardless of whatever obstacles Satan and the world might throw at us, we would continue to stand together and trust Jesus to help us overcome.

One afternoon I asked Joy's dad for his permission to seek his daughter's hand in marriage. I explained that although I had little money, I was determined to follow the Lord regardless of the cost. Although he realized we would be living on the other side of the world, he still gave me his blessing. Later that day I asked if I could borrow his car, and I snuck out to a jewelry store and bought an engagement ring.

I remained in my room on the evening of 11 January 1994, praying and preparing for the following day, when I planned to ask Joy to be my wife. I decided to propose by writing a poem expressing the love I felt in my heart for her, and my hopes that our union would bring much glory to the Lord Jesus Christ.

The next day I was a bundle of nerves as I readied myself for one of the biggest moments of my life. When I told Joy I had composed a special poem for her she brimmed with excitement. After tenderly reading the words from my heart, I went down on one knee, looked into her eyes, and asked Joy if she would consent to be my wife.

Her gorgeous eyes sparkled as she said, "Yes!"

* * *

Joy: Although I thoroughly enjoyed working with the teams of Bible couriers from around the world, other aspects of my final year in Hong Kong were horrible. It was a great relief to get away from that sick environment. Not only was Calvin harassing me, but the Canadian missionary who worked for him was also like a leech that wouldn't leave me alone. I was being stalked by two creeps who claimed to be ministers of the gospel. For some months after returning home to Idaho I struggled to come to terms with what had taken place in Hong Kong.

One day, out of the blue, Paul phoned. He was traveling in the United States and asked if it would be okay to come to Idaho for a brief visit.

I had only shared what happened in Hong Kong with a few people since arriving home, and they didn't seem too concerned or interested. It was eating me up inside, and even though I had done nothing at all to encourage Calvin's behavior, I felt stupid and worthless for finding myself in a position where a man older than my father could behave in such an inappropriate manner. Many times I had wanted to leave Hong Kong early, but Calvin threatened that if I left he would spread malicious rumors about me and my family among mutual contacts in Idaho.

Paul and I went out for a meal, and I felt I couldn't hold my secret in any longer. I shared everything with him, and a great weight lifted from my shoulders. Paul listened carefully as I relayed my experiences. I appreciated that he took it seriously and that he cared so deeply for me.

Paul remained in Idaho for a while. We prayed fervently together and he did his best to encourage me. Paul hadn't been raised in a Christian environment, so he simply didn't care about church traditions and protocols. He openly expressed his disgust at what had happened to me, and the Lord gradually helped me realize that it was the sin of a depraved old man that was to blame, not me.

It was obvious Paul was planning to ask me to be his wife. I was both excited and scared at the same time. Although we came from different ends of the earth, I had admired and respected him since the day we met. He knew what the Lord wanted him to do, and was already doing it with all his strength. From the start, our relationship had been based on a very strong friendship. We enjoyed one another's company, and we had no problem talking freely about the Lord. We also laughed a lot when we were together.

On the day Paul proposed, we went for a drive together before returning to my parents' home. He gave me a beautiful card and said he would like to read a poem he had composed especially for me. His words were so heartfelt that I cried as he read them. I would like to share the poem with you. It is entitled "Will You Marry Me?"

Joy, what words can I use to express
Just what you mean to me?
How I waited for that awesome time
When you knew we were meant to be.

From times eternal I waited
For a moment in your embrace.
The wait was all worth it and more
To see the smile on your face.

When our time presented
All my expectations were surpassed.
You are the partner God set aside
Whom I shall love unto the last.

Please take my hand my lovely one
And let me lead you through.
Each moment lost is tragic
When I could spend it here with you.

Forever I will hold you,
And forever you will be
The loveliest of ladies,
The only one for me.

To know you, precious Princess,
To love you intimately,
Is the greatest joy abounding
Like the crashing of the sea.

Will you be my partner,
My companion in the fight?
Will you join me in the work
Of spreading Jesus' light?

Through China and the world,
Over mountains, land, and sea,
Let's find the hurting captives,
Reach out and set them free.

May we always put His interests
Above those that are our own,
To go wherever He leads us,
His will to be our home.

Let's win those sin-bound nations
And build a church for them to meet,
Then take the crowns He gives us
And lay them humbly at His feet.

Will you commit to me the moments
As the months fade into years?
I promise always to protect you
And to wipe away your tears.

To have, to hold, and to cherish
To share with you my life.
Daily I will thank the Lord
For my darling, precious wife.

If you have a peace from God
And you know we're meant to be,
I have for you a question:
Joy, will you marry me?

CHAPTER 24
STRUGGLING TO THE ALTAR

August 1994

Love does not delight in evil but rejoices with the truth. It always protects, always trusts, always hopes, always perseveres.

1 Corinthians 13:6–7

A successful marriage requires falling in love many times, always with the same person.

Mignon McLaughlin

Joy and I had already experienced enough opposition to know that Satan wouldn't rest in his attempts to destroy our relationship. We planned our wedding to take place in Idaho the following August, and I returned to Asia. The eight months we spent apart left us bruised as the enemy threw everything he could muster at us. The battering we received was so severe that it almost sunk our fledgling relationship.

News of our engagement soon reached Hong Kong, where Joy's former ministry leaders, Calvin and Rhonda, voiced their strong disapproval and began to influence others against us. A few of our mutual contacts suddenly stopped supporting me and my work. When I asked a friend from one church in Oregon why they had discontinued their support, he replied, "Calvin spoke at our service recently and shared some things about you that give us great concern." When I asked what he meant, he replied, "We have known Calvin a long time, and we trust him." I never heard from that friend or his church again.

Now we were separated by thousands of miles, and Joy was already being placed under great pressure. Calvin even traveled all the way from Hong Kong to Idaho in an attempt to persuade her to call off our engagement. He told Joy she was making the biggest mistake of her life, and that our marriage wouldn't last six months. I was deeply upset when I learned that this man had gone to see my future bride, but there was little I could do about it from the other side of the world.

One day my pastor phoned from Australia. "Hey, mate, what's going on?" he asked. "Some guy with an American accent called the church and demanded to speak to 'Paul Hattaway's spiritual leader.' He was boiling with rage, but when he refused to tell me his name, I informed him I don't talk with people too cowardly to identify themselves, and I hung up!"

Three years had elapsed since I first met Joy. Most of that time had been excruciatingly difficult and heartbreaking, and now, right as God was giving us a great victory, my engagement was under severe assault thousands of miles away.

Aware that it would be extremely stressful to live as newlyweds in the same city as our enemies, I decided to relocate from Hong Kong to a new base in northern Thailand. I rented a small town house on the outskirts of Chiang Mai, and made plans to move in with my new bride after our wedding on 27 August 1994.

The weeks and months passed incredibly slowly. It was the longest eight months of my life. Our relationship was being opposed from three different continents as various people connected to Calvin and Rhonda rose up and voiced their opposition to our marriage. At one stage, Joy was under such heavy strain that I feared she would buckle before we made it to the altar. I canceled all other commitments and traveled to Idaho to try to rescue our relationship.

From the moment we were together again things were better. During my short stay in America, Joy and I were so emotionally drained from the fierce battle raging against us that we just tried to relax and enjoy each other's company. At the end of my fleeting visit, Joy hugged me tightly and assured me she wouldn't waver. By God's grace, I was now confident that we were going to make it.

In the weeks leading up to our big day, Joy put the finishing touches to the wedding arrangements while I fulfilled my final commitment as a single man – hosting a large team that had come to carry Bibles and to distribute evangelistic material among unreached ethnic groups in western China.

Some of our team members were riding in the back of a truck. Just hours into our mission, they handed several gospel booklets to a group of people standing on the side of the road. A police car happened to be following the truck. They pulled over and inspected what had been distributed, and before long our entire team was placed under house arrest. Our passports were confiscated and we were confined to a guest house. Officers from the Public Security Bureau searched the bags of every team member and found an enormous amount of Christian literature, which they stacked up on a large desk as evidence of our "crimes."

I was soon identified as the main leader and troublemaker, and we were informed that we had violated Chinese law and faced possible imprisonment. That area of China was so remote that when the chief of the prefecture's security forces was summoned to deal with the situation, it took him eighteen hours to drive to the town where we were being held. He wasn't at all happy with the interruption to his schedule.

An interpreter was summoned from the provincial capital and we were fingerprinted, photographed, and interrogated. At the start we complied with the officers' demands and showed as much respect as possible. We told them, "We came to your country because we love the Chinese people and we want them to know Jesus, who is the Creator of everything." When many of the young team members were told to "confess their crimes," they boldly testified of the difference Christ had made in their lives.

I had previously been arrested several times in other parts of China, and on each occasion the local authorities desired to resolve the situation as quickly as possible. It was a hassle for them to deal with all the paperwork involved with the arrest of a foreigner. On this occasion, however, we appeared to be locked in a stalemate, with the local officials unable to decide what to do. One afternoon I managed to escape from the guest house and used a payphone to call the US embassy in Beijing, to inform them that a large group of young American citizens were being held in a remote part of Sichuan Province. A lady at the embassy explained that there was nothing they could do and wished us the best!

On the third day I told the chief interrogator that I needed to leave because my wedding day was fast approaching on the other side of the world. He laughed out loud and said mockingly, "We will hold you here as long as we wish, and there's absolutely nothing you can do about it!"

Finally, after much prayer, I decided our deferential approach wasn't working and we needed to change tactics. I told the chief officer that they were illegally detaining us and had violated numerous international laws by refusing to notify our governments. I informed him that we would leave town the next morning whether they liked it or not, even without our passports if necessary. He angrily replied, "If you leave the front gate of this compound I will order my men to shoot you in the back!"

After the long struggle Joy and I had endured just to get this far, I thought it would be a cruel irony if our wedding was canceled because I was shot in the back in a remote part of western China! All I wanted to do was get out of there and fly to America to see my precious bride-to-be.

Our standoff was about to end, one way or another. The next morning we packed our bags and calmly walked through the compound gate and into the town. I rented a bus to take us all the way to the provincial capital. The local authorities realized we had called their bluff, and told us we had to report to the central police station when we reached the city of Chengdu. There, the provincial police ordered us to write a confession before they would return our passports to us. We couldn't agree that sharing the gospel of Jesus Christ was a crime, so we wrote in English, "We are sorry we got caught." This appeased the police and allowed them to "save face," and we were free to leave!

The next day our plane took off from Chengdu Airport. A great sense of relief washed over me the moment we touched down in Hong Kong. It felt as though I had escaped from the clutches of the enemy. I called Joy and told her I was coming to get married!

A short time later I found myself waiting at the altar of a church in Idaho, as Joy's dad led my beautiful bride down the aisle.

At long last, three years after the Holy Spirit had first impressed on my heart that Joy was to be my wife, the Lord had helped us overcome every obstacle. For most of those three years it felt as if we had been wrestling the armies of hell. The wedding ceremony itself wasn't a wonderful occasion for us. Joy and I were emotionally and mentally exhausted, but by the grace of God we made it to the altar!

* * *

Joy: The months Paul and I were apart during our engagement were very difficult. Although we spoke on the phone as much as possible, it felt like my emotions were in a tumble dryer, being continually tossed and turned as pressure mounted against us from people opposed to our marriage.

At one stage I wondered if the whole thing was a big mistake, as I believed that when God is involved in something then all of the details should fall perfectly into place. Paul's thinking was totally different. He pointed out that if God was truly involved in our union, then Satan would relentlessly target us and do everything possible to keep us from being together.

One way Paul encouraged me was by composing poems, which deeply touched my heart. He reassured me that even if the entire world tried to stop us, we would make it with God's help. He often reminded me of the Scripture, "If God is for us, who can be against us?" (Romans 8:31).

One poem Paul wrote during our engagement struggles is entitled "Ten Thousand Miles:"

Ten thousand miles between us, my love,
Ten thousand reasons to weep.
Only you and I and the heavens above
Know the extent of our love so deep.

Where did you come from that sweet winter day,
And how did you capture my heart?
I wish I could hold you; I have much to say,
But we're ten thousand miles apart.

Where did you go to, my love,
When you vanished into the night?
I searched for your smile to brighten my day,
But you're ten thousand miles from sight.

My life has an ache that's too hard to mend.
Deep longing for you floods my heart.
The love and prayers that I'm able to send
Seem forlorn 'cause we're so far apart.

I long to hold your hand, my love,
There's so much to say and do.
But it's hard when my soul is being torn to shreds
Ten thousand miles from you.

CHAPTER 25

HELL BREAKS LOOSE

> There is a war between the saint and Satan, and that so bloody a one, that the cruellest which ever was fought by men will be found but sport and child's play compared to this. The stage where this war is fought is every man's soul.
>
> **William Gurnall (1616–79)**

I have met many Christians who only like to hear positive stories, and whenever a "negative" report emerges they prefer to plug their ears and sweep it under the carpet. The Bible, thankfully, never paints a false picture, but presents people and situations as they really are.

The events described in the following chapters proved to be one of the most intense and important battles of our lives. To leave them out would leave readers without a reference point as to why the Lord Jesus Christ opened so many amazing opportunities to us in subsequent years, while empowering Asia Harvest to grow at such an astonishing rate. Tragically, the kinds of things I am about to share are all too common in Christian circles today. If sharing this part of our testimony provides comfort to any readers, or if it helps even one person to avoid the kind of dire situation we encountered, then it is all worthwhile.

Calvin and his family were highly regarded by many people in the mission world. They held a weekly prayer breakfast in Hong

Kong, at which many ministry leaders and missionaries gathered for prayer and fellowship. Calvin often wept as he prayed for the lost, and everyone considered him to be a model Christian. Calvin's son, whom I will call Wendell, possessed an engaging personality, just like his father. They were smooth operators, loved by many and looked up to as successful ministers of the gospel.

After saying goodbye to her family, Joy and I traveled to Asia to begin our new life together in Chiang Mai, Thailand. A few months passed, and we knew that what Calvin had done and said to Joy could not be ignored. The biblical pattern required that Calvin be confronted and given a chance to repent, and if he refused, then we had a responsibility to warn the Body of Christ (Matthew 18:15–17). We arranged a trip through southern China, which would culminate in a visit to Hong Kong, where we planned to confront Calvin. We were about to discover, however, that his lustful behavior toward Joy was just the tip of a large iceberg.

We were invited to dinner at the home of Calvin's son Wendell and his wife. Calvin was away traveling in China, but his wife Rhonda came along to dinner. The atmosphere was tense, but we all struggled through. Calvin's family had heard that Joy hadn't appreciated part of her experience when she had worked for them, so they asked her to share what had happened.

Joy calmly recounted how Calvin had tried to groom her and had acted inappropriately toward her over the course of a year, culminating with his sick attempt to seduce her at the airport just days before she returned to America.

Rhonda's face grimaced with pain as Joy recounted the details of her experiences. "I'm so sorry," Rhonda sighed. "I thought this kind of thing was over."

After washing the dishes, Calvin's son and daughter-in-law provided deeply disturbing details about the old man's past behavior. Decades earlier he had been a missionary in Africa, but had fled the mission field when accusations of child abuse surfaced. Calvin and Rhonda returned to America for a while, but were expelled from their denomination after further claims of child molestation. They ended up living in Germany, where they ministered to the families of US military personnel. Once again, this well-respected mission leader – a man who publicly wept when he prayed for the lost – moved on from Germany after a prepubescent girl complained that Calvin had sexually abused her.

Calvin's family members told us that not only had he abused his young victims, but in an attempt to protect his name, he had also spent years destroying the young girls' reputations. Calvin's daughter-in-law detailed how some of the victims' lives had been ruined. Unable to cope with his character assassinations, by the time they reached adulthood their lives had crumbled into depression and despair.

Joy and I left the dinner in shock. We sat in stunned silence as we caught the train back to the place where we were staying. We had never imagined that such ghastly criminal behavior could be found among people professing to be servants of God.

By the very next day, it felt as if hell had broken loose. Calvin had phoned home from China to discover that his wife, son, and daughter-in-law had shared details of his crimes with us. Calvin canceled the remainder of his trip and flew to Hong Kong on the next available flight, which would arrive that evening.

By the following morning Calvin had managed to track down where we were staying. He was beside himself with rage and on the warpath, and attempted to intimidate us into silence. His wife Rhonda called Joy and launched a vicious tirade against her, saying she ought to be ashamed for making up lewd stories, and she accused Joy of "trampling on the blood of Jesus" for telling the truth about her perverted husband. Calvin's son and daughter-in-law also completely changed their attitude from just two nights earlier, and they began attacking us as well.

At that moment, we recognized how much power and control this serial pedophile held over his family members. In less than forty-eight hours they had gone from expressing sorrow and comfort to Joy, to being Calvin's staunch defenders and attack dogs. Some experts say that serial offenders like Calvin need "enablers" to help them get away with their crimes. His enablers were his own wife and son, and we had become their targets.

Calvin angrily demanded a face-to-face meeting with us. We consulted our friend and ministry mentor Keith Kline, who wisely advised us to stay well clear of the man, and that we had no biblical requirement to meet with such a person on his own terms. We left Hong Kong as scheduled and returned to our home in Thailand.

In the following months all kinds of nasty tricks were implemented by Calvin and his family. We were threatened with a lawsuit for defamation, which we simply ignored, and news regularly reached us from other ministry leaders and missionaries that our names were being dragged through the mud by Calvin and Wendell. They adopted a "scorched earth" policy in an attempt to annihilate our reputations before we could reveal the truth.

Joy and I found ourselves in a tricky position. We had been given information – by his own family members – that this well-respected mission leader was a serial pedophile who had committed crimes against young girls on at least three different continents, not counting Asia. His family members, however, now strongly denied they had shared anything with us. They claimed we were liars and slanderers who would be severely judged by God. At the same time, Calvin launched a charm offensive, to convince mission leaders that he was a humble servant of God who was being persecuted by "an angry New Zealander and his deceived wife."

As newlyweds, Joy and I were supposed to be investing time getting to know each other without the kind of stress this situation brought. We felt we didn't have much choice, however. Ignoring it wasn't going to make it go away. All we could do was cry out to the Lord Jesus for justice and deliverance. We knew that our battle was not just against a sick old man and his family of enablers and co-conspirators, but with a host of very powerful demons. The Bible reminded us where our aim needed to be:

> For our struggle is not against flesh and blood, but against the rulers, against the authorities, against the powers of this dark world and against the spiritual forces of evil in the heavenly realms.
>
> **Ephesians 6:12**

As Joy and I continued to be attacked from all quarters, most of the Christians we shared our struggles with simply didn't believe us. They found it easier to think we were slanderers than to entertain the possibility that the sweet old mission leader they had grown to love and respect was actually an unrepentant child abuser. If only we had had a recording of what Calvin's wife, son, and daughter-in-law had told us that night in Hong Kong, but there was no recording, and the situation had become our word against theirs.

****

> I was friendly with Calvin and his family, as well as with Paul and Joy. I tried to set up a meeting with everyone, but Calvin only agreed to attend if he could control the format in every way. His conduct was so agitated and odd that it became clear to me he was merely trying to cover his tracks. There is a biblical precedent for people using God as a cover for evil, and anger is usually a sure sign of guilt.
>
> It became difficult for Paul and Joy at this time. Nobody else wanted to believe them. Over the years, Calvin had gained a respected place among the Christian community, and no one wanted to be immersed in an ongoing scandal. It was the word of an older, respected mission leader against a young, newlywed couple.
>
> I received some of the same treatment that Paul and Joy experienced. When I attempted to warn other Christians about Calvin's abuses and his son's complicity, I received nothing but avoidance and even rebuke – no one wanted to hear it. I was

thirty-seven at the time, and the "co-dependent" reaction of God's people was surprising to me.

Likewise, Calvin's son and the other family members lacked the courage to stand up to Calvin. Like Eli's passive response to his sons' sins (1 Samuel 2:12–25), the Church chose to remain on the sidelines. The incident taught me that, unfortunately, the modern Church is lacking believers like Phinehas (Numbers 25:1–13), who choose truth over expediency.

Keith Kline

CHAPTER 26

LINES IN THE SAND

Rescue those being led away to death;
hold back those staggering towards slaughter.
If you say, "But we knew nothing about this,"
does not he who weighs the heart perceive it?
Does not he who guards your life know it?
Will he not repay each person according to what they have done?

Proverbs 24:11–12

To sin by silence when they should protest makes cowards of men.

Abraham Lincoln

Months went by, and the conflict with Calvin and his family continued unabated. We knew the truth about Calvin's criminal past, and our heavenly Father also knew the truth. Ultimately, we realized, that would be enough on Judgment Day. In the meantime, however, we needed a lot of grace just to survive the relentless onslaught that was coming against us.

Everything seemed upside down in the Body of Christ. We were shocked when many ministry leaders took the side of our adversaries and attacked us. They considered that revealing the presence of a wicked threat was a worse sin than the wickedness itself. Most missionaries were totally unconcerned by the news of such evil in their midst. Because Christian leaders didn't have the courage to do what the Bible demands, this man Calvin and his complicit family members had been able to carry on committing their repugnant abuses for decades.

Recognizing that Calvin was doing everything possible to try to destroy us, Joy and I needed to make a decision. We could either just "move on with our lives and leave it in God's hands," as some were advising us to do, or we could draw a line in the sand and say, "Stop! This is unacceptable!"

The stress of our situation drove us to search for answers in God's Word. Many of the other missionaries we spoke with based their advice on two Bible verses. The first was, "Do not judge, or you too will be judged" (Matthew 7:1). The implication was that we should be quiet and do nothing, but this advice didn't make sense to us and was inconsistent with God's Word. Jesus also instructed His followers to "judge with righteous judgment" (John 7:24, NKJV), and the Apostle Paul wrote, "The person with the Spirit makes judgments about all things" (1 Corinthians 2:15).

Paul, Peter, John, and other New Testament leaders didn't hesitate to judge wicked behavior in the Church. Paul even instructed Christians:

> You must not associate with anyone who claims to be a brother or sister but is sexually immoral or greedy, an idolater or slanderer, a drunkard or swindler. Do not even eat with such people.
>
> **1 Corinthians 5:11**

The second Bible verse people frequently quoted to us came from the account of the woman caught in adultery. Jesus declared, "Let any one of you who is without sin be the first to throw a stone" (John 8:7). To apply this verse to our situation didn't make sense either. If we were to take that verse at face value, the apostles would never have judged anyone else, because they were not "without sin." Only Jesus would be able to judge anyone or anything, because He alone is sinless.

I studied Bible commentaries on this passage and learned that in ancient Israel nobody was permitted to testify in court if they had committed the same crime as the accused person. Jesus obviously wasn't implying that only sinless people can act against wickedness, as many believers suppose. Rather, He was rebuking the hypocrisy of a group of men about to kill a woman caught in the very same act they indulged in.

As Joy and I meditated on God's Word and considered our course of action, we gained a greater understanding of what the Lord thinks of this kind of sin. Nothing makes Jesus as angry as the abuse of a child. He declared:

> "If anyone causes one of these little ones – those who believe in me – to stumble, it would be better for them to have a large millstone hung round their neck and to be drowned in the depths of the sea. Woe to the world because of the things that cause people to stumble! Such things must come, but woe to the person through whom they come!"
>
> **Matthew 18:6–7**

Bible scholars say a millstone at the time of Christ could weigh up to four tons. Jesus' feelings on this matter were quite clear.

It felt as if God had drawn a line in the sand of our lives. We could stand up and tell the truth, or we could timidly draw back and suffer the consequences. The Holy Spirit challenged us with this Scripture as we wrestled with our decision: "'I take no pleasure in the one who shrinks back.' But we do not belong to those who shrink back and are destroyed, but to those who have faith and are saved" (Hebrews 10:38–39).

Gradually, as we continued to seek God, it became clear what He wanted us to do. The Lord was calling us to take up the cross and follow Him. Taking up the cross in this situation meant we couldn't stand by and say nothing while an unrepentant pedophile remained an active leader in the Body of Christ.

We were fully aware that by speaking out we would invite prolonged attacks and more conflict, but we had no choice. If we compromised we would displease our Lord, and He would lift His hand of blessing from our lives. Rather, the Lord Jesus wanted us to "have nothing to do with the fruitless deeds of darkness, but rather expose them" (Ephesians 5:11).

One evening, Joy and I knelt together beside our bed and prayed to our heavenly Father, asking Him to strengthen us and to help us survive what was to come. Even if the whole world turned against us, we decided we would rather die with our integrity intact, having done what Jesus wanted us to do, than live as cowards.

Even if our reputations were totally destroyed and it cost us our ministry, we would choose to stand and fearlessly testify to the truth. We placed our lives in God's hands, and whatever eventuated we would continue to cling to Jesus.

* * *

In February 1996, Joy announced the wonderful news that she was expecting our first child! Before our baby arrived, however, God arranged a special meeting for us – one that was extremely important and proved to be a dividing line between what had taken place and what was yet to come.

One afternoon we went to the old part of Chiang Mai to get our hair cut. As Joy and I walked out of the salon we immediately bumped into Calvin. He noticed that Joy was pregnant and said, "Why are you telling so many lies about me? Don't you know that you are touching God's anointed? What kind of baby do you expect to bring into this world when you two are spreading so much slander everywhere? If you don't repent, your child is never going to amount to anything!"

I immediately recalled the heavy spiritual oppression that came upon me the previous time I failed to stand up to this man. I considered Calvin's words about our unborn baby as a direct curse, so I looked straight at him and firmly stated, "In Jesus' Name, I reject your wicked curse! The Word of God says, 'An undeserved curse does not come to rest' (Proverbs 26:2), and 'Whoever digs a hole and scoops it out falls into the pit they have made' (Psalm 7:15). I rebuke your filthy words, and I declare that our child will be blessed by the Lord!"

Calvin's face turned red with rage. He pushed up against me and started jabbing his index finger into my chest while continuing to spew out threats. It was obvious he was trying to provoke me to anger in the hope I might lose my temper and strike him, but the Spirit of God helped me remain completely calm.

Despite all the pain Calvin had brought to our lives, as I stood there allowing him to jab me in the chest I surprisingly didn't feel any hatred or anger toward him at all. In fact, I felt great pity for him. I was overwhelmed with sadness that another human being – someone created in the image of God and a professing minister of the gospel – had allowed himself to fall so far into sin that he had become a tool of wickedness in the hands of Satan.

Calvin completed his rant against me by saying, "I want you to promise to stop spreading lies about me. It's just not right. Now go ahead and promise me!"

Looking directly into his eyes, I said, "Calvin, I will promise you just one thing. We know you are a dirty old man, and a danger to innocent children. I promise that we are going to warn as many people as possible about you!"

Seething with indignation, Calvin turned and walked off down the road. It was the last time we saw his face.

That impromptu meeting was a huge turning point for us. By standing up to Calvin, we realized he no longer had power to intimidate us. We were starting to get free!

* * *

Joy: I was disappointed to learn that although some Christian leaders knew about Calvin's lustful past, they hadn't bothered to warn me when I went to work for his ministry. I didn't want to be responsible for any other girls or young women being abused by this predator. If we refused to warn others, I knew the Lord would hold us accountable. I had to learn to trust Paul's leadership in this, because my natural inclination was to avoid controversy and conflict at all cost.

One day we bumped into Calvin on the street, and he tried to curse our unborn child. His curse, however, seems to have rebounded onto himself. Our son Dalen was born in Chiang Mai in November 1996, and has grown up healthy and strong. From the time of his birth, the Holy Spirit has had a beautiful touch on Dalen's life. Today he loves the Lord Jesus with all his heart, and is serving Him in a special way.

CHAPTER 27

STUCK IN A COBWEB

For the next several years, Joy and I continued to serve the Lord as we launched strategic projects in China, in Southeast Asia, and on the Indian subcontinent. A large missionary organization graciously provided us with office space on the third floor of their building, and God sent several people to help share our workload. The ministry grew quickly during this time.

The Lord blessed our family as our home in Chiang Mai became a place of refuge from the storms of life. Our little son brought much joy and laughter to our lives, and the love we had for one another grew stronger over time. As a couple united under God, Joy and I were infinitely more effective than I had been as a single man. I understood why God said one man can cause a thousand enemies to flee, but "two [can] put ten thousand to flight" (Deuteronomy 32:30).

The onslaught from Calvin and his family continued, but it helped greatly that there was a thousand-mile buffer between us in Thailand and our adversaries in Hong Kong.

One day I noticed that the foundation of a new building was being laid on the same property, just a stone's throw from our office window. I spoke to the owner of the property and asked him who was planning to move into the impressive new building. His answer struck me like a sledgehammer. Calvin and his entire ministry were leaving Hong Kong. Their new ministry base was going to be in Chiang Mai, Thailand, in the new building right next to our office!

I immediately spoke with the leader of the missionary organization that leased our building, and shared some of our experiences of Calvin and his family. Alarmed at the news, the mission leader told us, "It's not right for a dangerous man like that to be involved in the Body of Christ." He encouraged us to warn the pastor of the Chiang Mai Community Church, a large fellowship attended by hundreds of missionaries.

We went to the pastor's office on a hot Friday afternoon, where Joy did most of the talking. She calmly and confidently shared her personal experiences, and recounted what Calvin's family members had told us about the child abuse he had committed around the world.

The elderly pastor listened intently to every word, and then shocked us to the core. After being informed that a pedophile would almost certainly be attending his church, he said, "Whatever you do, I charge you not to share this information with anyone else. There's already enough disunity among the Christians in this city."

I was so taken aback by the pastor's feckless response that for a moment I was speechless. The pastor then indicated that our conversation was over and motioned that we should leave. I couldn't remain silent, however, and pivoted before going out of the door. "Listen carefully to me," I said. "We have told you that a dangerous man is moving here and will likely be part of the congregation you shepherd, but you couldn't care less about protecting your flock. We have warned you, and now you are responsible before the Living God. If anything happens because of this wicked man, the blood of his victims will be on your hands!"

I was disgusted by the insipid stance of that cowardly pastor. What a stark contrast there was between his attitude and that of the Apostle Paul, who once dealt with sin in the church by writing:

> When you are assembled and I am with you in spirit, and the power of our Lord Jesus is present, hand this man over to Satan for the destruction of the flesh, so that his spirit may be saved on the day of the Lord.
>
> **1 Corinthians 5:4–5**

Calvin, his wife Rhonda, his son Wendell and his family, and other co-workers duly moved to Chiang Mai, where they received a warm welcome into the Body of Christ from the pastor and the missions community. That day, any hope we had of a more peaceful existence flew out the window.

In a bid to smooth their transition to Chiang Mai, Calvin and Wendell hired a hotel conference room and invited about twenty key mission leaders to an important meeting. We were not invited. Two of our missionary friends did attend the meeting, and afterward they were very hesitant to reveal what had transpired. One of them finally gained enough courage to tell me, "Calvin and Wendell began by sharing how they have faithfully served the Lord on several continents, recounting their great successes. They were very warm and personable, and made everyone feel at ease. After a while they said that a rebellious couple named Paul and Joy Hattaway were doing their very best to destroy Calvin's reputation by spreading lies and monstrous false allegations."

I asked the missionary what the other people in the room had thought. Looking down at the ground, he replied, "I'm sorry to inform you that only two people challenged their claims. Everyone else seemed to be firmly on their side, and several even said that you need to be punished and ostracized from the missions community because of slander."

Even worse was to come. When one mission leader asked Calvin what he thought motivated us to make such claims, Wendell stepped in and answered on behalf of his father. With a straight face he said, "The truth is that Joy is a slut."

When someone challenged them to present evidence for their vile claim, Wendell replied, "We are not at liberty to share that information with you." Then he added, "And Paul is a former pimp who learned mind-control tactics during his time in charge of prostitutes."

At that, the meeting concluded. Our friends thought their claims were ludicrous, but the rest of the attendees appeared convinced by what they had heard, and found Wendell's explanations plausible.

That evening Joy and I tucked our precious son into bed, and we lay down to consider the events of the day. With heavy hearts we prayed, "Lord Jesus, we don't know what to say. You heard everything that was spoken against us at the meeting. We ask You to record every word, and to reveal the truth. If it pleases You, Heavenly Father, please help us experience Your promise that 'no weapon forged against you will prevail, and you will refute every tongue that accuses you. This is the heritage of the servants of the Lord, and this is their vindication from me' (Isaiah 54:17)."

As we prayed together that night, an unexpected thing happened. Instead of feeling crushed by the evil words that had been used to describe us, we found the whole situation so ridiculous that Joy and I began to laugh out loud with the joy of the Lord. My precious wife even joked that I should have hired a pin-striped suit and a gold necklace and turned up to the meeting unannounced just to convince everyone that I really was a pimp!

Our enemies had moved to our city, and they were far more skilled and clever than we were. They knew how to lie and manipulate others, while we were ordinary people who didn't like to get involved in such games. The incessant attacks and threats against us had continued unabated for several years. God had allowed us to be crushed. In our darkest moments it felt as though we were being repeatedly run over by a freight train, and soon all that would remain of our lives and reputations would be a pile of dust to be blown away by the wind.

At times, I recalled how in Australia a decade earlier I had prayed, "Please give me real Christianity! I don't care what it costs, Lord; please help me have a real faith and teach me to fear You!" I wondered if our painful experiences were God's answer to my prayer. All we could do was to trust that one day the Lord would bring the truth to light, whether in this life or the one to come.

Often, we as a family felt completely alone, and we struggled in the knowledge that we had become lepers to many within the missions community God had called us to serve. I had previously been invited to teach at large mission conferences focusing on ministry to unreached peoples. Eventually, because of the incessant slander of our enemies, I was not even invited to attend conferences – a situation that has lingered to the present day. Meeting organizers told me that some delegates even demanded to know if I was planning to attend their gathering, and they threatened not to attend if the response was in the affirmative.

Although being rejected by most of the missions community was a challenge, the most difficult aspect for me to overcome was the public claim that my precious wife was a "slut." Joy was known as a sweet, modest, and pure-hearted young lady with a deep love for Jesus. Having these people trash her purity in a bid to cover up their own perversions angered me.

As Christians, we knew that God required us to forgive all wrongs committed against us. On many occasions we poured our hearts out before the Lord Jesus, forgiving Calvin and his family for their sins and malicious words. Despite my best efforts, my heart began to grow bitter from all the conflict. I tried to hand all my burdens to the Lord, but the constant drip of being attacked and lied about slowly eroded my fellowship with God.

Joy and I had grown frustrated and exhausted from the long ordeal. We felt like insects stuck in a big, sticky cobweb. The more we struggled, the more entrenched we became.

* * *

In 1999, at one of our lowest points, I was invited to speak at a mission conference in Bangkok. One of the other scheduled speakers was a Chinese house church believer I had been hearing about for many years. Brother Yun had a powerful testimony, forged from years of brutal persecution at the heart of the Chinese revival.

In the 1980s, Yun was captured when the police raided a large Christian gathering. They demanded to know his name and home address, so in a bid to warn the other believers of the imminent danger, he shouted at the top of his voice, "I am a heavenly man! My home is in heaven!" The believers heard his shouting and fled to safety. As a mark of respect for his courage and love for the Body of Christ, Brother Yun was given the nickname "The heavenly man."

On the final night of the Bangkok conference, Brother Yun and his translator invited me to their room for a time of fellowship and prayer. Yun was keen for me to share my vision for unreached people groups with the house churches in China. This was a great opportunity, but I knew the devil would try to stop it in its tracks. On numerous occasions doors had been slammed in our faces because of the backlash from the ongoing conflict with Calvin and his family.

I told Brother Yun that he and his co-workers needed to be aware that my name was not very popular among many Christians, and that he shouldn't be surprised if he heard some bad things about me and my wife.

"Please tell me more," he requested.

Yun sat on the edge of his bed as I summarized the worst of our experiences. He listened intently, and when I said, "And now their entire ministry has relocated from Hong Kong to our city of Chiang Mai," Yun smiled and let out a sigh. The more I shared, the more Brother Yun seemed to be amused. I found it strange, and although I wasn't looking for sympathy, I never expected him to find mirth from the account of our darkest struggles.

I reached the part about how Joy and I had been publicly slandered and labeled with vile terms. As his translator interpreted those words into Chinese, Yun's reaction caught me completely by surprise. He leaned back and began to laugh out loud. He laughed so hard that at one stage he even held his sides! I was shocked, and wondered if the translator lacked the correct vocabulary to accurately communicate my painful account. I thought that if he had understood correctly, then Brother Yun must be the least empathetic person I had ever met.

When I finished everything I had to say, Yun's countenance suddenly changed. He stopped laughing and became intensely serious. Indeed, he had understood my story correctly, and he was now about to share why he found it so funny.

Brother Yun stared directly at me, his eyes blazing with fire. Then he loudly declared, "Blessed are you when people insult you, persecute you and falsely say all kinds of evil against you because of me. Rejoice and be glad, because great is your reward in heaven, for in the same way they persecuted the prophets who were before you" (Matthew 5:11–12).

I now understood his reaction. Yun hadn't been laughing at our misery. Instead, he was rejoicing because of all the rewards God was storing up for us every time people lied and spoke evil against us.

We prayed together for some time that night, and I left the room a different man from the one who had walked in. Something had broken in the spiritual realm. At the end of our time together, Yun said, "Now I am certain that you are meant to work with the persecuted churches of China. We welcome you, for you are called to walk in the way of the cross, just as we are."

I rushed back to my room, eager to share what had happened with Joy. I had spent hours with Yun, and she was wondering what had happened. "We are free!" I announced as I walked through the door. "We don't need to battle that family anymore. While they have surely been a tool of Satan against us, that's not the full story. The Lord Jesus said we should rejoice and be glad because we have a great reward in heaven!"

Joy was amazed at the difference she saw in me. A heavy burden had been lifted off my back. I stayed awake for hours that night, processing my thoughts and quietly thanking the Lord Jesus while Joy slept.

Before that decisive meeting, I hadn't dealt very well with the attacks against us. They had been poisonous darts that lodged in my soul, causing much pain and giving rise to a root of bitterness in my heart. Now, the words of Jesus had completely altered my perspective and turned the situation on its head. Unbeknown to us, while we had struggled to see any benefit from the years of fierce conflict, our loving heavenly Father had been blessing us in a special way. As Paul wrote, "It has been granted to you on behalf of Christ not only to believe in him, but also to suffer for him" (Philippians 1:29).

The next morning, as we caught the lift down to the hotel lobby, I told Joy, "Last night, while you were sleeping, I believe God showed me that I am to write Brother Yun's biography. I haven't discussed it with him, and I don't plan to tell him at all. If I'm correct, then the Holy Spirit will tell Brother Yun directly. Let's wait and see what happens."

We returned home to Chiang Mai with a radically new perspective. Each fresh slander against us no longer carried the sting that the previous ones had. We realized that through the years of heartache and pain, God had never let go of us. We had been privileged to partake in the "fellowship of His sufferings" (Philippians 3:10, NKJV), and had been "counted worthy of suffering disgrace for the Name" (Acts 5:41).

CHAPTER 28

THE TRUTH COMES OUT

Brother Yun's prayers and advice helped Joy and me to gain a heavenly perspective of our ongoing battle. Our loving Savior had walked with us through the storm. He had never left our side, and had kept His promise made many years earlier on the night I was called to be a donkey for Jesus. He had truly been a "friend who sticks closer than a brother" (Proverbs 18:24). During the times we were overwhelmed, God reached down, picked us up, and carried us. By the power of the Holy Spirit we overcame all the turmoil and came out stronger on the other side.

The Lord encouraged His disciples, "In this world you will have trouble. But take heart! I have overcome the world" (John 16:33). The Spirit of God helped us overcome all the obstacles in our path, and as we drew closer to the heart of Jesus, we found that we became more like Him. If having our names dragged through the mud for years meant less of us and more of Jesus, then it was all worthwhile.

Time continued its relentless advance, and soon a decade had passed since we had first encountered problems from Calvin and his family. For much of that time, Joy and I thought that forgiveness was all about us conjuring up positive feelings toward our adversaries. Now we understood that forgiveness was really about releasing the burden of retribution to our heavenly Father. He would take care of it, not us.

Before the crucial meeting with Brother Yun, we had struggled with the fact that Calvin and his family never acknowledged any wrongdoing whatsoever. It was hard to forgive someone who insisted there was nothing to forgive, and each time the situation arose it was like picking a fresh scab off a festering wound. It was a huge struggle which never seemed to end.

Finally, we decided enough was enough, and we simply had to let go. While God still wanted us to warn others when necessary, it was time to disengage and let the Lord Jesus Christ take over the battle.

A remarkable thing took place a short time after we relinquished our struggle for justice. One day, a Southern Baptist missionary named Russell Minick came to our home. He explained that he had heard contrasting stories in the missions community which had caused him great alarm, so he had decided to investigate the matter personally.

A few days after meeting with us, Russell Minick met with Wendell to get his side of the story. Their meeting was shocking. Perhaps because of an overwhelming burden of guilt, Wendell openly shared details of his father's crimes that he had committed over many years. The situation was even worse than we had imagined. Wendell freely provided the names, dates, and locations of even more of his father's abuses than we were aware of.

A short time later, Minick sent out a general warning to the Body of Christ in Chiang Mai. His message calmly set out the facts that Wendell had shared about his father, as well as the cover-up his family had been involved with.

After many years of Joy and me being isolated and viewed as liars and slanderers, the truth had finally entered the public domain, via the dramatic testimony of Calvin's own son.

Some may presume that as we read Minick's letter, we felt jubilant and relieved that what we had claimed all along had now been independently documented. Instead, our main emotion was one of intense sadness. We were grieved that the Name of Jesus had been slandered among the nations by people claiming to be His disciples, and we felt distressed that the lives of precious children had been destroyed. Furthermore, we bemoaned that such vile crimes had been allowed to take place for decades while the Body of Christ stood by, either unwilling or unable to stop them.

In the aftermath of the letter, Calvin and his family still never acknowledged any wrongdoing, but reverted to type by attacking Russell Minick, who had simply reported what Wendell had told him. Legal action was even threatened against Minick's mission organization. Lamentably, some of the missions community in Asia saw no problem in continuing to partner with Calvin and his family, even after learning of their sordid criminal behavior.

To this day, Joy and I continue to warn others who ask us about that situation. The Lord has taught us how to do so without a vindictive spirit, but with a motive of wanting to help others avoid their trap. If by speaking out we have prevented even one child from being ensnared in that family's sticky cobweb, then all the pain we endured for years was more than worthwhile.

The Lord watches closely the reactions of His servants to news of wickedness in their midst. Those who are too cowardly to take a stand may place themselves on the side of evil and come under God's judgment. The Bible cautions, "Rebuke your neighbour frankly so that you will not share in their guilt" (Leviticus 19:17), and, "Do not share in the sins of others" (1 Timothy 5:22).

This type of evil in the Church is deadly serious, and it is backed by very powerful demonic forces. Looking back, it is astonishing to see how many Christian leaders who willfully closed their ears to this matter are no longer involved in Christian ministry. Some experienced dramatic events that swept them out of God's service – marriages broke up, finances ran dry, and ministries split. Some organizations were decimated as if a tornado had swept through. Few, if any, of those ministry leaders are able to see any connection between their demise and their refusal to take a stand for righteousness on this matter.

The Living God knows that for many years Joy and I did everything we could to warn the Body of Christ of this danger lurking within. We did so even though we were fully aware that by taking a stand we risked losing our entire ministry.

We believe the Holy Spirit honored our stance. From the time the truth was exposed until today, God has blessed us and the work of our hands in an astonishing way. This long and intense struggle proved to be a springboard that catapulted Asia Harvest forward.

* * *

Looking back at my meeting with Wendell, I'm amazed that anyone could be so shameless. We met at a cafe and I explained that I wanted to give him an opportunity to state the truth. What followed was a series of disturbing stories with specific names and places.

In graphic detail, Wendell told me the disgusting acts his father Calvin had done to girls, some as young as eight years old. He also revealed a long pattern of abuse and intimidation by his father, and how he himself had also aggressively gone after others in a bid to protect his father's reputation. When I asked what he had done to protect his own children, Wendell was eager to sound responsible. He and his wife hadn't hesitated to protect their children from their grandfather. Wendell appeared startled and bemused when I asked what he and his wife had done to protect other people's children from Calvin.

From that point on, Wendell made an effort to back-pedal and to shift blame. Confused and concerned, he bizarrely began to focus on how Paul and Joy were slanderers who had tried to ruin their ministry. We explored that line of reasoning, and Wendell began to speak as if I was hearing everything for the first time. I was amazed at his short-term memory loss, so I reminded him that he had already told me he knew his father had been a sexual predator for decades. I reminded Wendell, "Paul and Joy didn't tell me about what Calvin did to those girls. You did. Just now."

I fulfilled my legal responsibility as a minister of the gospel by contacting the police and notifying them of what Wendell had told me. I also contacted his local church in Chiang Mai and asked if there was a way to deal with this situation in private. Neither Wendell nor the church offered a way forward. Next, I sent an open letter to the ministries that had asked if I recommended working with Wendell and Calvin's organization.

The word spread, and what followed was a sickening silence by most, and a crazed rationalization and rebuke by others. I was disturbed by the inability of many Christians to see or care about the severity of the problem.

At the time the media was full of stories about abuse that had been performed by Catholic priests. The missions community rightfully found those accounts repugnant, yet when they were informed that there was a person among them with a long history of doing the same acts, many appeared completely unconcerned and didn't want to know about it.

Wendell and Calvin threatened to sue me. I referred to Matthew 5 and told them I would give them all my worldly possessions, a motorcycle and a laptop, if they felt they needed them, but that I would not be silenced. They then took their legal threats to my mission board. I concluded that the board might have been frightened, because they sent me a letter instructing me to say nothing more about Calvin and Wendell's ministry.

By this time the missions community had access to what Wendell had told me. I stopped initiating information, but remained available to testify to the accuracy of what had been shared if anyone wanted to know. Many people did not want to know.

To the disgrace of the Body of Christ, this family continues to live in Chiang Mai today, where they still appear as cheerful servants of God. Many missionaries decided it was convenient to continue working with a ministry led by charming and pleasant people, even though they knew whom they were partnering with.

Russell Minick

CHAPTER 29

"GO HIDE YOURSELF"

> In those countries where the church of Jesus Christ is being suppressed, persecuted, and almost wiped out … believers are under divine obligation to step in and do things their governments object to and consider illegal. We have got to do it for the sake of Christ and for the sake of the whole world for which He died.
>
> **Brother Andrew**

Over the years we have met many Christians who believe that obeying a nation's laws is of supreme importance to God – even more important than rescuing the lost and setting the captives free. Those who insist it is always a sin for a Christian to disobey the law of the land have never explained to us how the gospel of Jesus Christ will penetrate the dozens of countries throughout the world where Christianity remains strictly outlawed.

Almost all the countries God has called us to reach do not permit open Christian activity. The believers in those nations are persecuted with various degrees of hostility, and it simply isn't possible for them to openly serve the Lord. Our approach has been to obey the law of each country as far as possible, unless those laws conflict with the commands of Scripture.

The early Christians also chose to obey the Bible. When they were hauled into court and commanded to stop preaching by the legal authorities, "Peter and the other apostles replied: 'We must obey God rather than men!'" (Acts 5:29).

Whenever we come across God's children who need Bibles but are unable to access them because of the laws of their land, we don't hesitate to obey God rather than that law. If the government of a particular country bans preaching of the gospel, we unapologetically continue to equip local believers to fulfill the Great Commission.

The Lord Jesus plainly told His followers, "You will be hated by all nations because of me" (Matthew 24:9). The stark reality of His words has struck home many times, and over the past twenty-five years more than fifty Asian Christians in ministries we work with have been martyred for their faith. Countless others have been imprisoned or tortured for the gospel.

Some of the most severe persecutions have not come at the hand of governments. One ministry we partner with in the Himalayas has seen seventeen believers murdered by Buddhist monks. The monks, worried about losing control as people found true life in Christ, attempted to stem the advance of the gospel by putting the Christians to death.

Every year in India, hundreds of Christians are killed by militant Hindus, Muslims, Maoists, and other enemies of the gospel. Because the persecution occurs at the village level and is not directly from the government, news of their deaths rarely reaches the outside world.

In 2008, one key Indian ministry we partner with was decimated after many of its key leaders were burned to death or buried alive. The Lord Jesus responded by imparting His life to the remnant. By the power of the Holy Spirit, that ministry rose from the ashes, and in the ensuing years it has seen many thousands of Hindus and Muslims transformed by Jesus Christ. It has been a great privilege to work with such believers. We have come to understand that the kingdom of God always advances through weak men and women who rely on the Holy Spirit, rather than by human strength and man-made programs.

The risks involved with Christian work in Asia are not only confined to Asian believers. An American co-worker was severely persecuted in Beijing just weeks after the conclusion of the 2008 Olympic Games – where China convinced the watching world that it is a modern and free society. Our friend was captured at a house church meeting and attacked by a dozen officers, who kicked him with steel-capped boots and beat him with batons until he passed out from the pain. His body was literally black and blue from his head to his feet, and he continues to suffer severe migraines and other ailments to the present day.

Many missionaries we have known over the years have been expelled from the countries God called them to reach because they were too casual with security. One man was detained while entering Vietnam and told he was banned from the country. When he asked why, an official showed the missionary a scan of a prayer card he had sent to family and friends back home. He has never been able to enter the country again.

When another friend was blacklisted from entering China, he was shown copies of his personal newsletters that had been pinned to church notice boards in America. Someone had pulled his newsletters off the wall and scanned them, and they were used as evidence against him in China. His missionary career ended that day, as have the ministries of hundreds of other foreign Christians who have found themselves blacklisted by China over the years.

Many Western believers often have a false sense of security in their own countries, thinking that persecution is something that only occurs in faraway lands. As our work expanded, we increasingly became an irritation to certain Asian governments. We were glad the Lord had led us to function discreetly, especially after several ministries with similar work to ours informed us that their offices in the United States had been broken into by unknown assailants, who only took computer hard drives and information from the filing cabinets, and left other valuable items untouched.

Since 1988, when God first called me to be a donkey for Jesus, I have learned that the only way to survive is to exercise caution and godly wisdom in the area of security. I first realized my need for security immediately after my initial six-month stint in China. When I returned to Australia to attend Bible College, a journalist from a local Chinese Christian newspaper phoned me and requested an interview.

I visited the journalist's apartment, where he asked increasingly probing questions about my experiences in China. At the conclusion of the interview the man thanked me, shook my hand, and assured me that the article would be a great encouragement to readers, who would enjoy learning about how Bibles reached the hungry believers in China. He said it would be published in the following month's newspaper and he would send me a copy. Several months went by and I didn't hear a word. One day, I asked a Chinese friend at church if she had read the interview. "What do you mean?" she replied. "There are no Chinese Christian newspapers in Australia."

The entire interview had been a hoax. The man probably worked for the Chinese government and had done his best to draw information from me that could be used against the churches in China. Thankfully, I had only shared in general terms and hadn't provided any names or specific information. That experience left a deep impression on me.

I realized that to survive and accomplish what God had called me to do, it was crucial that I maintained a low profile and worked as anonymously as possible. I needed to acquire godly wisdom and heed Jesus' warning to the disciples: "I send you out as sheep in the midst of wolves. Therefore be wise as serpents and harmless as doves" (Matthew 10:16, NKJV).

One decision we made was to never share photographs of ourselves or the leaders we work with in our newsletters or publications. This is the reason you won't find our photograph anywhere in this book.

Adopting such a low-key profile goes directly against what many Western believers regard as basic requirements for Christian service. Ministers are expected to put their names and faces forward to promote their work as widely as possible. People who adopt such an open approach don't last long in the restricted countries of Asia.

In the military, details are shared on a "need to know" basis, and we have adopted the same principle in our work. If people don't need to know sensitive information that could potentially place others at risk, then we don't share it with them.

We thank God for His power and grace. After more than twenty-five years working in hostile environments, the Lord has supernaturally protected us and enabled us to serve Him.

* * *

There are different seasons in a Christian's life which require us to be flexible, so that we can adjust our path as God directs. In 1 Kings 17:3, God told the prophet Elijah to go and hide himself. The prophet did as instructed for three years, much to the frustration of King Ahab. When that time was up, however, God gave a new command to Elijah: to go and show himself (1 Kings 18:1).

Preaching in churches around the world had become a major part of my ministry. Joy and I traveled extensively as I shared our vision throughout North America, Asia, Europe, and Oceania. The Holy Spirit anointed me to preach, and I believe many good things resulted from the meetings. People often remarked how God had challenged and encouraged them by what was shared.

One day, as I relaxed in a hot bath, these words suddenly and unexpectedly leapt into my mind and spirit: "Stop speaking and start writing."

I told Joy what had happened, but we weren't sure what to make of it. I thought it couldn't possibly be God telling me to "stop speaking," so I put it to the side.

Several weeks later I flew from our home in Thailand to the city of Melaka, Malaysia, where I had been invited to speak at four meetings over the course of a weekend. The Saturday evening meeting went well, and I had two churches to share at on Sunday morning, before a final Sunday evening service. Trips like this had become a regular occurrence in my life.

My second Sunday morning meeting was in progress, and a packed congregation had gathered to worship the Lord. The pastor warmly welcomed me to the pulpit, handed me the microphone, and took his seat in the front row.

When I stood before the expectant crowd, something took place that had never happened to me before and has never occurred since. My mind went completely blank! I wasn't fearful of speaking to that many people, nor was I having a medical emergency. I simply didn't know what to say or do next. As I stood there motionless for a minute, I had a deep sense that God was displeased with me, but I wasn't sure what I had done to offend Him.

The church members thought my silence was odd, and they waited patiently for me to begin. Another minute passed, and I still hadn't opened my mouth. People began to recognize that something was wrong. A concerned look came across the pastor's brow, and I noticed a number of believers had stretched out their hands toward me in prayer. I bowed my head and asked God to help me. Immediately these words came to my mind: "I told you to stop speaking and start writing."

I realized I had ignored the instruction the Lord had given me several weeks earlier. With my eyes closed, I whispered, "Heavenly Father, I repent for disobeying You. Please forgive me and cleanse me from my sin. If You will, please allow me to fulfill my commitments here, and I promise when I return home tomorrow I will obey Your command to stop speaking."

The moment I finished praying, I returned to normal. My tongue was loosened and my thoughts were clear. I gathered my notes, and the Holy Spirit enabled me to deliver a strong message to the Malaysian believers. After the meeting, I shared a meal with several of the church leaders, but none of them commented on my long silence. They may have already forgotten about it, but it was a lesson that would never escape my memory.

I flew back to Thailand the following morning and told Joy what had happened. I thank God for giving me such a gracious and godly wife. She simply said, "That's okay, the Lord knows best. Our job is to obey Him and not to try to figure everything out with human reasoning."

I didn't understand why the Lord had commanded me to stop speaking. From a human perspective it was a huge blow to our work. It also presented a personal challenge. We received no salary, and most of our income stemmed from offerings that churches gave when I ministered. When I told an American missionary what had taken place in Malaysia he strongly rebuked me, saying, "You're crazy! How do you think you can run a ministry without speaking in meetings? That's the most stupid thing I've ever heard!"

I wondered what kind of ministry God wanted us to have. He had already led me to establish a totally non-traditional organization with no visible headquarters and as few staff as possible. I understood our need to maintain a low profile, but now I was even forbidden to speak in meetings. It seemed like a joke. Nobody had ever heard of a missionary who didn't speak in churches. That's what missionaries are supposed to do.

Through this experience, I was reminded that what matters most to God is my obedience. He wanted to know if Jesus was truly the Lord of my life, or if I was really the one in control, only willing to do things that suited me and which lined up with my own plans and desires. I couldn't have it both ways. When the Holy Spirit first called me to go to China I jumped with excitement and raced off to serve Him. Now that the same Holy Spirit had told me to hide myself, I also had to accept it. I needed to ask myself:

> Am I now trying to win the approval of human beings, or of God? Or am I trying to please people? If I were still trying to please people, I would not be a servant of Christ.
>
> **Galatians 1:10**

It took some time and much fervent prayer before I was fully assured that I had indeed heard from God and had not been deceived. I concluded that the Lord wanted me to stop speaking in nations where the Church is visible and institutionalized, but I was still permitted to teach in small, low-key gatherings in Asia. Once I was sure that I was following God's will, I wrote a standard letter, which was sent to people whenever I received a speaking invitation. It said:

> Thank you for your kind invitation. For years I traveled the world and spoke at numerous meetings, and God blessed those efforts. Recently, however, I believe the Lord has told me to stop speaking and to concentrate on writing. This was an unexpected development, and when I disobeyed God's command I felt His strong displeasure, even while standing in a church pulpit. Although I don't fully understand His reasons, I know the Lord requires my unreserved obedience, and I am learning the meaning of the Scripture: "To obey is better than sacrifice, and to heed is better than the fat of rams" (1 Samuel 15:22). I therefore respectfully decline your invitation, and hope I don't offend you by doing so.

Most church leaders responded graciously after receiving my letter, although my resolve was soon tested when invitations to speak at a number of large churches came in, some with congregations of several thousand members.

After God retired me from public speaking, I came to appreciate several main benefits that resulted from the change. The first benefit was that a major source of temptation was removed from my life.

Public ministry has brought about the demise of multitudes of Christian leaders over the years. It's difficult for people to remain humble when people regularly pat them on the back and tell them what great servants of God they are.

I had also struggled greatly with the social aspect of public ministry. I wasn't good at meeting people after a service. After a series of meetings I would often be so emotionally depleted that it would take me several days to recover. Now I had more time to seek the Lord in prayer, and my fellowship with Him became richer than ever before. I learned that the more responsibility I was given, the more I needed to sit at the feet of Jesus to receive His grace and power.

Our family life also became stronger after I reduced my travel schedule and spent more time at home. I was now able to take better care of my family, and Joy and I developed a much stronger marriage than we would have otherwise had.

Joy was especially thankful for this dramatic pivot in my life. It was easier to deflect the enemy's fiery darts when we were together. Our most difficult times had invariably come when I was away from home and Joy was left to fight by herself. Those times apart were now history. We decided that as far as possible, and finances permitting, whenever we needed to go somewhere we would travel together as a family unit.

The third benefit we experienced was in the area of security. As the Lord continued to expand our work into nations that oppose the gospel, our need for anonymity increased. God removed me from public view before my ability to visit many Asian countries was jeopardized.

Although I was no longer speaking in public meetings, my heart continued to desire an outlet for fruitful service, and to exalt the Name of Jesus Christ among the unreached peoples of Asia. With the benefit of hindsight, I am deeply thankful that the Lord shifted my focus from speaking to writing. Whereas even the best spoken messages tend to have a limited span of influence before they are forgotten, a good book can impact people's lives for years, decades, or even centuries after the author has gone.

By His wisdom and power, the Living God gradually formed Asia Harvest into a ministry that was far more fruitful than I ever thought possible. If I had used "common sense" and continued to preach, none of this would have happened. Truly, it's better to obey the Lord than to sacrifice.

CHAPTER 30

OPERATION CHINA

When God commanded me to stop speaking and start writing, I was unaware that the Holy Spirit was about to supernaturally open doors for me to author various books which would glorify the Name of Jesus and encourage the Church around the world.

Since the early 1990s I had been gathering information and taking photographs of many ethnic groups throughout China. In the early years, my research was more a personal hobby that I pursued between other ministry activities.

My writing career got off to an inauspicious start. In 1996, a mission leader asked me to write a collection of one-page prayer profiles of unreached people groups, which he intended to distribute to thousands of delegates at a large conference in South Korea. I set to work compiling as many profiles as possible in time for the conference. I worked day and night to complete twenty profiles. Each one contained information and prayer points about a specific unreached group, accompanied by a picture and a map.

I was disheartened when the mission leader failed to circulate any of the profiles at the conference. Even though I was exhausted and feeling frustrated at having wasted my time, I decided to continue to produce more profiles. After a while I had compiled enough to self-publish my first book, *The 50 Most Unreached People Groups of China and Tibet*.

After printing an initial quantity of a thousand books in Thailand, I believe the Lord showed me how He wanted them to be distributed. We were to employ three main methods to help get them into people's hands. First, we sold the books for $10 each, including postage. Next, if people wanted a book they could send a donation of any amount to one of our projects and request a complimentary copy.

Thirdly, based on Jesus' instruction "Freely you have received; freely give" (Matthew 10:8), anyone who wanted a book but genuinely couldn't afford to either buy one or give a donation could ask, and we would send them a free copy. This three-pronged approach became the template for all of our later books. We put the kingdom of God first by helping anyone who wanted a book to obtain one, regardless of their financial status. I believe the Lord was pleased with this strategy and bestowed His blessings upon us.

We sent out an email notifying people of my first book, and the response was staggering. Orders came flooding in, and within a few months our first print run had completely sold out. Readers commented on how crucial the information was, and many intercessors used it as a prayer guide. We printed another thousand books, and they also quickly sold out. Within a year we had distributed almost 5,000 copies of our little prayer book.

Encouraged by these developments, in 1997 I wrote *The Peoples of Vietnam*, followed a year later by *Faces of the Unreached in Laos*. These books were a breath of fresh air to many in the mission world. At the time, little information had ever been published on unreached people groups.

God also used the distribution of these books to raise awareness of our work, and the Lord began to open the floodgates of heaven on our ministry. Despite doing no fundraising at all, God blessed us as we busied ourselves with projects dear to His heart – providing Bibles to hungry believers and helping Asian missionaries take the gospel to the unreached. In those years the Lord also connected us with godly Christians in other parts of the world, who became the representatives of Asia Harvest in their countries. Our ministry suddenly had people of integrity representing us in the United

States, Germany, the United Kingdom, Australia, New Zealand, and Malaysia.

Encouraged by the impact of my small prayer books, I continued to research the peoples of China. I traveled extensively throughout the country, learning all I could about its fascinating people. I felt it was crucial for someone to bring these unknown groups to the attention of the global Body of Christ, so that they might experience His salvation. The Lord Jesus had died for them; His blood had "purchased for God persons from every tribe and language and people and nation" (Revelation 5:9). I couldn't imagine how these precious tribes and nations would ever hear the gospel if nobody knew they existed.

The Chinese government to this day claims there are only fifty-five "minority nationalities" in China, but it didn't take me long to conclude that their figure was massively understated. By the end of 1999, after almost a decade of research, God had enabled me to collect information and photographs of almost 500 distinct ethnic groups in China! I had personally visited many of them, and had consulted as many sources as possible in a tireless pursuit to bring their existence to light.

I hoped my research would be turned into a book that believers would be able to use to reach each group for Jesus. Such a large book required an official publisher, but I didn't know where to begin. I presented my research to several Christian publishers in the United States, but they saw little value in it. I also showed it to a number of mission leaders. They were more enthusiastic, but nobody thought I would be able to find a publisher for such a huge tome.

When I traveled to Virginia and met David Barrett, a renowned scholar and the chief editor of the massive *World Christian Encyclopedia*, he was keen to know which university I had graduated from. After all, I was an unknown missionary asserting that China was deliberately understating the ethnic composition of its country. Furthermore, I claimed to have discovered and documented nearly ten times as many groups as the Chinese government acknowledged.

I didn't want to come straight out and tell Dr Barrett that I was a high school dropout, so I jokingly told him, "I'm afraid all I have is a BA, which stands for Born Again!" Despite my lack of academic credentials, Dr Barrett was so impressed by my research that he wrote a wonderful endorsement for my book, describing it as "The most significant new contribution to missions research in twenty years."

After returning home to Thailand, I felt increasingly frustrated by my lack of progress in finding a publisher. Each day that passed without the Church knowing about the unreached groups was a day of lost opportunities. Tens of thousands of Buddhists, Muslims, animists, and atheists had died and crossed into eternity during the months I had struggled to find a publisher. It felt as though I had discovered a goldmine for God's kingdom, but nobody else was interested in sharing the plunder.

One evening, a thought crossed my mind that I should contact Patrick Johnstone, the British author of the best-selling *Operation World* books. I phoned Patrick and shared my dilemma. Patrick casually asked, "Have you heard of my friend, Pieter Kwant? This is the kind of project he might be interested in."

Pieter Kwant, a Dutchman based in northern England, had recently launched his own publishing company. As soon as I heard his name I sensed the Lord wanted me to travel to England to meet him. Joy and I had about $1,000 in our bank account at the time. A return ticket from Thailand to England, plus other expenses, would exhaust all the funds we possessed.

I told Joy that I believed God wanted me to fly all the way to England to meet a man whose name I had just heard a few minutes earlier. After explaining that we would have no money left when I bought my tickets, my precious wife immediately replied, "Go for it! If the Lord is leading you, don't think twice. He will provide all our needs."

A week later I pulled up in my rental car outside the home of Pieter and Elria Kwant in the English town of Carlisle. I knocked on their door with a large box of papers and photographs tucked under my arm, and was given a warm welcome. Our meeting was scheduled to last forty-five minutes, but after five hours of rich fellowship I departed, with my box remaining in Pieter's possession. He realized that the task of turning my decade of research into a book would be a gigantic and costly undertaking. The book would need to be 700 to 800 pages in length, and would include almost a thousand photographs.

As I left his home, Pieter stood in the doorway and asked if I had any last requests. I turned around and replied, "Yes, I have two. My first request is that the book must not be too expensive, otherwise it will only be used by a few mission fanatics and will be beyond the reach of normal believers."

"What else?" Pieter enquired. I took a deep breath and told him, "The entire book, all 700 to 800 pages, must be in full color! The peoples of China are full of vibrant color, reflecting the creativity of God. If the book is in black and white it will appear boring and drab, and the images won't touch readers' hearts or motivate them to pray and get involved."

Pieter thoughtfully stroked his long beard, and appeared to be a little flustered as he pondered my two contradictory requests. As I climbed into my car he called out, "Thanks for coming, Paul. I can't promise anything, but I'll see what I can do."

As I drove away from Carlisle toward the Scottish border, I cried out in fervent prayer, "Dear Lord Jesus, if You want this book to be published, please perform a miracle. Please make a way where there seems to be no way. Let Your favor rest on Pieter and Elria, and use them mightily to glorify Your Name."

God answered my prayer, and in due course the beautiful *Operation China* emerged. It was 706 pages in length, a stunning visual representation of all the people groups of China, and printed in full color throughout. Somehow, Pieter and his team had managed to keep the price at an affordable level.

When *Operation China* hit the market, it shook many mission groups, as readers were confronted with the stark reality that of the nearly 500 distinct nations living in China, 438 were yet to be reached by the gospel.

It was both satisfying and humbling to be notified of efforts that were launched to reach many of the groups profiled in the book. Both foreign mission organizations and Chinese house church networks used the book to send workers to the unreached.

Although the Christian status of hundreds of groups in China remains little changed since the book's publication, dozens of others have experienced dramatic transformations. The 50,000 Mosuo people, for example, had a mere handful of Christians among them at the time *Operation China* was released. They were one of the new groups whose existence was brought to light by the book. Today there is at least one Christian fellowship in every Mosuo village. Similarly, the 10,000 Baima people had never heard the gospel, but today there are many strong and vibrant churches in their midst. Even as this chapter is being written, I have just been shown a video of new believers from small ethnic groups like the Tagu, A Che and Pumi being baptized in southwest China. I praise God for His love and mercy.

Since then I have written many other books, but I still consider *Operation China* to be my favorite. It was the culmination of a decade's work, undertaken against a backdrop of unceasing personal struggles and attacks, and it was a result of the vision God had given me on the mountain in Nepal all those years earlier. It also represented the first project in a long and fruitful partnership with Pieter and Elria Kwant, which endures to the present day. The book was a glimpse into the heart of the Lord Jesus Christ and the outworking of His plan of redemption for all nations. He did it!

* * *

When Paul first contacted me, our company, Piquant, had not yet been properly launched. His call was welcome, but we had nothing to offer him at that time.

Paul stacked a huge pile of papers and photographs on our kitchen table, and as he passionately presented his work to us we caught the vision. The next day I organized a trip to meet with a number of large publishers. I planned to see if any of them would be able to turn the manuscript into a book worthy of the many years of loving effort Paul had put into it.

Two weeks of travel and very frustrating meetings followed. I was upset, having exhausted all our money on a trip and with nothing to show for it. The large affluent publishers were not willing to take a risk. It was like talking to a brick wall. They told me the market for such a book was tiny, and there was no way they would be able to sell more than a thousand copies worldwide. They also insisted there was no chance it could ever be done in color, as it would be far too expensive.

When I returned home, my wife Elria asked, "Why don't we publish it ourselves?"

My short answer was, "We have no money and no publishing house."

She encouraged me to look deeper to see if God might be leading us to take a step of faith.

A week later I had completed my calculations. To publish the book would prove to be a very expensive exercise because of all the color mixing costs required for a project of this nature. All up, we needed £100,000 (about US$150,000) just to produce and print the book. I estimated that we would then need to sell 13,500 books just to break even. Such a quantity seemed impossible, especially after a host of publishing executives had assured me they would struggle to sell a thousand copies.

Elria and I had no capital to put into the project at all. When Paul turned up at our door, I had recently resigned from my job and was seeking God about what to do next. All paths to publish Paul's book seemed to lead to a dead end, until one day my phone rang, and a friend from church surprised me by asking, "Do you need anything, Pieter?"

"Just £100,000!" I answered.

He told me that although he didn't have that much money, he could give me a £20,000 interest-free loan for one year. God was starting to answer a prayer I had scarcely begun to pray.

Next, a friend in the publishing world asked if he could assist me with anything. I shared the challenges I was facing and he offered to extend me £80,000 credit for nine months. He also offered to provide his technical expertise to help us produce the book.

All of a sudden, the impossible was taking shape! We commenced the editorial and production process, and I traveled to the United States, Asia, and elsewhere to see if organizations were interested in buying bulk quantities of the book. Amazingly, before many months had passed we had pre-sold 12,500 copies!

Operation China was printed, and my friends in the publishing world were astonished that we had been able to produce such a high-quality, beautiful, coffee-table style book. It was the first of its kind, and broke the mold for Christian mission books.

When feedback started to come in, I was glad Paul had insisted the entire book be produced in color. It made all the difference. The Overseas Missionary Fellowship, established by Hudson Taylor in 1865, called it "The China book of the decade!" Dr Ralph Winter, the founder of the US Center for World Mission, described *Operation China* as "A remarkable graphic visualization of the urgent reality of the unreached peoples," while Paul Eshleman, the president of The Jesus Film Project wrote, "The color photos help to give a greater vision and appreciation for the unreached."

The book was later translated into Korean and Chinese. By the hand of God, sales of the English version soared past the break-even point, going on to sell more than 25,000 copies! The £20,000 loan was paid back within the year, and my trade partners were repaid their full £80,000 well before the due date.

God had done it! *Operation China* was the first book published by Piquant Editions, and the project led the way for us for years to come.

Pieter Kwant

CHAPTER 31

A NEW MILLENNIUM

January 2000

A few weeks into the twenty-first century, I found myself in a small town in northern Myanmar (Burma), where a group of twenty senior Chinese house church leaders had come across the border for an important time together. Brother Yun had invited me to participate in the meeting, and it turned out to be one of the most blessed and transformative experiences of my life.

I felt deeply unworthy when I was asked to share God's heart for the unreached peoples of China with those leaders of several house church networks, each of which contained millions of believers. Most of these Chinese leaders had spent considerable time in prison for their faith, and they had all been key participants in one of the greatest revivals in Christian history.

After sharing how God had enabled me to find almost 500 ethnic groups in China, I challenged the leaders to mobilize their churches to reach every group for Jesus. Sharing statistics and words seemed to have little impact on the Chinese leaders, but when I began to show photos of the groups on a projector, the whole atmosphere of the meeting was energized. Seeing the faces of men, women, and children from unreached people groups within their own country struck them with great force. Bread and grape juice were fetched from the kitchen, and we shared an impromptu Communion together as the house church leaders cried out in fervent intercessory prayer. They dedicated themselves afresh to God, seeking His power to take the Good News to all of China's peoples.

After our Communion and prayer time, the meeting resumed and I was asked to share my personal testimony. I recounted how the Lord had saved me when I was nineteen, with no education, money, or prospects. I testified how the Holy Spirit had thrust me onto the mission field just months after my conversion, and had miraculously provided as I stepped out in faith. The Chinese leaders nodded and said, "Amen!" Some had tears in their eyes.

When I finished speaking, one man stood up and spoke on behalf of the whole group. He said, "Brother Paul, we are your family in Christ. We understand and accept you. Many Westerners desire to work with us, and while we appreciate their efforts, it often feels like we come from two different worlds. Your testimony, however, is just like ours. We also are nothing in the eyes of this world, and we possess nothing but Jesus. He called us by His grace, and we simply stepped out in obedience."

It felt as though a heavenly shower had refreshed us from above. Arrangements were already being put in place for me to visit regional hubs throughout China, to teach house church leaders the necessity of reaching every nation before Jesus can return.

One thing about the Chinese church leaders that left a lasting impression on me was their genuine humility. One of the younger participants was Joseph, a small man in his late twenties from Henan Province. Joseph was one of the few leaders who hadn't spoken in the meetings up to that point. I wondered if he was there in an administrative capacity, or if perhaps he had come along to carry the bags of one of the more senior leaders.

I ended up sitting next to Joseph at lunch one afternoon. Huge pots of rice and steamed vegetables were placed on a table at the far side of the courtyard, and everyone was invited to help themselves. I decided to serve Joseph, so I took his plate and headed toward the table. I only made it a few steps, however, before Joseph jumped to his feet and ran after me. He grabbed me by the shirt and pulled me back with all his might, determined to serve lunch to me, and not the other way around!

I was delighted when Joseph was asked to share his testimony on the final day of the meeting. I was keen to learn more about this humble brother. He began by telling of the time he had been arrested and incarcerated in 1993. Upon arriving at the prison, Joseph received a savage beating from the guards, who knocked him unconscious and broke his ribs and collarbone. His bloodied and battered body was then thrown into an overcrowded cell that already contained about thirty prisoners.

The cell had just one bed, and a single bucket served as the only toilet. The leader of the cell was a notorious gangster, and nobody was allowed to sit on his bed. When the guards threw Joseph's unconscious body onto the cement floor, however, even that hardened criminal had compassion on Joseph and laid him on his bed.

According to the other prisoners, at around two o'clock in the morning a supernatural light appeared in the cell and hovered over Joseph's body for several hours. The other inmates were terrified and backed themselves into a corner. They were so scared that they shouted for the guards to let them out. The guards came and also saw the supernatural light, and they too were afraid.

By sunrise, Joseph had regained consciousness. He had not seen the light. Despite the serious injuries he had suffered the previous night, he felt much better and his broken bones had been healed.

Still terrified by what they had seen, the first question the prisoners asked Joseph was, "Who are you?"

He replied, "I am a servant of Jesus Christ," and he went on to boldly preach the gospel to the men. That day, this unassuming brother led twenty-eight of the prisoners to faith in the Living God!

In the years since that meeting in Myanmar, Joseph has become the leader of one of the fastest-growing house church networks in China, with millions of believers under his leadership.

My time in Myanmar concluded, and I felt like a changed man as I boarded my flight back home to Thailand. Joy picked me up at the airport and drove me home. As soon as she saw me, she remarked, "You look different!" I tried to explain the powerful things that had taken place in Myanmar, but I struggled to speak through the tears that were welling up in my eyes. I felt I had made a deep connection with those Chinese leaders, and something powerful had taken place in the spiritual realm.

* * *

The months leading up to the meeting in Myanmar had been a testing time for Joy and me. Our personal financial support came from a small number of individuals and several churches the Lord had connected us with. In late 1999, however, three of the churches wrote to say they were discontinuing their support. One of them was my home church in Australia, who wrote to say that they wished us the best, and they had decided to head in a new direction at the start of the new millennium.

Although the money they had sent over the years was greatly appreciated and being cut off so abruptly was a blow, it wasn't totally unexpected. The pastor had suggested I should visit Australia more frequently to speak to the congregation. I did my best to explain that God had told me to "stop speaking and start writing," but my stance was too unconventional for the pastor to accept. We had no choice but to thank the church for the great blessing they had been to our family, and we continued to follow the path the Lord had laid out for us.

A few months after the Myanmar gathering, I found myself in central China, meeting with a group of about forty house church leaders in a town located at the heart of the revival that was sweeping millions of people into God's kingdom. One evening, a senior leader asked me unexpectedly, "Tell me about your church situation. Did any congregation send you to the mission field? Do they help you financially?" It was the first time I had ever been asked these direct questions by an Asian believer. I shared how a church in Australia had laid hands on me and sent me to the mission field with their blessing and oversight, but they had recently decided to stop supporting us.

The leader immediately went to consult some of his colleagues. A few minutes later a group of eight or nine men emerged from their dormitory. They asked me to come to the meeting room, as they believed the Lord wanted them to pray a special blessing over me and my family.

Seating me on a chair in the center of the room, the leaders laid their hands on my head and cried out to the Lord in unified prayer, as they typically do in China. After praying intensely for about ten minutes, the senior pastor said, "Brother Paul, we consider you a true brother in Jesus Christ. If the church in your own country won't cover you, we will! We recognize the special gifts God has given you, and we commission you to the service of the Lord. We ask the Holy Spirit to pour His blessings upon you and your family. May you be anointed with the power and presence of Jesus Christ, and may His favor rest on the work of your hands, so that millions of people will hear the gospel!"

I greatly appreciated their special blessing that evening. I have never claimed that the Chinese Church officially ordained me or anything like that, nor was I ever asked to serve them in any kind of formal capacity. It was simply a spontaneous moment when a group of believers felt led to embrace me. The Chinese leaders' love and acceptance of my family and our ministry was a precious encouragement.

In hindsight, it is clear that our work took off exponentially after that powerful prayer of blessing in China. The quantity of Bibles we provided experienced a dramatic and sustained increase, while the number of evangelists we supported also grew markedly.

Although God had instructed me to stop speaking in churches around the world, the total income for Asia Harvest greatly increased. In 1999 we received a total of $158,450 for our projects. This figure rose to $199,362 the following year, but in 2001 – the year after the prayer of blessing by the Chinese house church leaders – we experienced a huge leap to $743,744. This enabled us to print and distribute hundreds of thousands of Bibles and to spread the gospel among Asia's unreached people groups through many strategic initiatives. All of this was achieved by the supernatural hand of the Lord.

In subsequent years, many Christians around the world have asked me to connect them with the house church leaders of China. Some have wanted to know how I, an uneducated nobody, have been able to win favor with the Chinese Church. Some pastors and missionaries have even told me how gifted they are, and informed me that it is my duty to open doors for them in China so they can spread their teaching far and wide.

I always respond to such people by truthfully telling them, "I can't help you. Only God can open those doors for you. I wasn't accepted by the Chinese Church because of any human effort or ability. It was a miracle of the Holy Spirit. He did everything. The Lord supernaturally opened the doors, and I just went along for the ride."

CHAPTER 32

THE HEAVENLY MAN

More than six months had passed since the time I spent with Brother Yun in Bangkok. On our final morning there, I told Joy I had a distinct impression that God wanted me to write Brother Yun's biography. I figured that if I had heard correctly from God, then the Holy Spirit was more than capable of telling Yun directly, so I didn't say a word to him about it.

One day Brother Yun said to me, "Paul, I have been busy traveling around the world and sharing my testimony in many meetings. In various places, authors have come up and offered to write my biography for me. However, I believe the Lord wants you to write it. What do you think?"

I told Yun how God had told me to write his book more than six months earlier, and asked why it had taken him so long to get the same message. We had a good laugh together!

Arrangements were made for Yun to visit Chiang Mai for ten days so I could interview him in depth and gain a better understanding of his testimony. To overcome the language barrier, we asked an excellent Chinese translator to fly in from Taiwan.

I was already aware of the highlights of Brother Yun's story, and I recognized it was vital to get the more dramatic incidents absolutely correct. For example, in 1997 he miraculously escaped from a maximum security prison when the Lord healed his crushed legs and allowed him to walk past several prison guards to freedom. Instead of merely asking Yun to explain what had happened, I took him to the stairwell of our office building and asked him to demonstrate each part of the escape. He showed me where the guards were stationed on each floor, and where the doors and gates were positioned. By spending time covering the details of his testimony in this manner, I was confident that I understood all the key events of his extraordinary story.

When I started writing Brother Yun's biography, I realized that several things were likely to occur. First, I knew it would be a best-seller. I was sure that Yun's testimony of the power and grace of Jesus in the midst of horrific persecution would greatly inspire and encourage Christians around the world. I also suspected that many unbelievers would come to faith through reading the book.

Desiring to reach as many people as possible and to bring much glory to the Lord, I began to ask our heavenly Father to bless the book and, if it pleased Him, for at least one million copies to be printed and distributed worldwide. When I mentioned this figure to a friend in the publishing world, he tried to temper my enthusiasm by explaining that very few Christian biographies had ever sold a million copies. The more I sought God's will, however, the more confident I became that He wanted to use the book to advance His kingdom.

I also knew that many people would be upset and angry at the book. Yun's testimony sat in stark contrast to the dry experiences of many churchgoers, and the words that would encourage one reader were likely to infuriate another. If my writing attracted criticism, I would need to count the cost and carry on. Compromise was not an option.

Recognizing that Satan would use every insidious weapon at his disposal in a bid to destroy the book's impact, I interviewed as many independent eyewitnesses as possible to verify the key events in Brother Yun's life. I traveled to China to speak with people, and I also consulted his wife Deling, who provided valuable insight into the story from her perspective. Many readers later commented on how important her contributions were to the book.

Speaking with others about Yun's life was very revealing. For example, every person who saw him immediately following his seventy-four-day prison fast was overcome with emotion as they recalled the moment Yun's abused and shriveled body was carried into the prison visitation room. Almost two decades after the event, the impact remained fresh in their hearts and minds, causing them to break into deep sobs.

I also spoke with three house church leaders who had witnessed Yun's miraculous prison escape in 1997. All three men were incarcerated with him at the time, and confirmed the details of his escape.

By the time I had completed my interviews, I was confident that I had done my due diligence. I concluded that it was highly improbable that all the people I had consulted – in various locations both inside and outside China – had conspired to lie to me about Brother Yun. I was therefore fully convinced of the veracity of his testimony. For that reason I gave the book the subtitle *The Remarkable True Story of Chinese Christian Brother Yun*.

Pieter Kwant, whom the Lord used to publish *Operation China*, played a key role in finding a suitable publisher for *The Heavenly Man*. After I sent him the completed manuscript, Pieter used his extensive contacts in the publishing world to gauge interest in the book. When he sent sample chapters to many publishers, he was surprised to receive little interest in return. Most publishers were extremely busy and would receive new manuscripts every day. It appeared that some of them hadn't even taken the time to read the material Pieter sent before they filed it in the trash.

Finally, when things were beginning to look forlorn, Pieter received a firm offer from Monarch Books in England. They were so enthusiastic about the book that they even sent an advance royalty payment to confirm their interest. What the executives at Monarch didn't realize was that they were the only Christian publisher to express the desire to publish the book! Monarch was clearly God's choice for the project, and they did a wonderful job promoting and distributing the book throughout the English-speaking world.

The Heavenly Man started flying off the shelves as soon as it was released. It was incredible to sit back and watch as God placed His supernatural blessing on the book. Sales were further boosted when it was voted Book of the Year at the Christian Booksellers Convention.

Brother Yun's story has continued to encourage Christians around the world to the present day. One of the greatest blessings has been to see it translated into almost fifty languages, ranging from the Amharic language of Ethiopia to Mongolian and Turkish. Thanks to Pieter's expertise, tens of thousands of copies have been circulated in difficult parts of the world. The Arabic version went viral in countries like Egypt and Jordan, and bootleg copies of the Farsi translation swept throughout Iran, where many Muslims were eager to read a testimony about real Christian faith under fire.

The Heavenly Man became a tremendous success, all thanks to the Lord Jesus Christ. It began by selling hundreds of copies each month, then thousands, and ultimately tens of thousands. The book inspired multitudes of Christians around the world to live for God wholeheartedly, and encouraged them to keep trusting Jesus even in the darkest of circumstances. Finally, after a few years, the worldwide sales of the book surpassed the one million mark. Once again, God had performed a miracle!

* * *

I have often been asked to share some personal insights into Brother Yun, something more than what is written in his book. I grew to respect him in many ways, but the greatest lesson I learned from observing Yun's life can be summed up with one four letter word: *love*.

Brother Yun has a genuine love for people. On countless occasions around the world he has stayed behind for hours to pray for people after the meeting has concluded. He looks into the eyes of each individual, praying as fervently for the last person in the line as he does for the first. Yun does this because he believes that if Jesus loves everyone, then he should do likewise.

Later, I was privileged to see Yun display an even greater kind of love – love for his enemies. I witnessed his reaction after other Christian leaders publicly slandered him. In the midst of those attacks, he lifted his hands to heaven and prayed with tears in his eyes and compassion in his heart for his attackers. Observing his faith and love made a tremendous impact on my life.

At the height of the Chinese revival it was said that every house church believer was an evangelist. There were no committee meetings to debate whether the gospel should be proclaimed, simply multitudes of believers with a deep burden to reach as many people as possible for Jesus. Many felt as though they had been thrust into action by God, and they could echo the words of the Apostle Paul: "I cannot boast, since I am compelled to preach. Woe to me if I do not preach the gospel!" (1 Corinthians 9:16).

Even after relocating from China to Europe, Brother Yun retained an extraordinary ability to win people for the Lord Jesus. I have never met a more gifted evangelist. Despite being frustrated in his desire to reach Westerners because of language barriers, whenever he spots a Chinese person – whether on the street, at a busy airport, or in a crowded restaurant – he walks straight over to them and shares his faith. More often than not, within a short time Yun can be seen kneeling on the floor with his arm around the shoulder of a new believer in Jesus. I can only explain his ability to lead people to Christ as a supernatural gift of the Holy Spirit.

The same gift of evangelism has also been on display in public meetings. In one predominantly Muslim country, Brother Yun was invited to speak to a large gathering of university students. That day, hundreds of Muslims were convicted of their sins and decided to follow Jesus. In response, the government barred Yun from returning to that country, but the impact of his short visit has endured.

Brother Yun possesses godly wisdom that results from his knowledge of the Bible and his intimate relationship with the Lord Jesus and it overflows to those he meets. Pearls of wisdom regularly manifest themselves in simple yet profound ways. For example, a female animal rights activist attended several of Yun's meetings during a preaching trip to Scandinavia. By the end of the third meeting, the woman had grown visibly upset that he had still not mentioned animal rights in any of his messages. She angrily confronted him at the front of the church, saying, "If you were a man of God, you would mention that God loves animals, and that we have a responsibility to treat them humanely."

Yun wasn't sure if the woman was joking, but when his translator assured him that she was deadly serious, Yun looked directly into the woman's eyes and said, "I intend to keep preaching the gospel. That way, people will be saved and Jesus Christ will give them a new heart. Once they have a new heart, they will automatically treat their animals better."

The lady walked away speechless, unable to counteract the simple wisdom behind Brother Yun's answer.

CHAPTER 33

THE OPEN LETTER

> Any story sounds true until someone tells the other side and sets the record straight.
>
> **Proverbs 18:17 (TLB)**

For the first eighteen months after publication, *The Heavenly Man* enjoyed great success. Christians in many parts of the world were deeply touched and challenged to a deeper walk with God, and we received numerous letters and emails from people telling of the difference Brother Yun's testimony had made in their lives. The book also spread like wildfire among the prison systems of many nations, bringing conviction of sin and revival to many inmates.

One pastor in the United Kingdom shared how his congregation of about eighty believers decided to read the book together. They were convicted of their lukewarm faith, rededicated themselves to Christ, and began to earnestly study God's Word. This produced a greater desire to reach others with the gospel, and within a year the congregation had tripled to almost 250 members.

Satan was not willing to stand back and let the book go forth unhindered, however, and he moved on many people to launch undeserved attacks on Brother Yun's integrity. The intensity of the attacks increased, until what had begun as a smoldering ember of discontent from a few disgruntled individuals was growing into a raging forest fire, fanned by the internet. Now that he had left

China to minister around the world, Yun experienced a new form of persecution, this time at the hands of other Christians.

Many church and mission leaders spewed forth violent condemnation and harsh criticism of Yun and his testimony. One church even arranged a public bonfire to burn copies of the book. It deeply bothered me that many people took obvious delight in trying to destroy Brother Yun. Displaying no fear of God, they gleefully tried to smash him to pieces over things they knew nothing about.

I believe the two main motivating forces behind the onslaught against Brother Yun were self-righteousness and envy. There were some who slandered him because his testimony made them feel uncomfortable about their own lack of progress in the faith. They hoped that by pulling down Yun it would make them feel better about themselves.

Others, including many who worked in China, were worried that all the publicity Yun was receiving might affect their ministry income, so they launched waves of blistering attacks against him, hoping to ruin his reputation. The criticisms became so fierce and personal that I found myself not wanting even to open my inbox at the start of each work day, as dozens of vitriolic messages were arriving daily. At one stage I told Joy I needed to take a break from my computer for a while because it had become a "portal to hell." The pure hatred emanating from some people reminded me of Jesus' warning, "The time is coming when anyone who kills you will think they are offering a service to God" (John 16:2).

When people contacted me with their accusations, I always encouraged them to obey the Bible by taking any complaint they had against Brother Yun directly to him. I also told them that if they were too cowardly to do this, then they should shut up and stop spreading false rumors about a fellow believer. Very few had the courage to meet with Yun, even though he was available to meet with anyone during his travels. The majority of his critics chose to remain hidden in the shadows, from where they could hurl their poisonous darts undetected.

The barrage against Brother Yun reached its climax when Samuel Lamb, a famous house church leader in south China, wrote a small booklet entitled *The Heavenly Man: China's Great Conman*. The booklet was a vicious rant against Yun's character and testimony, based entirely on lies that had been told to him. Lamb had never personally met Yun.

Having spent twenty-one years in prison for his faith, Samuel Lamb was frequently held up by Western mission organizations as a hero of the persecuted Church. Consequently, many believers assumed there must be substance to the rumors. They couldn't imagine that a man who had spent decades in prison for the gospel could possibly slander another Christian without cause, even though Lamb had previously done the same to other Chinese house church leaders.

The situation was starting to spiral out of control. I thought the false charges against Brother Yun would die down over time, but the opposite seemed to be happening. By the time he was invited to speak in South Korea, the issue had grown to such ridiculous proportions that the attacks on his testimony were even reprinted in the national newspaper on the day he arrived. Sales of the Korean translation of the book had been strong up to that point, with thousands of believers blessed and strengthened in the faith, but the controversy caused sales to plummet dramatically.

At one stage I traveled to the country of my birth, New Zealand, where a series of meetings had been arranged for Brother Yun. During our time together, I sensed it was time for someone to stand up and attempt to put a stop to the onslaught against him. For his part, Yun steadfastly refused to defend himself. When I asked him if he thought it would be a good idea to issue a statement to help clear up people's misconceptions, he quoted the Apostle Paul:

> I do not even judge myself. My conscience is clear, but that does not make me innocent. It is the Lord who judges me. Therefore judge nothing before the appointed time; wait

> until the Lord comes. He will bring to light what is hidden in darkness and will expose the motives of the heart. At that time each will receive their praise from God.
>
> **1 Corinthians 4:3–5**

Several days into our trip to New Zealand, an incident took place that put the attacks against Brother Yun into perspective for me. We had some spare time as we passed through the beautiful Queenstown region, so I decided to drive Yun up a mountain that overlooks the pristine lake. Strangely, at the summit of that mountain sits an abandoned replica prison, which had been built as part of a 1980s movie set for a film about the Korean War.

As we began to ascend the mountain, I told Yun about the amazing views from the summit, and that we would also see an abandoned Korean prison. He went quiet, and a tense atmosphere filled the vehicle. I glanced at Yun and saw that he had broken out in a cold sweat and was shaking. He had been happy until the moment I mentioned the prison. It had touched a raw nerve in him because of his prolonged experiences of torture while imprisoned in both China and Myanmar.

I attempted to clarify that the building had never been used as a real prison, but was only a movie set. He understood, but continued to struggle emotionally. We pulled over for a moment to pray, and Yun lifted his hands to heaven and declared, "Hallelujah!" In an instant he returned to his normal, cheerful self. It dawned on me that for all the heavenly parts to his character, Brother Yun was also human, with the fragilities we all share.

* * *

A short time later I traveled to Hong Kong, where I met with a number of Brother Yun's friends and co-workers. I told them I believed it was time for someone to stand up and set the record straight, because people would continue to believe the lies about

Yun until the truth was set out to counteract them. With one voice, the men told me it was best to say nothing, and that God would vindicate him at the right time.

One of the men quoted Gamaliel, a Pharisee who had once cautioned other Jewish officials against persecuting the apostles. He advised,

> "Let them go! For if their purpose or activity is of human origin, it will fail. But if it is from God, you will not be able to stop these men; you will only find yourselves fighting against God."
>
> **Acts 5:38–39**

The other men in the room nodded their heads in agreement. They all believed it was best to say nothing in defense of Brother Yun, and that God would fight for him and sort it out.

That night I gave much thought to what had been said in the meeting. The advice of Brother Yun's friends sounded so pious and reasonable, but something didn't sit right with me. I asked the Lord to grant me insight and to share His heart on the matter. The longer I prayed, the more troubled I became in my spirit.

I thought about how fourteen centuries ago a young man named Mohammed introduced a new teaching in the Middle East. Perhaps the Christians at the time didn't consider it a serious enough threat to oppose it. Maybe they heeded Gamaliel's advice to do nothing. The new teaching took root and grew, and today Islam holds more than one and a half billion people captive, separated from the saving grace of Jesus Christ.

The next morning I returned to the meeting and announced, "I have decided to write an open letter in defense of Brother Yun. It's time to clear up this mess. I also intend to name names and lay out the facts, so that fair-minded people can decide the truth for themselves. This nonsense has gone on long enough. It's time to take a stand!"

The men reluctantly agreed that I should write the letter if I was sure the Lord was prompting me to do so, but they cautioned me against using people's real names. "Be careful, Paul," they said. "We don't want you to be entangled in a lawsuit."

A few weeks later I completed my article, which I entitled "An Open Letter Regarding the Heavenly Man." We sent it to everyone on our email list and posted it on our website, inviting anyone who wanted to circulate it to do so freely. We also had it translated into Chinese, Korean, and German.

In the letter I provided a summary of the accusations against Brother Yun and refuted them one by one. I also decided not to bow to intimidation or threats of a lawsuit, so I publicly named the key individuals who were the driving forces behind the character assassinations.

The part of the open letter that riled many mission leaders was my public exposé of Samuel Lamb's baseless slanders. Many considered it a terrible sin to say anything against Lamb. I had personally met Lamb many times over the years and I had no desire to disparage him at all. I simply quoted what he had written against Yun and set the record straight.

Before releasing the letter, I called Lamb at his church in Guangzhou, China. I wanted to give him a chance to explain why he had so spitefully maligned another believer. The call was bizarre. I started by enquiring if he had ever met Brother Yun.

"No, no, I don't think so," Lamb replied.

When I asked why he had openly attacked a man he'd never met, Lamb chuckled and said, "He's a bad man! No good. I don't want to meet him. He's a troublemaker!"

I calmly yet firmly told Lamb that he had been deceived and was spreading lies. I reminded him that if he didn't repent, one day he would have to stand before God and give an account for his words. Lamb didn't sound in the least bit concerned, and our conversation concluded.

Samuel Lamb has since passed away. Brother Yun never said a word against him, but he prayed for Lamb often and forgave him from his heart.

The open letter had an immediate impact. Many websites and Christian publications reprinted the letter, and thousands of people finally got to hear the other side of the story. Extraordinarily, about 90 percent of the attacks against Brother Yun instantly ceased, as many of his slanderers lost courage and ran for cover. I was told that some were afraid of being publicly named in a future letter if they continued in their efforts to destroy Yun.

A few months later, I saw Yun again in another country. He smiled and thanked me for writing the letter. He explained that he didn't think a Christian should ever defend his own reputation, but that it is the responsibility of other believers to defend a brother or sister when they are wrongfully accused.

As I look back at this episode, my one regret is that by listening to the human wisdom of Yun's circle of friends, I failed to write the open letter much sooner. Because of the ferocity of the prolonged attacks, to this day many people continue to think Brother Yun's testimony is false. Sales of the book took a major downward turn at the height of the onslaught. Tragically, in places like the United Kingdom where the book had brought a spark of inspiration to the dry lives of tens of thousands of Christians, the slanders snuffed out the spiritual spark that had been ignited by the Holy Spirit.

It angers the Lord Jesus Christ when Christians try to destroy one another. To those like Brother Yun who are the targets of undeserved attacks, the Bible says, "God is just: he will pay back trouble to those who trouble you and give relief to you who are troubled" (2 Thessalonians 1:6–7). Looking back, it's amazing to see how many of the ministries that led the blitz against Yun are no longer in existence, and the lives of more than a few of the individuals who indulged in character assassination have since fallen into disrepute.

Brother Yun and Deling, meanwhile, continue to serve the Lord from their base in Germany. God has used them to bless millions of people. Both of their children are now married and in full-time service for the Lord.

Almost fifteen years have elapsed since *The Heavenly Man* was first published, and nearly two decades have passed since he left China. In recent years, some of the Westerners who have been associated with Yun are not those I would endorse as of godly character, and some of the churches he has spoken at would certainly not be my choice. Regarding the veracity of the book, however, I remain confident that Yun's testimony is true, and there is nothing in the book I would retract.

I am deeply thankful for the connection the Holy Spirit formed between me and Brother Yun. I was honored to help write his testimony, and whatever trouble eventuated was insignificant when compared to the great spiritual blessing God brought to the lives of countless people around the world.

CHAPTER 34

A GLORIOUS MESS

Following the success of *The Heavenly Man* book, God greatly increased awareness of our ministry and the projects through which we help to advance the kingdom of God in Asia. The finances generated by the book gave a boost to all our projects, enabling us to print more Bibles and to support more workers.

Over the next few years I visited China frequently. Whereas my previous trips had primarily been to research unreached people groups, now I traveled there to minister to house church leaders. It was a tremendous honor to be welcomed into the heart of the largest revival in Christian history, and to fellowship with believers whose simple faith had shaken their country. I have many precious memories from those times, and they will remain with me for the rest of my life.

As I traveled around China ministering in house churches, I also spent hundreds of hours recording the testimonies of many church leaders, for use in future books. I was fascinated with the Church in China, but nobody was sure how many Christians lived in the world's most populated country. Most estimates were wildly inconsistent. Consequently, I decided to launch the first exhaustive survey into Christianity in China since the advent of Communism in 1949, when the country was home to about 750,000 Protestant believers.

I wanted to start my research from scratch, so I placed all assumptions aside and collected every scrap of information on Christianity in China that I could find. I scoured books, magazines, and websites, and I collated the information the house church leaders shared with me. It was a massive undertaking, but in the end the Lord enabled me to make Christian estimates for all of China's 2,371 cities and counties.

My research was published in an article on our website. The total number of Christians in China, across all denominations, came in at 105 million. More than half were house church believers whom the Lord had called us to serve.

Because it was the first survey of Christianity in China to be conducted in such detail, the statistics began to be quoted by both the missions world and the media, including the BBC and CNN. Some people complained that my figures were too high, and others said they were too low. While only God knows the true extent of His kingdom in China, it was clear that the Chinese Church had grown about hundredfold in the decades under Communist rule!

The growth of the Church in China was so extraordinary that people can only begin to understand it if they first recognize that it was not a natural event. The revival was a supernatural partnership between the Living God and broken vessels whose only desire was to exalt the Name of Jesus.

A few stories spring to mind that provide a glimpse into the phenomenal power and grace that God unleashed in some regions of China. The city of Daqing sits on a barren plain in the northeast of the country. In 1991 it was home to just a few hundred house church Christians. Around the same time, a severe persecution broke out hundreds of miles away in Henan Province. To flee the persecution, a small group of Henan church leaders fled their homes and moved north to Daqing. After arriving in the city, the pastors trained thirty local Christians in the ways of the Lord. Many of the Daqing believers worked in factories. They took the gospel to their workplaces, where they found receptive hearts. Revival began to sweep through the factories and apartment blocks of Daqing.

Incredibly, between 1991 and 2003, the house church movement in Daqing grew from 200 people in a handful of fellowships to at least 200,000 believers in 2,500 house churches – a thousandfold increase in a dozen years! The city became a hub for the gospel in northeast China, and many evangelists took the fire of the Holy Spirit into neighboring provinces like Inner Mongolia, where the revival also spread quickly.

Equally remarkable was the success of the "Gospel Month" initiative, which was launched in 1992 by a single fellowship in central China. Between Christmas and the Chinese Lunar New Year, each church member was expected to lead at least three people to the Lord. A greater responsibility was placed on church leaders, who were required to lead at least five people to faith.

The vision was embraced by many other churches in the region, and soon thousands of Christians had been mobilized to win their lost neighbors. The results were astonishing. A total of 13,000 new believers were baptized at the conclusion of the first Gospel Month program in early 1993.

Those new Christians were trained to participate in the same outreach the following year, but many realized there was no point confining their efforts to just one month each year, so they became full-time evangelists. At the conclusion of the Gospel Month in early 1994, the house churches baptized 123,000 new believers in Henan Province alone!

One senior house church leader told me, "Previously, during our open air meetings, few people would pay attention. Now, everywhere we went, crowds of people stopped whatever they were doing to listen. As we preached, many cried out, 'We have never heard such good news in all our lives! Why hasn't anyone told us this before?' The people set aside all other activities and listened attentively to the gospel for hours. This was a sovereign work of God, and the Holy Spirit confirmed His Word with many signs and wonders."

Following the 123,000 baptisms that were recorded in 1994, the number of people saved during the Gospel Month outreaches in subsequent years grew too large to keep track of. What began in a single fellowship in an impoverished farming area spread to almost every province of China, and many millions of people were transformed by the Lord Jesus Christ.

* * *

While statistics from the Chinese revival may sound impressive, many people have asked me to describe a typical house church meeting. They have read stories of miracles and mass conversions in China, but it is difficult for them to picture the revival on a practical level.

I would normally be collected at a prearranged location by a Chinese believer in a van with tinted windows. We would drive into the countryside, often for many hours. I was instructed to sit in the back, to wear a coat with a hood, and to keep my head down, especially when we approached a roadblock or intersection.

After arriving at our destination, I would be given a short time to settle in, before being taken to a meeting room that had been soundproofed by egg cartons affixed to the walls, while triple-glazed windows prevented the sounds of singing and preaching from reaching the streets outside. Waiting for me in the meeting room would be thirty, fifty, or sometimes even a hundred house church leaders, many of whom had traveled long distances to be there. With faces brimming with the love and light of Jesus, I was invariably welcomed like a long-lost brother.

I was usually required to teach God's Word in three- to four-hour blocks, separated by meal breaks. Although the Lord had restricted me from preaching in other parts of the world several years earlier, the restriction did not apply to the countries in which I was called to serve. I love teaching the Bible, and with God's help I didn't have much trouble speaking for eight hours or more per day. The Chinese would tell me how surprised they were to discover that many foreign preachers could only teach for thirty or forty minutes at a time before they ran out of things to say. The normal pattern of my teaching was to walk the believers through the Scriptures, revealing God's master plan to save all nations from Genesis to Revelation.

Each day would normally start at seven o'clock in the morning and conclude late in the evening, or even after midnight if the Holy Spirit was still moving. We would go to sleep after the meeting finally finished. As the guest teacher I would be given my own room, while the Chinese laid down on mats side by side and head to toe, with the brothers and sisters staying in separate rooms.

The new day would dawn, and the routine would repeat itself after breakfast. I was always greatly impressed by how well organized and resourceful the believers were. In those days of cassette tapes, they had a line-up of machines to record every message. As technology advanced, the tape recorders were replaced by CD players, and later by smartphones.

If the teaching was believed to have been anointed by the Spirit of God, the recordings were taken to a central location, where mass duplicating machines quickly produced hundreds of copies. They would be distributed far and wide, and recopied until they had made their way throughout the house church networks. Within days of a message being taught, tens of thousands of believers throughout China may have already listened to it.

Personally, I found the most difficult part of the meetings to be the intense prayer sessions, which often continued for hours. Every believer would kneel and cry out to God at the top of their voice, and to fully participate in the meeting I also knelt on the hard floor, which often became slippery from the tears and mucus of believers while they engaged in fervent intercession.

To be honest, at times I had tears in my eyes during those long prayer meetings, not from compassion, but because it felt as if I was close to passing out from the pain in my knees, especially in the winter, when my lower legs went completely numb from kneeling on the cold cement floor. My spirit was willing but my flesh was weak.

Someone once asked me to describe the Chinese revival in a few words. I thought about it for a moment and replied, "A glorious mess!"

Many people assume that a church in the midst of a heaven-sent revival must be clean, structured, and highly unified – a near perfect representation of Christ's Body on the earth. The reality, however, is that the Chinese Church in revival had plenty of problems, temptations, trials, and weaknesses. There were various theological debates, members who fell into sin, and people who caused division, just like there were in the Church of the New Testament.

Being exposed to the Church in China helped me to realize that we are all jars of clay. While there is much to admire and learn from the revival, I caution people against idolizing persecuted Christians. I have been troubled by letters we have received from people who say if they could just visit a Chinese church then all their troubles would be over. This mindset is misplaced and dangerous. It can be a form of idolatry, where people look to other human beings to satisfy their needs, instead of falling to their knees and seeking Jesus Christ with all their hearts.

The Lord Jesus provided a balanced view of persecution. In His letter to the believers in Pergamum, the Lord described their town as "where Satan has his throne" (Revelation 2:13), and where one of their members, Antipas, had already been put to death because of his faith. False teaching and compromise had entered the church, however, and the Lord didn't hesitate to rebuke and threaten them with severe judgment if they didn't take care of the problem.

Likewise, while there are good things we can learn from the persecuted Church, we should never place our hope in it. Being persecuted for the gospel is no antidote to sin, and no guarantee of holiness. The reality is that the revival in China was not the work of men and women. It was a sovereign act of the Almighty God, who chose to manifest His glory through weak vessels, "so that in all things God may be praised through Jesus Christ. To him be the glory and the power for ever and ever" (1 Peter 4:11).

* * *

A characteristic of fire is that it must always have new fuel added to it, or it will die. Most revivals throughout history have only lasted a short time, as mortal men and women have struggled to cope with God's consuming fire. The Israelites were also often stuck in a cycle of revival and backsliding. God summed up their plight this way:

> "I cared for you in the wilderness,
> in the land of burning heat.
> When I fed them, they were satisfied;
> when they were satisfied, they became proud;
> then they forgot me."
>
> **Hosea 13:5–6**

I am deeply thankful for every experience I had during the blessed years when the Almighty God descended on China and saved people by the millions.

The years rolled on, and many swift changes came to both the society and the Church in China. By 2008 the revival had begun to wane. Materialism gradually took hold of the masses, making it increasingly difficult to reach people with the gospel. The nature and intensity of persecution gradually subsided, and the flame of revival began to flicker less brightly than before. The kingdom of Jesus Christ continued to advance, but sadly, the intense, white-hot revival that consumed many parts of China from the 1970s to the mid-2000s – when the power of God fell from heaven and multitudes repented of their sins and were empowered for gospel service – became increasingly difficult to find.

For decades the Church in China had been tested by hardship and persecution, and it came through with flying colors. Now it was being tested by prosperity. Christian history shows that this test is much more difficult to overcome.

Then unexpectedly, in mid-2016, the Chinese government reversed its course and launched a brutal and sustained crackdown in yet another bid to eradicate the house church networks. In many parts of the country pastors were bundled into vans and not seen again, while others were mercilessly tortured in secret 'black jails.' Intense pressure was placed on Christians who refused to join the government-approved churches and even the children of Christians were punished with new laws that threatened their futures. My hope and prayer is that once again revival fires will be rekindled across China, and the Body of Christ will continue to grow in both size and grace. God has gained much glory through His children in China, and it's clear their baptism of fire is far from over.

* * *

At one time I faced a difficult personal decision. Around the time that Joy was about to give birth to our second child, one of my brothers called from New Zealand to inform me that my father was dying of kidney cancer and was unlikely to survive much longer.

My dad had shown no interest in the gospel on the several occasions I had spoken to him about God. He was lost, and would soon face eternity having spurned God's offer of salvation.

My initial reaction was that I should jump on the first available flight and go to my father's bedside. But Joy also needed me. Having a baby in a foreign land with no family members or relatives to assist can be a lonely experience.

I faced a difficult dilemma, and I needed God to reveal whether I should remain in Thailand or travel to New Zealand. I sent an email to a small group of prayer partners, explaining the situation and asking them to pray for clarity. One man replied to say it was a "no-brainer" that I should go to my father's bedside. He even offered to pay my air fare, expressing disgust that I would even think twice about going to share the gospel with my dying father. I had a hesitancy in my spirit, however, and when I didn't immediately accept the man's offer to pay for my ticket, he wrote back angrily, telling me to take his name off our list and to never contact him again.

A second friend committed to pray for our situation. After a few hours of fervent intercession, she shared that God had given her a deep sense that I should remain in Thailand and take care of my family. She wrote, "I believe the Lord has your father's situation under control, and He wants to encourage you with this Scripture: 'God is not unjust; he will not forget your work and the love you have shown him as you have helped his people and continue to help them'" (Hebrews 6:10).

Our doctor in Thailand decided Joy would need a Caesarean delivery, and a date was scheduled for the birth. I had previously committed to go on another house church teaching trip into China. Joy agreed that I should keep my commitment as long as I returned to Thailand in time for the birth.

In China, the first two days of the meetings went well. During the prayer time on the third day, the house church believers asked if I had any prayer requests to share with them. "Yes," I replied. "My father is dying, and he doesn't know Jesus as Savior. He has strongly opposed the gospel all his life. Please ask God to perform a miracle and save him before it's too late."

My request galvanized the forty Chinese Christians into action. They cried out in unified prayer, interceding with great fervency and battering down the demonic forces over my father's life as they begged God to have mercy on him. I was reminded of what the Lord once said: "From the days of John the Baptist until now the kingdom of heaven suffers violence, and the violent take it by force" (Matthew 11:12, NKJV).

After forty-five minutes, the uproar of prayer suddenly subsided and the believers went quiet. They believed their job was done, and that all spiritual hindrances to my father receiving the gospel had been removed. It was now up to him to decide whether to submit to Jesus or not.

I returned to Thailand and phoned an elderly New Zealand pastor who lived about an hour's drive from my parents' home. I explained that my father was close to death and needed to repent and believe in Jesus before it was too late. The pastor said he would try to visit him.

The next day I received an email informing me that my dad had become a Christian! Overjoyed, I called the pastor to hear the rest of the story. He had driven to my parents' home to find my dad in a deep sleep owing to the heavy medication he was taking. After waiting patiently for more than an hour, it looked as though my father was not going to wake up, so the pastor thanked my mother for her hospitality and put on his coat to leave. At that moment, a fly buzzed around my father's head and landed on his nose, waking him up. Hearing the pastor and my mother talking in the hallway, my dad said in a faint voice, "Tell him to come in."

The pastor sat at my father's bedside and shared the gospel with him. He also read a letter I had written, encouraging him to repent and to give up his stubborn rebellion against God. All his life he had been a cynical man who treasured his intellect and boasted that he would always remain an agnostic.

Now, as he drew near to death's door, the fear of God gripped my dad's heart. He prayed with the pastor, renounced his sins, and asked God to have mercy on him through the shed blood of Jesus Christ.

The pastor took a photograph, which remains on the wall above my desk to this day. When I first saw the picture I was shocked to see my father's emaciated, cancer-ridden body, but his beaming face revealed a man who had finally made peace with his Maker.

Two days later I received another message from my brother. My father was dead. He had gone to stand before God, a convert to Jesus Christ at the very end of his seventy-two years on earth.

A short time later our second son was born in Chiang Mai. We called him Taine, a name derived from a native Maori word meaning "mighty warrior." We were now a family of four. Joy and I rejoiced in God's grace and mercy. He had performed two miracles of life that week: one a natural birth, the other a supernatural birth.

I knew that if it had not been for the powerful intercession of the Chinese house church believers, my father would have died without faith and been lost for all eternity.

CHAPTER 35

CHURCH ON A STAGE

> You feel sorry for us in India because of our great poverty in material things. We who know the Lord in India feel sorry for you in America because of your spiritual poverty. We are praying that you also might come to church with a hunger for God and not merely a hunger to see some form of amusement.
>
> **Bakht Singh, Indian church leader**

Several years ago the Smithsonian Institute displayed an exhibit of Thomas Jefferson's Bible. Jefferson had taken a pair of scissors and cut out all the parts of the Bible he didn't like, including God's moral laws which he felt were outdated. He also removed all mention of hell, and because he didn't believe in miracles, he chopped those passages out too!

While most Christians would agree that Jefferson's actions were ridiculous, I've met numerous believers who do exactly the same thing to God's Word, albeit not usually with a pair of scissors. By picking which parts of the Bible they want to accept, people invariably choose those verses that make them feel good about themselves, while ignoring the rest.

During the years when I spoke in hundreds of meetings around the world, I found it increasingly difficult to effectively communicate testimonies from the Church in Asia to believers in "free" countries. Often when I spoke in meetings, people looked at me as if I had just dropped in from another planet.

I became aware that the spiritual dynamics of the persecuted Church in Asia were completely different from those in Western Christianity. The differences were so stark that I sometimes felt I was interacting with two different faiths. Even the most basic understanding of God's character appeared to be fundamentally different.

For example, on one occasion in China I shared a powerful testimony from the Mru tribe of Myanmar. The Mru number about 25,000 people, most of whom are Buddhists. The gospel had recently experienced a breakthrough among them, and several Mru villages had turned to Jesus Christ. The Buddhist monks were furious when they heard about it, so they hired two gangs of thugs and sent them to the Christian villages to beat the believers, rape the women, and burn down their houses.

Armed with chains and machetes, the first group of thugs made their way on foot to the Christian area. Before reaching their intended destination, however, a freak electrical storm descended on them as they traversed a mountain pass. All of the men were killed by lightning. The lightning also struck the 400-year-old Buddhist temple in the Mru township, burning it to the ground.

The second mob of would-be persecutors traveled to the Christian villages aboard a large raft. As they made their way down the river, a thick fog suddenly enveloped them, making it impossible to see where they were going. A barge sliced through the fog, struck the raft, and hurled the thugs into the rapids, where they all drowned.

When news of these events reached the Mru communities, the fear of God fell on them. Realizing that the Living God had displayed His awesome wrath, hundreds of people turned to Christ and repented of their sins.

When I shared this testimony with the Christians in China, they literally jumped up and down with joy and shouted "Hallelujah!" at the top of their voices. They rejoiced in the judgments of God, as the Bible says, "Zion hears and rejoices and the villages of Judah are glad because of your judgments, Lord" (Psalm 97:8).

Just a few weeks later I found myself standing in front of a congregation in Texas. As I shared the same testimony from Myanmar, I looked out at a sea of grim faces staring back at me. There was no rejoicing in that meeting, and not a single "Hallelujah" was uttered.

After the service, an elderly lady came forward to confront me on behalf of the other church members. She strongly rebuked me with the words, "Our God is not like that, brother. Our God is a loving God!" I noticed many people behind her nodding their heads in agreement.

Like that congregation in Texas, many believers imagine God to be a cuddly, teddy bear-like figure whose main purpose is to encourage and bless them. They think God is so gentle and loving that He would never harm a fly, and Christians who dare to mention His wrath or coming judgment are often pushed into a corner and considered a threat to the peace of the Church.

With such a skewed, chummy attitude toward God, it is no wonder that many Christians no longer fear Him. They love to hear about how John reclined at the dinner table by leaning against His best friend Jesus, but few remember that the two men met again many years later. This time the resurrected Lord was dressed in the robes of a Roman judge. John, who was absolutely terrified, wrote, "When I saw him, I fell at his feet as though dead" (Revelation 1:17).

As followers of the Lord Jesus, we need to cultivate a deep, loving intimacy with Him, while not becoming so familiar that we lose a healthy fear of God. May we never forget that one day the anger of the Lord Jesus will be so fierce that people will call "to the mountains and the rocks, 'Fall on us and hide us from the face of him who sits on the throne and from the wrath of the Lamb! For the great day of their wrath has come, and who can withstand it?'" (Revelation 6:16–17).

I once shared at a home meeting in New Zealand about the need for every Christian to take up their cross and follow Jesus. To illustrate my message, I shared the testimony of Sister Yuen of Shanghai. It is a favorite story of the house churches in China, and touches a deep chord in believers' hearts whenever they hear it.

Sister Yuen, a widow with two small children, was arrested and thrown into prison because of her faith. In a bid to make her renounce Christ, the guards brought her children and had them stand outside the prison gate. With their arms outstretched, they begged their mother to come home.

The guards taunted Sister Yuen by asking, "Doesn't your God want you to take care of your own children? You can return home today if you just sign a statement declaring you will no longer be a Christian."

Like any mother, Sister Yuen's heart was torn at the sight of her crying children, and she asked the guards to bring her a sheet of paper and a pen. They hurriedly fetched the items, thinking they had finally found a way to break her faith in God. Sister Yuen calmly wrote on the paper and handed it to the prison warden. A moment later his face turned red with rage. She had written in large letters, "Jesus can never be replaced! Even my own children cannot replace Jesus!"

Sister Yuen was sentenced to twenty-three more years in prison. By the time she was released her children were adults, having been raised by the atheistic state. She spent months trying to locate them, and was finally able to be reconciled with her daughter. Her son, however, had become a policeman and his heart was filled with hate for his mother and her God. He wanted nothing to do with her ever again.

As I shared this powerful testimony with the small group of New Zealand believers, a married couple, who were well regarded in the Christian community of that town, threw their heads back and began to sigh and moan. After the meeting, coffee was served. The couple marched straight up to me, obviously wanting to get something off their chests. "Your story is stupid!" they protested. "If we were in that woman's position, we would have signed the paper. Of course God wanted her to take care of her own children!"

"So are you saying you would willingly deny the Lord Jesus to get out of prison?" I enquired.

"Yeah, we would," they stated matter of factly. "God would understand and forgive us."

I was astonished that a pair of professing Christians could openly admit that they would willingly deny their faith under pressure, and that they didn't see anything wrong with that. I asked if they were concerned about the words of Jesus, who said, "Whoever disowns me before others, I will disown before my Father in heaven" (Matthew 10:33).

"God wants us to take care of our children," they reiterated.

Following that incident, I was more careful about who I shared precious testimonies with, and was reminded of the warning the Lord gave to His followers: "Do not give dogs what is sacred; do not throw your pearls to pigs. If you do, they may trample them under their feet, and turn and tear you to pieces" (Matthew 7:6).

* * *

Some years ago a passenger boarded a flight in Los Angeles, intending to fly to Oakland, California. He expected the flight to take about an hour, so several hours into the journey he started to suspect something had gone wrong. Somehow, owing to a mix-up, instead of being on a flight to Oakland, he had boarded an international flight to Auckland, New Zealand!

Many Christians today presume they are heading to heaven. They believe they have secured their ticket and are confident of reaching their final destination. Could it be that many will one day discover, to their horror, that they have been heading the wrong way for years, having acquired a skewed understanding of the Christian faith and of God's Word?

In many parts of the world today, Christianity has been reduced to weekly stage performances. The gospel has been stripped of its power, and believers have fashioned an idol of a false, sentimental God. The Bible accurately predicted the state of many churchgoers today:

> The time will come when people will not put up with sound doctrine. Instead, to suit their own desires, they will gather around them a great number of teachers to say what their itching ears want to hear. They will turn their ears away from the truth and turn aside to myths.
>
> **2 Timothy 4:3–4**

Many large Christian gatherings are similar to attending a football game, where you can find a select group of men exerting much energy, while thousands of spectators sit on their backsides, watching from the comfort of their seats. Some wish they could be involved in the action, but most are content to remain on the sidelines while offering the occasional cheer or criticism.

God never intended His Church to be a social club, or for it to be an institution where people rise to leadership positions because of a "successful" image or charming personality. The Church was created to be a spiritual family where the faithful are strengthened by God's Word, and where disciples are trained and sent forth to engage in spiritual combat.

The "Church on a stage" type of Christianity will not endure. In the day of testing, Christians who are happy to sit in their pews and let pastors spoon-feed them will discover that their faith isn't strong enough to withstand the storm.

Anyone who wants to be a true Christian must first get to know who Jesus Christ really is, as revealed in the Scriptures. It may surprise them! Many churchgoers have created a sentimental image of God in their minds. They imagine Him according to how they want Him to be, and not as He really is.

Our lives must be shaped by the Word of God, and we should ensure we never shape the Word of God according to our lives. Possessing a self-made image of God is a dangerous form of idolatry.

My prayer for our family and our co-workers, and for all Christians, is that we would have a correct, biblical view of God. We must abandon all views of His character that do not conform to Scripture, for if that is distorted, the rest of our faith will be warped. The Bible instructs us to "consider therefore the kindness and sternness of God" (Romans 11:22).

For years the Lord had been stripping me of wrong ideas about His nature. The Holy Spirit gradually opened my eyes to see God as He really is in the Bible, and not how I think He ought to be. As I studied His Word, I obtained a more balanced view of the two sides of God's character. Just from the *New* Testament I discovered that God is love, but He is also an all-consuming fire (Hebrews 12:29).

I learned that the heavenly Father is building a heavenly mansion for those who belong to Him, but He has also created a dreadful lake of fire for all who "refused to love the truth and so be saved" (2 Thessalonians 2:10).

I read how the love of God has been revealed in Jesus Christ, but also that the wrath of God is being revealed against mankind (Romans 1:18).

I saw that the Lord delivers people from sin but can also hold people under His punishment (2 Peter 2:9), and that while the Holy Spirit softens hard hearts, He is also able to harden people's hearts (Romans 9:18).

I trembled to learn that while God loves to display the riches of His glory through vessels of mercy, He may also display His power by patiently preparing vessels of wrath for destruction (Romans 9:22–23).

Finally, I realized that in the New Testament the Living God opened blind eyes, but He also blinded seeing eyes (Acts 13:11), and while He brought the dead back to life, He also struck some people dead (Acts 5:1–10).

The good news is that if we still have breath in our lungs, it's not too late to change! Whether it's the persecuted Church in Asia or the "Church on a stage" in other parts of the world, "the eyes of the Lord range throughout the earth to strengthen those whose hearts are fully committed to him" (2 Chronicles 16:9).

CHAPTER 36

GOD'S GREATEST MISSIONARY

"So shall My word be that goes forth from My mouth; It shall not return to Me void, But it shall accomplish what I please, and it shall prosper in the thing for which I sent it."

Isaiah 55:11 (NKJV)

The greatest missionary is the Bible in the Mother tongue. It never needs a furlough, and is never considered a foreigner.

Cameron Townsend

There is a huge need for the Word of God in Asia and throughout the world today. Of the 7,000 languages on earth, only 513 have the full Bible available. In Asia, 1,600 languages have no Scripture available at all – not even a single book or portion of God's Word.

Since the moment God first called me to be a donkey for Jesus in the 1980s, providing Bibles to hungry Asian believers has been a major focus of everything I have done. Now that we had connections deep within the Chinese house church networks, our role in providing Bibles to them moved forward in leaps and bounds.

Until the late 1990s, all the Bibles we provided to Christians in China were carried in from outside the country. We hosted numerous teams in pursuit of that goal, and they exerted much sweat and expense hauling thousands of Bibles across the borders and throughout China.

It was clear that the need for Bibles among the rapidly growing Chinese Church had far surpassed the number that Christians could carry in. It was simply too slow and costly to keep doing it that way. With the Church in China expanding by thousands of new believers each day, a more effective approach was desperately needed.

In the late 1990s, friends of ours took an audacious leap of faith by boldly attempting to print Bibles inside China without government permission. It had never been done before. The plan succeeded by the miraculous hand of God, and that success inspired other ministries to attempt to print inside the country. Soon we were involved too.

Each Bible produced for the house churches was, and still is, considered illegal. Anyone caught printing or distributing Bibles faces three years in prison without trial. Over the years, many Chinese Christians involved with this crucial project have been arrested and punished, and some have even been called to lay down their lives for Jesus. They willingly sacrificed themselves for the kingdom of God, motivated by the cry of millions of new believers facing spiritual starvation without the Bread of Life.

After much prayer and research, our Chinese co-workers found a way to secretly print high-quality, full Chinese Bibles for just US$2.25 each. The house church networks took full responsibility for the distribution, and after a few years they had fine-tuned the process to such an extent that the cost was reduced to just $1.80 per Bible.

Ironically, when we began to print and deliver the Scriptures this way, some mission groups criticized us, complaining that the cost of our Bibles was so low that it made them look bad. Their prices for similar Bibles ranged from $3 all the way up to $10. The reality was that many organizations loaded their operational costs, salaries, vehicles, rent, and other expenses into the "cost" price of the Bibles they produced. Consequently, some ministries ended up raising significantly more money for Bibles that actually cost them about $2 to print.

Because God had led us to structure Asia Harvest differently, our overhead expenses were negligible, and this enabled us to use incoming funds to produce the maximum number of Bibles for the persecuted Church. We never anticipated that a torrent of criticism would come our way for providing God's Word, free of charge, to starving Chinese Christians! In response, we simply let the petty criticisms slide by, and we got on with the task of providing as many Bibles as possible.

Because of the diligence of our Chinese co-workers, a system was established that helps us keep track of every box of Bibles and allows us to produce detailed reports and distribution maps that show exactly where the Bibles end up. Ministries that partner with us have expressed their appreciation of our detailed reporting.

We have seen two main benefits from our Bible projects. First, providing the Word of God to hungry Christians has proven to be a highly effective form of evangelism. In China, feedback indicates that on average, two to three people come to faith in Jesus as a result of every Bible delivered to the rural house churches. Numerous reports tell how Christian communities have doubled in size after receiving a shipment of the Scriptures. Most of the growth occurs after believers read the Word of God and understand the necessity of sharing their faith with their lost neighbors and relatives.

The second major benefit of providing Bibles may not sound as exciting, but it has also been crucial to the health and development of God's kingdom. Asia is full of numerous cults and sects, and Christian leaders are engaged in a constant battle to keep dangerous heresies from infiltrating and destroying their flocks. Before they had access to the Scriptures, many new Christians were easy prey to deception. Thankfully, by providing tons of Bibles through our projects, the Lord has established the faith of multitudes of new Christians on the solid rock of His Word.

As the years have progressed, one of the largest challenges we have faced has been the belief widely held by many Christians that Bibles are freely available in China today. Some of the biggest names in Western Christianity have spent years telling the Christian world that China has all the Bibles it needs. This is one of the biggest deceptions believed by the Body of Christ in the past fifty years. Some Chinese pastors have told me they feel they are persecuted from two sides – from the Communist authorities in their homeland, and also from Western church leaders who spread lies and misinformation about the situation in China.

While it is true that a limited number of Bibles are available to members of the government-approved Three-Self Church in China, the house churches have been left to fight for the few crumbs that fall from the table of the registered churches. The house churches, which contain at least sixty million believers, have been deliberately starved of Bibles in a bid to force them to register with the government. Most refuse to comply, despite intense pressure to do so.

I am not ashamed to say that we serve the illegal house churches of China, even if other Christians don't consider it politically correct to do so. There are no second-class citizens in the family of God.

* * *

Before I left Australia to return to the mission field in 1991, an elderly believer told me, "Young man, the greatest ability you will ever have is your availability." Joy and I made ourselves available to God, and asked Him to use our lives to provide His Word to His children throughout Asia. The Lord Jesus Christ granted us the desire of our hearts, and by His good pleasure has accomplished more than we ever asked or imagined.

From a human perspective, our ministry had no chance of producing significant numbers of Bibles. Other organizations hired professional fundraisers and employed all kinds of techniques to elicit donations. The Holy Spirit never allowed us to get involved with anything like that. He even restrained us from public speaking.

We did have one special advantage, however, which tipped the scales in our favor. The Lord Jesus Himself decided to be our fundraiser! As this crucial project blossomed, the Holy Spirit moved in the hearts of many people to pray and give so that Chinese Christians – especially new believers from impoverished rural areas – would have access to His Word.

Over the years, some people have noted the large quantity of Bibles we have distributed and assumed we must be connected to some rich and famous people. The reality is that we have been joined to the richest and most powerful individual in the universe, Almighty God, who once declared, "If I were hungry I would not tell you, for the world is mine, and all that is in it" (Psalm 50:12).

Instead of connecting us with a few large donors, the Lord chose to link us with hundreds of normal believers throughout the world. We marvel at the wisdom of God in leading us to function in this manner. A few individual snowflakes can easily be brushed aside, but a multitude of snowflakes can join together to stop trucks and derail freight trains.

Overall, the median size donation we have received over the years is $52, but by forming Spirit-led connections with many members of the Body of Christ, our Bible projects rapidly grew in scope, and God gained much glory for His Name.

We receive many touching letters from Christians who sense the Holy Spirit prompt them to support our Bible projects. Children have broken open their piggy banks and sent their savings. One young American lady mailed a check for $5,000, with a note explaining that she had been saving for her wedding, but the Lord directed her to give the money to print Chinese Bibles instead. When we shared her precious letter with the Chinese believers, they openly wept with joy and appreciation.

The tragic reality is that the rural churches of China still experience a massive famine of God's Word today. Several years ago, an extensive survey by many church networks revealed a shortage of thirty-four million Bibles, just for each member of their congregations to personally own a copy of God's Word.

After receiving this report from China, I imagined how wonderful it would be if God were to provide enough funds to enable all thirty-four million believers to have their own Bible. Because the cost per unit would be lower for such a large quantity, we estimated we could print and deliver thirty-four million Bibles for about US$40 million. If that were ever to happen, the impact on China would be immense. The Body of Christ would be greatly strengthened, and tens of millions of new believers would come into God's family.

A short time later we visited friends in Tennessee. They drove us around their city before pulling over to show us their magnificent church building. When they told us that a new auditorium was to be built alongside the existing one, I naively asked, "Why? What's wrong with the one you've got now?"

"Oh, nothing's wrong with it. It's just a little outdated," our friends explained. "The church leaders want more space for programs and activities, so our church is expanding the facilities. They have already purchased several adjoining houses which will soon be demolished to enable us to expand our parking area."

"Wow," I said. "How much will all this cost?"

"$40 million," came the reply.

I thought about the strange Christian world we live in. While tens of millions of believers in China were struggling to survive without God's Word, this one evangelical congregation of several thousand believers in Tennessee was planning to spend exactly the same amount of money on a building they didn't really need.

I wondered what the pastors and elders of that church would have said if I had asked them to cancel their building project and instead use the money to provide a Bible for every house church

Christian in China. Would they believe me if I told them that by doing so, tens of millions of people would experience Christ's salvation? Would they care? I wonder what the Lord thinks when His followers invest so many resources in buildings, to worship the God whom the Bible says "does not live in temples built by human hands" (Acts 17:24).

A few years ago we received a letter from a huge British organization which claims that China is awash with Bibles. In the margin of the letterhead the patron of their organization was listed as "Her Majesty the Queen." While I have great respect for the Queen, I smiled to myself because our ministry has never been able to boast of connections to anyone the world considers famous or influential.

As I thought about the letter, the peace of God flooded my heart, and the Holy Spirit reminded me, "You may not be connected to the Queen of England, but you are connected to the King of kings and Lord of lords!"

Against all odds, God has taken our small, insignificant ministry and has provided millions of Bibles to His Church in China and throughout Asia. Perhaps one day in the future, things will change and God's Word will be freely available to all Christians throughout Asia. Until that time, as long as the Lord Jesus enables us, we will continue to supply as many Bibles as possible.

Hallelujah! All glory belongs to Him.

CHAPTER 37
REAPING THE HARVEST

> Do not pray for easy lives; pray to be stronger men. Do not pray for tasks equal to your powers; pray for powers equal to your tasks. Then the doing of your work shall be no miracle, but you shall be a miracle.
>
> **Phillips Brooks**

God never promised to keep His followers out of trouble. It is a heresy that teaches no harm can befall a child of God. Millions of martyred Christians over the centuries make that clear. Thankfully, our heavenly Father knows when to draw a line beneath the trials His children are called to endure. Hardships don't last forever, lest we be crushed, for "God is faithful; he will not let you be tempted beyond what you can bear. But when you are tempted, he will also provide a way out so that you can endure it" (1 Corinthians 10:13).

Joy and I are able to look back and marvel at how God turned our trials into stepping stones that advanced the work He called us to do. He helped us not to give up during the most difficult times, when we were greatly distressed. Many Christians give up hope when the hour is at its darkest, not realizing that if they hold on in faith just a little longer, light will come into their situation, for the Bible promises that "at the proper time we will reap a harvest if we do not give up" (Galatians 6:9).

By 2006 Joy and I had been married a dozen years and our relationship was stronger than ever. As a family we were growing in the grace and knowledge of God, and we had learned to trust the Lord and to encourage one another through the difficult times. God taught us that our chief responsibility was to stay connected to Jesus, who said, "I am the vine; you are the branches. If you remain in me and I in you, you will bear much fruit; apart from me you can do nothing" (John 15:5).

For many years we had faithfully sown seed for the kingdom of God throughout Asia, and the Lord had knitted us together with many godly Asian church leaders. Now our ministry was entering a new season, and the work of Asia Harvest was growing exponentially. Instead of just writing about unreached people groups, we were now helping to reach dozens of them. Instead of providing thousands of Bibles to Asian believers, the Lord was enabling us to provide hundreds of thousands.

On numerous occasions we witnessed God's miraculous provision. Time and again, projects that were low on funding received a surge of donations without us saying a word to anyone. Operating our ministry this way boosted our faith, and reminded us that Jesus truly is the leader of His work. It also encouraged us to know that many believers around the world are in tune with the Holy Spirit. They are able to hear His voice and obey when He prompts them to pray or give to a specific need.

As our ministry became more fruitful, my personal role became more clearly defined. Many Christians desire great spiritual gifts from God, but I believe the Holy Spirit gave me one of His lesser known gifts – the gift of administration (1 Corinthians 12:28, NKJV) – which has greatly benefited the work He called us to do. The Greek word translated "administration" refers to the captain of a vessel whose role is to guide a group of people toward a goal.

It was no longer necessary for Joy and me to travel as extensively as we previously did. Our projects were now overseen by godly leaders who had proven themselves to be capable ministers of the gospel over many years. They took care of the frontline work, while our role was to take a step back, to continue to share the vision through writing, and to ensure that the ministry functioned in a manner pleasing to God.

As we entered this new season of harvest, the Holy Spirit breathed life into our projects, and they experienced startling growth that can only be explained as a supernatural blessing of God. The China Bible Fund was a prime example.

In the early 1990s, Joy and I met in Hong Kong as two single missionaries carrying Bibles into China. By 2004, after fourteen years of doing all we could to provide the Scriptures, we passed the milestone of 500,000 Bibles distributed to believers in China.

A pivotal event took place in 2006, in the small town of North Bend, Washington. We had traveled to the bedside of a dying man, Brother David, who wanted me to record his testimony. Brother David's emaciated body was literally being eaten up by diabetes. He was partially blind and deaf, and had suffered multiple heart attacks over the years.

Over the course of a week, David shared his remarkable testimony, beginning with the early 1980s when he had led a bold and courageous project to deliver one million Bibles by ship to a beach in mainland China. David and the crew had literally risked their lives, and by the hand of God, 232 tons of Bibles were delivered ashore to thousands of waiting Chinese believers who had been starved of God's Word for decades. Brother David's story was published in my book *Project Pearl*.

Before I left his home, David shared how as a young man God had given him a vision to provide ten million Bibles to Christians in China. For years both before and after the risky boat delivery in 1981, he had led initiatives toward achieving this goal, but then failing health took its toll. In total, he told me, he had been involved in providing about two million Bibles to China, but he knew he would not be able to reach the target the Lord had given him.

David prayed for me and asked the Lord to transfer this vision to Asia Harvest, for the glory of God and the expansion of His kingdom in China. With tears in his eyes he prayed that the Holy Spirit would anoint our lives and work, and that through us at least ten million Chinese Bibles would be distributed to believers in China.

Brother David died in May 2007. At the beginning of that year, the total number of Chinese Bibles we had printed and delivered surged past the one million mark. In less than three years, God enabled us to match the output of the previous fourteen years.

Then things really took off!

* * *

The final week of each year is an important time for me. During that week I dedicate myself to seeking God's will for the coming year. Before praying, I empty my thoughts of any preconceived notions of what I think the Lord wants to say to me, and I try to present a blank canvas for Him to communicate whatever He wishes. My simple prayer is: "Speak, Lord, for your servant is listening" (1 Samuel 3:9).

As I waited upon the Lord during the final week of 2007, I gained a distinct impression that He wanted us to stretch our faith and provide more bread to His hungry children in China. At the end of 2007, the total number of Chinese Bibles God had enabled us to print and deliver stood at just over 1.2 million. Joy and our sons joined me in prayer. We knelt down around our living room table and solemnly asked our heavenly Father to double the number of Bibles in the following year.

To double the number from 1.2 million to 2.4 million Bibles in a single year would require US$2,160,000 to come in for our China Bible Fund throughout the following twelve months. This was in addition to the support we required to implement all of our other projects in Asia. As usual, we were not permitted to ask anyone to give, nor had the Lord released me to speak in any public meetings. We simply presented our request to God and asked Him to provide according to His will.

I knew the enemy would not stand idly by while this project took a massive leap forward. With an average of two to three new believers resulting from every Bible we delivered to the house churches, an increase of that magnitude would potentially result in two to three million people being delivered from the kingdom of darkness into the kingdom of light.

I spoke with my family members individually and collectively, reminding them that we had a real enemy who would seek to do anything to prevent us from reaching the goal. I asked them to pray and think about what I had shared, and to let me know if they still felt we should accept God's challenge to double the number of Bibles.

Joy, Dalen, and Taine came to our family Bible study the next day and said in unison, "Yes! We are willing to count the cost for the Lord!" We rededicated ourselves to God, and asked Him to continue to use our lives to glorify Jesus.

A while later we got into our car. I was driving, Joy was alongside me in the passenger's seat, and our sons were in the back seat. We had a green light as I approached an intersection near our house, so I drove forward. Suddenly, out of the corner of my eye I saw a car hurtling toward us at high speed, barreling straight through a red light!

Joy shouted, "Lord, save us!" as the car smashed into the side of our vehicle. There was a surreal moment when time seemed to stand still. My side of the car was up high in the air, and I was looking down at Joy below me. Our car was hit with such velocity that it almost flipped onto its side before finally coming to rest on the far side of the intersection. The police and an ambulance arrived. They were amazed when we all walked free from the wreckage with just a few scrapes and bruises.

The attending police officer pointed at the impact spot on our crumpled doorframe. "You're extremely lucky," he said. "If the other vehicle had struck you a few inches nearer the front, it would have smashed into the driver's door and you would probably be dead. And if it had struck you a little further back, it would have killed your son in the back seat. As it is, the impact occurred precisely on the frame between your two doors, which spared your lives."

The experience shook us, but we knew our survival had nothing to do with good luck. An angel of the Lord had preserved our lives. The battle lines had been drawn. Satan was not going to idly stand by while we printed enough Bibles to reach millions of people in China. At the time, it felt as though it would take a lot of prayer and perseverance just to survive the year in one piece.

During the next twelve months we received donations for the China Bible project from hundreds of different people. Most were gifts in the $20 to $200 range, with occasional larger donations. The world financial crisis struck during the year, and many large mission organizations experienced great difficulty. When their funds dried up they had to lay off staff, pull missionaries from the field, and stop recruiting new workers. Because our operating expenses were already at a bare minimum, we were able to function as previously.

The morning of 31 December 2008 dawned, and we were still a very long way from having enough funds to double the number of Chinese Bibles that year. We had printed a little more than 200,000 during 2008, well short of the 1.2 million we had prayed for. "Oh well," I thought to myself. We had much to be thankful for. We had prayed and done our best, and a great number of Scriptures had still been produced.

That afternoon we went to the post office to check our mailbox for the final time in 2008. A small stack of letters had arrived, which we took home to open. Some late Christmas cards had come, along with some regular donations. As we neared the bottom of the stack of letters, we found one from a man we had never met, and with whom we had never previously communicated about the China Bible Fund.

The man's letter shared how the Holy Spirit had burdened him to send his donation months earlier, but it was such a great sacrifice that he had been wrestling in prayer for a long time, wanting to make sure he had heard correctly from God before sending it to us. Finally, after an intense spiritual struggle in which he said it felt like every demon in hell tried to stop him from giving, the man finally knew it was God's will to send his donation.

I rubbed my eyes in astonishment as I stared at his gift on my desk. Sitting before me was a check for $1,800,000, to print one million Bibles for the house churches of China! It was by far the largest donation we had ever received.

We recorded this amazing gift in our ministry database and found that when we closed our books at the end of 2008, God had provided enough funds for us to produce a cumulative total of 2,483,198 Chinese Bibles, up from 1,212,860 at the end of the previous year.

We had not told anyone that we were hoping and praying for a doubling of Bibles that year, but Jesus had done it! On the last day of the year and in a totally unexpected way, the Living God had more than doubled the number of Bibles for His children in China. I called our project leader in China and broke the extraordinary news to him. He simply shouted, "Hallelujah!"

For the next several months the printing presses were cranked up to full speed, as one million brand new Chinese Bibles were printed and delivered to multitudes of appreciative Christians.

* * *

In subsequent years, our Bible projects have continued to flourish under the blessing of God. His provision has been so remarkable that at times we gained a sense of what it must have felt like when the Lord miraculously fed 5,000 men and their families with five loaves of bread and two fish.

By the end of 2008 we had printed and delivered a total of just over 2.4 million Chinese Bibles. The Holy Spirit continued to breathe on the project, and in the next four years, to the end of 2012, the total tripled to 6.6 million Bibles. During that year alone, the Living God enabled us to produce one full Bible every eighteen seconds!

Some people assume that printing illegal Bibles inside China must be a fairly straightforward task. We encourage them to try it, and they will soon discover the truth! China has crafted one of the most sophisticated and intrusive security mechanisms of any country on earth. They are determined to control the population, and they don't hesitate to crush any perceived threats to their authority. Large quantities of Bibles cannot be safely produced and delivered inside China apart from the supernatural power of the Almighty God, and it requires hundreds of intercessors praying for divine protection over every step of the process.

Amazingly, in 2016 we passed the milestone of ten million Chinese Bibles produced for the house churches of China. Each one has been a miracle.

Although China has been the main focus of our Bible projects, we have also printed Bibles in numerous other languages throughout Asia. Tribal Christians in countries like Vietnam, Laos, and Myanmar have been deprived of the Scriptures for decades. This project, which we call the Asian Bible Fund, has also grown exponentially as God bestows His blessings.

At the start of 2007 we had produced 94,000 Bibles in twenty-one different languages through the Asian Bible Fund. By the start of 2017 the number had risen to more than 720,000 Bibles in seventy-two languages, all under the protective hand of our loving and merciful God.

Many of the testimonies we receive from around Asia are both inspirational and humbling. In 2016 we distributed thousands of Bibles in the Sqaw Karen language of Myanmar (Burma). Those wonderful Karen Christians, who have endured decades of brutal treatment from the Burmese military, were overwhelmed with gratitude to God.

One woman of eighty-five recalled how when she was growing up there was only one Bible in her village, and it belonged to the pastor. In 1945, at the age of fourteen, she prayed to God, begging him for her own copy of His Word. For many years Myanmar was closed off to the world, and it wasn't until 2016, seventy-one years after she first prayed, that this dear saint received her own copy of the Scriptures. She wrote, "By the grace of God, today I received the full Bible from you. This is amazing. Only God can do this. He answered my seven decades of prayers. It was well worth the wait. He is so good to me! My favorite Scripture is Psalm 23. Thanks to all who donated and brought my precious Bible. I will always read it. God bless you all."

In the bookcase above my desk I keep a sample copy of every Bible we have produced in the various languages. I'm always humbled when I look at these blessed Scriptures. They represent decades of prayers and toil by faithful men and women. Someone diligently translated God's Word into each language, others helped establish the Church, and we have been blessed to play a part by meeting the current needs of thousands of hungry believers. All the glory belongs to the Lord Jesus, for it is "from him the whole body, joined and held together by every supporting ligament, grows and builds itself up in love, as each part does its work" (Ephesians 4:16).

CHAPTER 38

SNIPPETS FROM THE JOURNEY

> It is not the critic who counts. The credit belongs to the man who is actually in the arena, whose face is marred by dust and sweat and blood; who strives valiantly; who errs and comes short again and again, who knows the great enthusiasms, the great devotions, and spends himself in a worthy cause; who at the best, knows the triumph of high achievement; and who, at the worst, if he fails, at least fails while daring greatly, so that his place shall never be with those cold and timid souls who know neither victory nor defeat.
>
> **Theodore Roosevelt**

I would love to report that my life as a servant of Jesus Christ has been trouble free and filled with one victorious experience after another. The Bible, however, often links trouble to fruitful service for the kingdom of God. The Apostle Paul once wrote, "I will stay on at Ephesus until Pentecost, because a great door for effective work has opened to me, and there are many who oppose me" (1 Corinthians 16:8–9).

From the moment I became a Christian I experienced trouble. When I dedicated my life to serve the Lord in Asia my problems multiplied, and at that time I began to accumulate enemies who sought my destruction.

One thing I have learned is that Christians shouldn't assume they need to be perfect before stepping out to serve God. We won't be perfect until Jesus returns. God doesn't call His children to sit around trying to preserve their salvation. As it is, the best way for a believer to keep their faith is to give it away. We need to get busy for the Lord. The line from an old poem attributed to C. T. Studd holds true: "Only one life, 'twill soon be past. Only what's done for Christ will last."

The Apostle Paul wasn't the kind of man to sit around while opportunities passed him by. He knew the Lord would transform Christians as they marched forward in faith, and that the Holy Spirit is able to shape a believer into the image of Jesus while they serve Him. Paul wrote, "I pray that you may be active in sharing your faith, so that you will have a full understanding of every good thing we have in Christ" (Philemon 6).

A number of years ago the term "friendly fire" was coined to describe casualties that an army inflicts upon its own soldiers. Unfortunately, there is too much friendly fire within the Body of Christ, and anyone who does an effective work for the Lord is guaranteed to be the target of much criticism. The key for believers is to be able to move forward without letting negative words harden their hearts. By the power of the Holy Spirit, I believe it is possible to maintain a tough exterior while still possessing a soft heart.

The Apostle Paul concluded the list of troubles he had endured in ministry by saying he was "in danger from false believers" (2 Corinthians 11:26). Our strongest opposition has also come from professing Christians who have an ax to grind. These people tend to be self-appointed "watchmen" in the Body of Christ. They are adept at trying to iron out everyone's faults except their own. I once told such a person that I thought he was a perfectly balanced individual. When he asked why, I explained it was because he had a chip on each shoulder!

Some friends who are aware of the intense attacks Joy and I have endured over the years have asked how we manage to retain our composure in Christ. To be honest, it's been difficult, and at times we've been tempted to retaliate, but the Lord has continually taught us to surrender, to forgive, and ultimately to love and bless those who treat us unkindly. Through it all, God has required us to be humble enough to listen to constructive criticism, in case He has wanted to correct or rebuke us through other people. In truth, we all have limitations and weaknesses, and we often need help to turn from our failures and receive the grace of God.

I have been privileged to meet many persecuted Christians who have spent years or even decades in prison for the gospel. Despite unmentionable cruelties being done to them, these men and women are free! They have learned that the only way for a believer to remove the stubborn root of bitterness from their hearts is to freely forgive.

The Lord has gradually subdued my stubborn heart and brought me to a place where I seek to obey the words of Jesus:

> "Love your enemies, do good to them, and lend to them without expecting to get anything back. Then your reward will be great, and you will be children of the Most High, because he is kind to the ungrateful and wicked. Be merciful, just as your Father is merciful."
>
> **Luke 6:35–36**

Occasionally, I like to head out on a long drive in the middle of the night after my family are all tucked safely into bed. I find a remote location, usually in the mountains, where I can pour out my heart to the Lord without being disturbed. One night I headed out on a prayer drive with a flashlight, a sheet of paper, and a pen.

After pulling over in an isolated spot I began to pray, asking the Holy Spirit to search my heart and reveal the name of anyone I needed to forgive. Some people immediately came to mind, so I wrote their names on my paper. When I thought of others, I wrote their names down too. Some of the people had engaged us in battles years earlier, and I thought I had already moved on and forgiven them. That night, as the Holy Spirit searched my heart, I realized I needed to pray for them again, lest any seeds of unforgiveness still remained in my heart where they might sprout back to life.

After praying for about an hour, I was shocked to find both sides of my sheet of paper filled with names! When I was sure I had recorded all the names on my list that night, I wept bitterly before God, asking Him to forgive me for holding grudges. I begged Him to help me forgive others as Christ had forgiven me, and then I began to pray for each person individually. I released them from all the wrongs that had been committed against me and my family, and asked the Lord Jesus to bless and use them for His kingdom, and to pour out His mercy and favor on their lives.

As life goes on, I'm sure it won't be too long before I again need to grab some paper and a pen and head out to an isolated place, to again pour out my soul before God and allow Him to reveal the contents of my heart. I think it's something all Christians need to do occasionally.

* * *

As I progress on my journey with Jesus, I have come to understand three things: how much God loves us, how much Satan hates us, and that we are just a layer of God's protective grace away from being utterly destroyed. Thankfully, that layer is very strong! The Lord Jesus once told Peter, "Satan has asked to sift all of you as wheat. But I have prayed for you … that your faith may not fail" (Luke 22:31–32).

Some people have told us they are baffled at how we have managed to remain involved in God's work for so long, especially as most of our activities are considered illegal by the powerful governments of the countries we serve.

For almost three decades we have experienced the Lord's supernatural protection, not only from "friendly fire," but also in myriad other ways. At times, the Lord Jesus has also protected me from myself. For example, after *The Heavenly Man* experienced a great deal of success, many Christians complimented me on the book and remarked how well written it was. I always deflected their compliments so I wouldn't get a big head, and I reminded them that I was merely the person privileged to write down Brother Yun's testimony. I had the simple part, while Yun's role had been to endure years of cruel persecution and imprisonment for Jesus!

One day a friend grabbed me by the arm, looked me directly in the eyes, and said, "Yes, Paul, Brother Yun's testimony is powerful, but you need to accept that your writing was exceptional, and that without it the book would never have done so well."

A strange thing happened when I began working on my next book a few months later. For weeks I experienced absolutely no blessing of the Holy Spirit on my writing. My mind and heart were cluttered, and it felt as if I was trying to swim upstream against a strong current. This was a new experience for me, and I was getting nowhere. I finally stopped and spent some time in prayer. The Lord showed me that I had allowed the words of my friend to seep into my heart, and a seed of pride had taken root. In the back of my mind I had foolishly told myself, "Well, maybe I am a skillful writer after all. People tell me so."

My merciful heavenly Father reminded me of my background, and how He had rescued me from the scrapheap of humanity. Despite the fact that I was a high-school dropout, the Holy Spirit had anointed me with a gift to write for God's glory. It had absolutely nothing to do with my own skill or ability. I could only write because of His empowering grace. I fell to my knees and repented of my foolish pride. Immediately, the blockage in my spirit was removed and the words began to flow again.

God has helped us survive many dangers. I have already shared some of them, such as when I nearly died in Nepal from altitude sickness. We have walked away from major car and bus crashes, and a train derailment. There have been times when we have been forced to flee pursuing authorities, and occasions when we have escaped the clutches of hostile people who intended to do us harm.

We are convinced the Lord sent angels to help us escape other perilous situations too.

Our faith in God has also been stretched by close calls during times of political turmoil. I was once in Bangkok during anti-government demonstrations, when dozens of protestors were shot dead by Thai soldiers just a stone's throw from where I was staying. On another occasion I narrowly missed a bomb blast that rocked the city of Colombo during the Sri Lankan civil war.

Over the years our work has meant we have caught more than 400 flights around Asia and to various parts of the world. God has kept us safe, although we have experienced many narrow escapes. It hasn't been the flights we took that are the most memorable, but the ones we thankfully missed. Just before Christmas 1999, our entire family traveled on Indian Airlines flight 814 from Kathmandu to New Delhi. The very next day the same plane, flying the same route, was hijacked by terrorists and diverted to Kandahar, Afghanistan. For seven days, the 176 passengers were forced to sit on board in dire conditions while Islamic extremists debated what to do with them. Some of the passengers were executed. We thankfully missed that horrifying experience by twenty-four hours.

On another occasion I boarded a flight from Colombo, Sri Lanka, to Madras (now Chennai) in India. The plane taxied to the end of the runway but never took off, and I was forced to remain in Sri Lanka for several days as all flights were canceled. At the very moment our plane was due to depart, the Indian Prime Minister Rajiv Gandhi was assassinated in Madras. For days the city was a diabolical cauldron of death as Muslim and Hindu mobs hacked one another to pieces. I was glad my flight had been canceled that day.

* * *

Joy: God has delivered us from many tight corners. Once, when I was heavily pregnant with our first son, I was sitting outside on the ground listening to Paul teach at a Bible School in Myanmar. All of a sudden, one of the Burmese students grabbed a wooden plank and violently smashed the ground right next to me! A large scorpion had snuck up beside me and was inches away from sinking its venomous tail into my arm.

Not all of our experiences have been so intense. We have also had many times of great laughter. My husband has a habit of doing embarrassing things at regular intervals. On more than a few occasions I have been left red-faced by his antics!

Paul sometimes finds himself in sticky situations because of cultural differences. Once, he visited the home of an American missionary family who had a toddler. The couple needed to pop out to the store to buy some supplies, and said they would return in a few minutes. Paul innocently told them, "Don't worry. I will nurse the little one until you come back." The couple looked at him with disgust, unaware that in New Zealand and Australia to "nurse" a child can simply mean to take care of them. Paul, on the other hand, wasn't aware that in American parlance he had just offered to breastfeed their toddler! Needless to say, that family has never invited him to their home again.

Another time, we traveled from our home in Thailand to Yangon, the capital of Myanmar, where a group of respected church leaders awaited our arrival. The pastors came to the airport wearing their best suits as a mark of respect, but just before we boarded our flight, Paul managed to split his trousers. It wasn't a normal split, but a mega-split from top to bottom! There was no chance of him buying another pair before the flight departed, and our luggage had already been checked onto the plane. We had no choice but to continue our journey and make the best of an awkward situation. At Yangon Airport the pastors patiently waited for Paul to emerge from the immigration area. He finally came through the doors, taking tiny steps with his cheeks tightly clenched as he attempted to minimize the spectacle for those walking behind him! The pastors graciously took us downtown so Paul could buy some new trousers.

Once, on a flight across America, Paul removed his shoes and pushed them under his seat. As our plane descended it was time to put them back on, so he reached down and felt under his seat. After a minute, Paul thought he had located one of his shoes and tried to pull it out. Unfortunately it was stuck, so he pulled harder. Convinced it was tightly jammed, he used both hands as he attempted to wrestle it free with all his might.

A man sitting in the row behind us tried to get Paul's attention by coughing politely. When that didn't work, the flustered man said, "Excuse me!" Paul had reached so far beneath his seat that he had grabbed the foot of the passenger sitting behind us!

CHAPTER 39
MY SECRET WEAPON

> Before marriage I loved her very much. After marriage she was no longer another person to be loved. We had become one. There was no place where "I" finished and "she" began. Even in matters in which we disagreed, she only expressed the part of my being that I repressed. We were one.
>
> **Vladimir Amburtsunov, Russian martyr**

As I near the end of my testimony thus far, I would like to reveal the secret weapon that has helped me through all of the exciting and turbulent parts of my journey. Alongside me during all the ups and downs has been the most wonderful and supportive wife I could have ever hoped for.

One of my favorite stories comes from the life of British Prime Minister Winston Churchill, who had his share of critics. One of them was Lady Nancy Astor, who told him, "Mr Churchill, if you were my husband I would poison your tea."

Never slow to offer a witty response, Churchill looked directly at his antagonist and replied, "And if you were my wife, I would drink it!"

I am glad to say that I have never had the same feelings toward Joy as Churchill had for Lady Astor! Like all marriages, Joy and I have experienced some difficult patches along the way, but as the years have rolled by I have grown in my love and appreciation for my hand-picked blessing from God.

I believe that from the start, Satan could sense the God-given potential of our union, and as detailed in earlier chapters, the enemy did all he could to stop us being united in marriage. Joy and I endured a fierce struggle just to make it to the altar, but in the end the Lord Jesus helped us overcome all the obstacles to get there.

The first time I met Joy she was a young lady in her early twenties. She radiated purity and beauty, and her countenance glowed with a deep love for Jesus Christ. I didn't realize it at the time, but the Living God had been separately preparing Joy and me, carefully arranging the moment when our paths would intersect while we served Him in China.

In His wisdom, the Lord decided to join a beautiful young Christian lady from Idaho together with a rough zealot from a dysfunctional family in New Zealand. Sometimes I still have to pinch myself that Joy said "Yes" and agreed to marry me! I was amazed that she loved me so much and was willing to trust my leadership as we learned to follow the Lord together.

We never dated in the way that most couples do. In fact, Joy and I hardly spent any time together before our wedding day. Our lack of dating turned out to be a blessing in disguise, and the opposition we encountered caused our eventual union to be even sweeter than it might have otherwise been. Since our marriage twenty-two years ago, we have done almost everything together and have rarely been apart for more than a few days at a time.

Joy is a naturally shy person who feels most comfortable when quietly encouraging and serving others in the background. Because she is softly spoken, she is sometimes misunderstood in those parts of the world where women are expected to be more forceful and domineering. At times she has been like a lily among thorns, and I have needed to step in to protect and encourage her.

Although she has never been out in front of a big crowd or had her name on the cover of a book, I know that every good thing God has accomplished through our work has been credited to Joy's account in heaven. She has not only tolerated me, but has also embraced God's plan and has become an integral part of it all, becoming my best friend and indispensable partner. Of the many gifts the Holy Spirit gave to Joy, her spiritual insight and discernment have proven invaluable.

It's difficult for any two people to become one, especially two stubborn hard-heads like Joy and me! As the Holy Spirit used our marriage to mold and shape our lives into the image of Christ, God gradually chiseled away our rough edges and selfishness, although we are still very much a work in progress today. Through it all, despite our faults, the Lord Jesus has bound us together with a strong love for Him, a deep love for one another, and a shared vision and purpose.

The secret to our blessed marriage is that ours has not been merely a partnership between two people, but also a union between Joy, me, and the Almighty God. This three-way bond has proven strong, for "Though one may be overpowered, two can defend themselves. A cord of three strands is not quickly broken" (Ecclesiastes 4:12).

Some Christians claim we can marry anyone we like, and that it's up to the couple to turn it into a successful marriage. I wholeheartedly disagree. There has only ever been one lady in the world for me. Joy's strengths, gifts, and weaknesses complement my gifts, strengths, and weaknesses, resulting in us being whole when we became one. She was uniquely knit together by the Lord in such a way that we have been able to walk hand in hand through the storms of life – storms so fierce that at times we would have been torn apart if our marriage hadn't been solidly anchored to the Rock.

In more than two decades since our marriage, Joy has endured many trials and difficulties as she has faithfully walked alongside me every step of our journey. While at times we have felt battered and bruised by the battles and challenges of life, God has caused us to triumph over all of them! Like the Apostle Paul, we can testify, "We are hard pressed on every side, but not crushed; perplexed, but not in despair; persecuted, but not abandoned; struck down, but not destroyed" (2 Corinthians 4:8–9).

I'm so thankful that my heavenly Father allowed me to launch out on this journey with my precious secret weapon by my side. Among all men I am most richly blessed!

* * *

In 2011, at the age of forty-three, I noticed that my heart would often race after a brisk walk. I put it out of my mind, but one day as I rested on our bed I could hear every surge of my heartbeat as if it was connected to a microphone. I made an appointment to see our local doctor, who listened to my heart for a few seconds before sending me to the hospital for tests.

An Indian cardiologist took X-rays and told me I had been born with a misshapen heart valve, and that it would need to be replaced. He explained that a lot of blood was flowing back into the main chamber of my heart because of the faulty valve, forcing it to work much harder than it normally would.

Without a flicker of emotion, the cardiologist informed me, "Don't worry, we do these surgeries all the time. First, we will knock you out and cut your chest open. Then we will break your collarbone to access your heart, which we will remove from your body and put on ice for forty-five minutes while we replace your valve. After that we'll shock your heart back to life, staple your broken collarbone together, and stitch you back up!"

His deadpan description shook me to the core. Up to that point I had considered myself somewhat invincible, and had never experienced any major health problems except my near brush with death from altitude sickness twenty years earlier.

"Okay, doc. When do I need to have the surgery?" I asked.

"At least two years ago," he replied. "Your condition is very advanced and you could drop dead at any moment!"

In a bid to make me feel more at ease, a second doctor was called into the room. "Don't worry," he said, with a strong south Indian accent. "You have a one in three chance of dying during the operation."

My heart skipped another beat upon hearing this grim news. There was one chance in three that my life on this earth was about to end, leaving behind a widow and two young sons. It wasn't the kind of news I was hoping for. Seeing my horrified expression, the doctor corrected himself, "Oh, sorry, my English is not so good. I meant there is a one to three *percent* chance you will die!"

My odds of survival had just appreciably increased, but in the weeks leading up to the surgery I was forced to face my mortality. On the night before my operation I hugged Joy and our beloved sons before we prayed together and sang "Great is Thy Faithfulness." They departed to a nearby motel and sent out an urgent prayer request, asking Christians around the world to pray for me.

Early the next morning I became unconscious after being administered a cocktail of powerful drugs. The next thing I knew I was in a recovery ward, being assured by nurses that everything had gone smoothly. I was told I would need to stay in the hospital for three days before being released.

After initially saying that everything had gone according to plan, the surgeon revealed that the procedure had encountered complications, and had taken four hours instead of the expected forty-five minutes. When I asked what had gone wrong, he refused to tell me and just said, "Don't worry, you'll be fine now."

By the second day, my recovery had gone so well that the doctors and nurses were considering letting me go home early. I shared the good news with Joy and the boys when they came to visit. Feeling relieved, they left for the night, and Joy planned to return to the hospital the following morning to check on me.

Almost as soon as my family departed, however, my heart began to beat quickly. After an hour, the nurses gave me medicine to stabilize my heart rate, but it had no effect. They increased the dosage, but it continued to beat frantically. Hours passed and my condition remained the same. X-rays were taken and the surgeon was summoned to the hospital in the middle of the night. He looked deeply concerned, and I knew something had gone wrong.

Throughout the night my heart continued to beat out of control at more than 100 beats per minute, rising to 140. Although it was a cold night, sweat poured off me, and by the morning I was totally exhausted. I felt as though I had run a marathon during the night.

The surgeon and nurses crowded around my bed and told me they had tried everything to slow my heart, but the new valve was malfunctioning. They said they would give it another fifteen minutes, but if it didn't calm down they would have no alternative but to make me unconscious again, cut my chest open, re-break my collarbone, and repeat the surgery. With worried looks on their brows, they returned to their office down the hallway from where they observed my vital signs on their monitors.

Just then, Joy arrived at my bedside. She had enjoyed a peaceful sleep and was completely unaware of the exhausting battle I had endured throughout the night. She took one look at me, saw the stress on my face, and began to cry. I was too weak to talk, but as I lay on my side I felt the soothing touch of a cool cloth as my beloved wiped the sweat from the back of my neck.

Through her tears, Joy gently placed her hand on my shoulder and, with a quivering voice, began to pray:, "Dear Lord Jesus, please rescue Paul. Please help him, Father. He needs a miracle. Thank You for your goodness to us. In Jesus' Name, Amen."

Despite feeling hopeless and distraught, Joy needed to return to the nearby motel to take care of our sons. I felt overwhelming love for my wife as she left my room. The Spirit of God had knitted us together so closely that every minute apart made me feel incomplete.

Within two minutes of Joy's departure I heard the pitter-patter of steps coming down the corridor toward my room. The surgeon and a team of nurses burst through the door, their faces brimming with relief. "It worked!" they exclaimed. "The medicine has finally worked! Just a few minutes ago, while we monitored you from our office, we saw your heartbeat return to normal for the first time in twelve hours."

I knew the truth. Whereas an entire night of strong medicine had failed to make any difference, my Lord and Savior, Jesus Christ, had healed me. My heart had returned to normal the very moment Joy laid hands on me and asked God to heal me.

Two days later I was released and I returned home with my family. My heart has not skipped a beat in the years since God healed me.

A while after arriving home, I downloaded my emails and was encouraged to read many messages from believers who had prayed for my operation. One message particularly stood out. A sister in America wrote, "The Holy Spirit led me to empty my soul in intercession for you during your operation. I fasted and prayed without ceasing, because I believe God showed me that the devil was trying to kill you. The Lord instructed me to engage in intense spiritual warfare in the heavenly realms until the danger passed."

CHAPTER 40

BUMPS IN THE ROAD

> Why, you do not even know what will happen tomorrow. What is your life? You are a mist that appears for a little while and then vanishes.
>
> **James 4:14**

Of the many strategic initiatives the Lord has led us to implement over the years, none is as dear to my heart as helping the gospel of Jesus Christ penetrate unreached people groups. As I continued to follow the Lord, my life and service increasingly revolved around this great goal, which I believe is at the very center of God's purposes on the earth today.

Many years ago I almost died on a remote Himalayan mountain, but God rescued my life and revealed to me His heart for the lost peoples of Asia. On a later occasion I received a vivid and life-changing dream, when I saw Asia's unreached people groups as boulders needing to be loosened by the gospel. In the years since that dream we have begun to see its fulfillment, with the kingdom of God taking root among numerous tribes and groups.

As 2012 drew to a close, I set time aside to seek the Lord's will for the following year. As I prayed, the Holy Spirit impressed on my heart that we should ask God to double the reach of the Asian Workers' Fund. This is the project through which we support Asian missionaries who are taking the gospel to the unreached.

At the start of 2013, we were supporting 359 workers among 172 different people groups. That year also marked the twenty-fifth anniversary since God had first called me to serve Him in 1988. It had taken a quarter of a century for the project to grow to the point we were at, but now the Lord was saying He wanted to double it in a single year!

To double the reach of the project by the end of 2013 meant we would need to be supporting in excess of 700 Asian missionaries among 350 different groups. God wanted to stretch our faith to trust Him for the increase. I asked our heavenly Father to breathe His life into the project, and for His will to be done on earth as it is in heaven.

Amazingly, before we had shared our new emphasis with anyone, people began to write in, telling us the Lord had burdened them to help Asian missionaries in the coming year. Some donors, who had been faithfully supporting other projects for years, suddenly redirected their gifts to the Asian Workers' Fund. It was reassuring to know that the Spirit of God was already speaking to the hearts of His children. Truly, "those who are led by the Spirit of God are the children of God" (Romans 8:14).

It's not a simple process to support hundreds of new workers. Each one has to be trained, evaluated, and sent out by their local church, with oversight and care structures in place to enable them and their families to be as effective as possible. Those vital components are implemented by a large network of more than seventy ministries with whom we partner throughout the length and breadth of Asia – from the deserts of northwest China and the frozen Tibetan Plateau down to the teeming slums of India and Bangladesh, and across to the steamy river deltas of Southeast Asia.

On the administrative side, we work hard at collecting and maintaining excellent records of every evangelist we support. This enables us to send laminated prayer cards to everyone who gives to the project, and we also provide bi-annual updates from the mission field for those who continue to support their worker.

The road toward reaching this God-given vision of doubling the Asian Workers' Fund in 2013 proved to be difficult and full of potholes. The journey was to take some unexpected detours that would almost cost my life.

A few months into the year I boarded a plane and rushed to the bedside of my ailing eighty-year-old mother in New Zealand. Although I had prayed with her to believe in the Lord a few times over the years, she had never progressed in her walk with God. My father had humbled himself at the very end of his life a dozen years earlier, but my mother had continued on without a vital relationship with Jesus Christ.

After arriving in Auckland, I again shared the gospel with my mother, encouraging her to repent of her sins and surrender her life to Christ before it was too late. Sadly, her heart had become hard against the truth, and her chilling last words to me before she became too ill to speak were, "Don't bother. You will never persuade me."

A few days later I sat at her bedside as she gasped for breath. I prayed out loud, asking God to have mercy on her, but my mother's time was up, and she departed for the judgment seat of Christ.

What happened next served as a stark reminder of the background Jesus had rescued me from. I had spent so many years away from my home country and culture that I had largely forgotten about my ungodly heritage. When news of my mother's death was relayed to our Maori relatives, a small group set out by car, driving several hours to the hospital. They called ahead and gave strict instructions to the doctors and nurses not to touch the body, even though it had already started to decay.

After offering condolences to me and my siblings, my aunt, a Maori spirit priestess, insisted on conducting a spiritual ceremony in a bid to guide my mother's soul to the realm of her ancestors. I excused myself from the room and prayed to the Lord Jesus Christ as my relatives chanted and prayed to the ancestral spirits. I had witnessed many similar rituals among the tribes of Asia during my twenty-five years on the mission field. Until that moment, it had never dawned on me that my own idolatrous family background was identical to that of the people I'd been called to reach with the gospel.

A few months after my mother's funeral, I woke up one morning feeling dizzy and was rushed to hospital in an ambulance. The next thing I knew, a doctor was leaning over me, saying, "Mr Hattaway, you have suffered a massive stroke. I'm sorry to inform you that half your brain has died."

As I shared at the beginning of my story, my heavenly Father once again delivered me from the clutches of the devil. I experienced a rapid healing after thousands of Christians in Asia and around the world fervently interceded for me. In the space of several days, I progressed from being wheeled around the hospital in a bed, to a wheelchair, then a walking frame, and on to crutches. Then finally, by the power of the Risen Christ, I began to walk around the hospital unaided, to the amazement of the doctors and nurses!

God graciously preserved my mind and speech throughout the ordeal. During the recovery process, with my family's assistance, I was able to write and communicate with people as normal, and we were able to complete all of our ministry duties.

One thing that did change after the stroke, however, was my hearing. I was fine with one-to-one conversations or in a small group, but I found it difficult to cope in places with competing noise, such as in a crowded restaurant, or in a location where people were talking with music playing in the background. After the stroke, I also discovered that my body's thermostat had unexpectedly rewired itself. I had always loved cold weather, but now I had to wrap myself in blankets just to keep warm.

My strength slowly returned as I saturated myself in God's Word, listening to the Bible and godly teaching for hours every day. It was to be a full year before I was permitted to drive again, but by the grace of God I have not suffered any other long-term detrimental effects from the stroke. The Lord has performed a miracle!

As I mentioned at the start of this chapter, at the beginning of 2013 we supported 359 Asian missionaries among 172 unreached people groups. Although the stroke slowed me down a little, I hadn't forgotten that God wanted us to double the impact of the Asian Workers' Fund. The Holy Spirit moved in the hearts of believers around the world to pray and give, and by the end of the year we found that Jesus had done it again! Without any publicity, and despite encountering some bumps in the road along the way, the Asian Workers' Fund had more than doubled in size. By the end of 2013 we were supporting 756 Asian missionaries among 378 different people groups.

In the last few years the project has doubled again, and it continues to expand. We are currently supporting more than 1,700 missionaries among more than 750 ethnic groups. In 2016 alone, the workers reported that 67,500 people came to faith in Jesus. Incredibly, in excess of 165,000 decisions for Christ have been recorded since the project began. Most of these new believers come from Muslim, Buddhist, and Hindu ethnic groups that are usually considered difficult to reach and hostile to Christianity.

When the Holy Spirit first revealed God's heart and plan for Asia's unreached peoples to me back in the early 1990s, I would have been overwhelmed and amazed if Jesus had used my life to help reach just one people group for His kingdom. Now we have a vision to help reach more than 1,000 unreached groups for the King of kings, and by His mighty power we will be able to reach that goal and beyond.

It's astonishing when I stop and consider what God has done. To be honest, it seems surreal at times, and it's a mystery how things have grown so quickly. All glory to the Lord Jesus Christ! When He commands something to grow, it can grow very quickly and bring salvation to many people. All of our projects have started like a mustard seed, which the Lord said "is the smallest of all seeds, yet when it grows, it is the largest of garden plants and becomes a tree, so that the birds come and perch in its branches" (Matthew 13:32).

Over the years I have learned that the Living God is in complete control of everything, so a child of God has no reason to fear. While this world appears to be falling apart at the seams, the Lord has been steadily reaping a mighty harvest among the nations, with hundreds of thousands of people experiencing God's salvation every day. The victory belongs to Jesus!

At the Tower of Babel, God created the first nations and languages to prevent mankind from uniting for evil purposes. At the end of the age, the same God who created the nations at Babel will complete His perfect plan by uniting the redeemed from every tribe, language, people, and nation around the throne of the Lamb! God's timetable will be completed, and He will close the curtain on this sick and sorry age. A trumpet will sound, and there will be "loud voices in heaven, saying, 'The kingdoms of this world have become the kingdoms of our Lord and of His Christ, and He shall reign forever and ever!" (Revelation 11:15, NKJV).

Until that glorious day, I plan to keep marching forward, lifting up the banner of Jesus Christ among Asia's unreached peoples. I can think of no greater privilege or joy.

* * *

Joy: Paul's stroke in May 2013 was a tough time for our family. All of a sudden our leader was taken down, and we found ourselves in disarray. God showered His love and grace upon us, however, and Paul experienced a supernatural touch from God.

From the first time we met, Paul had always been a steady and relaxed person. He took everything in his stride, and very little bothered him. After the stroke it seemed as if his thoughts and emotions had been rewired, and he had to learn to conquer things that had been alien concepts to him before the stroke, like fear, anxiety, and insecurity.

Paul experienced many good days and battled through the bad, but over time the Holy Spirit helped reprogram his mind with the Word of God. He gradually recovered and, amazingly, there is now nothing God called him to do that he is unable to do, although some things are now done at a slower pace.

Paul has an overwhelming desire that all people groups in Asia will know the Lord Jesus. In the months following the stroke, his passion for the unreached motivated him to design a huge spreadsheet, listing and profiling the thousands of Asian people groups in their respective countries. He did this so we could keep better track of the workers we support, and to help us select new workers as strategically as possible. While to some people this kind of work might seem tedious, to my husband it was relaxing and therapeutic.

Very few people are aware of this, but Paul has Asperger's Syndrome. Asperger's is a form of autism that runs through the male side of his family. Experts describe it as a kind of high-functioning autism, meaning that on the surface people who have it usually don't appear different from everyone else.

People with Asperger's, however, are wired very differently from other people in the way they think and act. They tend to possess an acute sense of justice, and they see things in very black-and-white terms. They are often socially awkward, and they find it nearly impossible to learn in a structured setting.

On the positive side, however, when someone with Asperger's Syndrome finds something they are good at, they are often able to achieve things that most neurotypical people cannot. This has been the story of my husband's life. He was going nowhere until he met Jesus. Paul was so overwhelmed by the love of God that he gave his life unreservedly to serve Him, in the hope that others might experience the same salvation in Jesus.

I feel greatly blessed to have been at Paul's side throughout our journey. I thank the Lord Jesus, and I give Him all the glory for the great things He has done.

CHAPTER 41

PLANS TO REFIRE

"I consider my life worth nothing to me; my only aim is to finish the race and complete the task the Lord Jesus has given me – the task of testifying to the good news of God's grace."

Acts 20:24

I've learned that life is like a roll of toilet paper. The closer it gets to the end, the faster it goes.

Andy Rooney

Thank you for taking time to read the story of my journey. I hope you gained a clear impression that anything good that has come from my life is entirely thanks to the grace of God, which He surprisingly lavished on me.

After my stroke, a friend asked if I had plans to retire. I was taken aback by his question as I was only in my forties, so I told him, "No way! I don't ever plan to retire. I plan to *refire* for the Lord! The world needs to know about Jesus, and we can only reach people this side of the grave!"

One of my favorite Bible characters is Joshua, who was a man of war and unquenchable zeal. He clearly harbored no thoughts of retirement when at the age of eighty-five he boldly proclaimed, "I am as strong this day as on the day that Moses sent me; just as my strength was then, so now is my strength for war, both for going out and for coming in" (Joshua 14:11, NKJV).

I would love, like Joshua, to live to a ripe old age and serve God wholeheartedly until my final breath, but none of us knows when our life will end. The health issues I experienced made me aware of the fragility of life, and have helped me treat each day as a precious gift.

I'm glad that since Jesus met me when I was nineteen, I haven't wasted much of the precious time He has given me. I remain incredibly excited about the future! The Spirit of God is continuing to move powerfully in many parts of Asia, transforming shattered lives and delivering entire communities from centuries of bondage to Satan.

China has clearly played a prominent role in my service for the Lord Jesus up to this point. I will always deeply love China, and I plan to continue helping the gospel go forth there in every possible way. If the Almighty God allows me to serve Him long enough for a second part of my testimony to be written, however, I suspect that India will be the main emphasis. We are connected with many godly ministries throughout India, and they are poised to bring in a mighty harvest for God's kingdom. Many signs of genuine revival are already apparent in rural areas, where Hindus are being saved by the thousands and a great hunger for the gospel is evident. We receive many testimonies from India that remind me of China in the 1980s and 1990s, when the revival was at its most intense.

I believe the Lord Jesus is about to do such a mighty work in India that the size of the Church there will surpass even that of China. Being an unreached people group fanatic, nowhere is more exciting to me than India, which contains almost 2,000 unreached groups – by far the largest number of any country on earth.

The Scriptures declare that one day every people group will have worshipers around the throne of the Lamb. It would be our great privilege to help the Church in India make this vision become reality.

* * *

An executive of one of the largest mission organizations in the world once told me that if I had tried to join their ministry my application would have been rejected, owing to my lack of formal education and my unconventional pathway to the mission field. I'm so glad the Lord Jesus Christ accepted me instead!

At various times in the past, people have approached me at the end of a meeting and said, "Thank you for sacrificing so much to serve the Lord on the mission field." I always chuckle to myself when they say that. What exactly did I give up to serve the Living God?

The truth is that I gave up nothing. Before I met Jesus I was deeply oppressed and my life was heading nowhere. My school principal had labelled me a "waste of oxygen," and I had started to believe it. When God first called me I had $5 to my name and was unemployed. My various jobs even included a brief stint as an Avon lady! My life was a joke, and all I had to offer Him was a miserable life of failure, loneliness, and depression. I carried all of my worldly possessions in a bag, and had been sleeping on the roof of a public toilet.

Amazingly, the love and mercy of Jesus Christ was showered on me. He even called me to be an ambassador for the gospel in the very same church building I had vandalized as a youth. Every good thing has been a result of His grace. Even the desire in my heart to serve God was put there by the Holy Spirit, "for it is God who works in you to will and to act in order to fulfil his good purpose" (Philippians 2:13).

I have been the beneficiary of a completely lopsided exchange. I handed Jesus my futile existence, and in return He gave me a life of purpose and fulfillment. He has blessed me in every conceivable way, joined me with a beautiful woman who happens to be my best friend in the world, and has given us two precious sons. His favor has rested on our family. We have never lacked, and His mercies have been new every morning.

I didn't have a clue what it meant to serve God when I took my first steps of faith in the 1980s, but He carried me along. Almost nothing God has called me to do has been conventional, but He has required me to trust Him and to go against the flow of conventional human wisdom. The results have been phenomenal. Like a surfer riding a powerful wave, the Holy Spirit has provided all the impetus and thrust, carrying me along on an exhilarating ride.

When I set out on my adventure with Jesus, I never imagined in my wildest dreams that God would allow me to be involved with printing millions of Bibles or supporting thousands of evangelists throughout Asia. Every success has been solely thanks to the love and grace of God. If we had tried to implement these projects in our own strength they would have failed miserably, and if we had tried to sustain the work by human effort, it would have disintegrated like a cardboard box in a hurricane. The Lord has structured our ministry in such a way that our entire existence depends on Him. As the Scripture declares: "'Not by might nor by power, but by my Spirit,' says the Lord Almighty" (Zechariah 4:6).

Asia Harvest will never be the largest ministry in the world, but that has not been our goal. Our ministry has never been an attempt by man to build something for God. It began as a work of the Holy Spirit for His glory, and will only continue if God desires to keep it alive. We have been careful not to ask the Lord to bless *our* work for Him, but rather the cry of our hearts has been that we might get to participate and watch some of God's amazing work, while hoping we never get in the way of the wonderful things He is doing.

After our many years of turmoil and conflict, my experiences with the revival in China were like healing balm to my soul. If all the pain and struggles we endured were necessary to open the doors to fruitful service for Jesus, then it was all worthwhile, and those experiences have proven inconsequential compared to the overall plan of God in my life. Like the Apostle Paul, I can testify that "what has happened to me has actually served to advance the gospel" (Philippians 1:12).

Whenever I have felt discouraged, the Lord has lifted my spirit and compensated in unexpected ways, like the occasion when the group of Chinese house church leaders laid hands on me and embraced my family and me as part of their vision. Something powerful took place in the spiritual realm, and from that day forward the Holy Spirit added a turbo boost to our work.

In the past I have spent much time and energy traveling around Asia, teaching hundreds of church leaders. I now believe I am required to invest the rest of my life by pouring the Word of God into a small number of key Asian leaders, in keeping with the instruction Paul gave to Timothy: "The things you have heard me say in the presence of many witnesses entrust to reliable people who will also be qualified to teach others" (2 Timothy 2:2).

I have come to understand that God doesn't need the big and powerful to achieve His purposes. Instead, He loves to display His power through weak vessels, "to show that this all-surpassing power is from God and not from us" (2 Corinthians 4:7). As I gradually learned the principle that in the kingdom of God, human weakness equals strength and human strength equals weakness, our work became more effective.

Some people have asked me what I did to "deserve" to be in Christian ministry, and what qualifications I possess to write so many books or to lead a ministry. The answer is: Absolutely nothing!

I am nothing! It's all about Jesus. He is everything! His wisdom is beyond compare, and He loves to choose the rejects of society and use them for His glory. I deserve none of His goodness. The only thing I deserve is an eternity in hell.

Perhaps my favorite Bible passage is this one from Paul's first letter to the believers in Corinth, because it perfectly summarizes my life:

> For the foolishness of God is wiser than human wisdom, and the weakness of God is stronger than human strength. Brothers and sisters, think of what you were when you were called. Not

> many of you were wise by human standards; not many were influential; not many were of noble birth. But God chose the foolish things of the world to shame the wise; God chose the weak things of the world to shame the strong. God chose the lowly things of this world and the despised things – and the things that are not – to nullify the things that are, so that no one may boast before him.
>
> **1 Corinthians 1:25–29**

* * *

If you are not yet a follower of Jesus Christ, I pray that you will commence your journey by bowing your knee and surrendering your life to Him. If you do, you won't regret it. All of life's answers are found in Jesus. Many things in this world can provide temporary pleasure, but only Jesus is able to satisfy the deepest spiritual and emotional longings of your heart, for in Him "are hidden all the treasures of wisdom and knowledge" (Colossians 2:3).

I'm not talking about joining a religion or obeying a set of man-made rules. That won't save you. I'm talking about a vibrant and transformative relationship with the Living God, who desires to be involved with every area of your life as a loving father cares for and nurtures his child.

To experience the matchless reality and saving power of Jesus Christ, however, you must do things His way. You must both repent of your sins and believe in Him. It isn't enough to do one without the other. Come to Him in humility, like a beggar asking for food. This is the only way to reconcile with the True and Living God, for the Bible says, "God resists the proud, but gives grace to the humble" (James 4:6, NKJV).

If you are already a Christian but the grind of life has caused you to grow weary and disillusioned, I encourage you not to give up! No broken life is beyond repair with Jesus. When the Living God turns up, He can inject Himself into the most hopeless situation and instantly turn it on its head. As long as you have breath, it's not too late to be transformed. Peter, in a letter written to Christians, said that God is "not willing that any should perish but that all should come to repentance" (2 Peter 3:9, NKJV).

Are you willing to open your heart to Jesus and trust Him to take control of your life? If you are, then you will no longer be just a believer. You will become a disciple of Jesus, and will gain the kind of confident assurance that John wrote about: "I write these things to you who believe in the name of the Son of God so that you may know that you have eternal life" (1 John 5:13).

The reason so many believers struggle through life is that although they understand the basic doctrines of the Bible, they have commenced their journey with the wrong person behind the steering wheel. Some people hear the gospel and want to see how Jesus fits into the plans they have already made for themselves. They are willing to bring Him along on the journey, but only if He stays quiet and doesn't try to take control. They will occasionally reveal Christ if it suits them, but most of the time they would rather keep Him gagged and hidden away in the trunk, where He can't be seen or heard. One day, the Lord Jesus Christ will ask such people, "Why do you call me, 'Lord, Lord,' and do not do what I say?" (Luke 6:46).

Many other Christians, including me on numerous occasions, claim that Jesus is the Lord of their lives, but they love to be back-seat drivers. Most of the time they're glad Jesus is behind the wheel, but if He heads off in a direction that makes them feel uncomfortable, they complain and do everything possible to change the route He wants to take them.

There are perilous times coming upon the world. Dark clouds are gathering on the horizon, and people instinctively know that much trouble lies ahead. Only those who have Jesus Christ behind the wheel of their lives will be able to endure to the end.

Is Jesus truly the boss of your life? Is He the one calling the shots, steering your life from the driver's seat as you submit to His authority and go along for the ride?

* * *

Finally, may I ask you to please pray for our family? We would be honored if you would take a moment to lift us up in prayer before God's throne of grace. Please pray that our lives would be pure, that our faith would always have the simplicity of a child, and that we would never cease to marvel at the goodness of God.

Please pray that our ministry will continue to walk in integrity, and that we will be faithful to accomplish everything our heavenly Father wants us to do. There is still much work to be done before the Lord Jesus will return to reign over the nations.

May God bless you and use your life to bring much glory to the King of kings. May you possess an intimate relationship with the heavenly Father, as He strengthens and enables you to become the kind of person He desires you to be. The Bible says that "the people who know their God shall be strong, and carry out great exploits" (Daniel 11:32, NKJV).

Our Master, Jesus Christ, will soon return and take possession of His earth. On that day, may we all be able to say, "We are unworthy servants; we have only done our duty" (Luke 17:10).

CONTACT DETAILS

Paul Hattaway is the founder and director of Asia Harvest, a non-denominational ministry which serves the Church in Asia through various strategic initiatives, including Bible printing and supporting Asian missionaries who are sharing the gospel among unreached peoples.

The author can be reached by email at **paul@asiaharvest.org**, or by writing to him via any of the addresses listed below.

To receive the free Asia Harvest newsletter or to order Paul's other books, please visit **www.asiaharvest.org**, or write to the address below which is nearest you:

Asia Harvest USA & Canada
353 Jonestown Rd #320
Winston-Salem, NC 27104
USA

Asia Harvest Australia
36 Nelson Street
Stepney, SA 5069
AUSTRALIA

Asia Harvest New Zealand
PO Box 1757
Queenstown, 9348
NEW ZEALAND

Asia Harvest UK & Ireland
c/o AsiaLink
PO Box 891
Preston PR4 9AB
ENGLAND

Asia Harvest Europe
c/o Stiftung SALZ
Tailfinger Str. 28
71083 Herrenberg
GERMANY

The Heavenly Man

With Paul Hattaway

The Heavenly Man is the intensely dramatic story of how God took a young, half-starved boy from a poor village in Henan Province and used him mightily to preach the gospel despite horrific opposition.

Brother Yun is one of China's house church leaders, a man who despite his relative youth has suffered prolonged torture and imprisonment for his faith. Instead of focusing on the many miracles or experiences of suffering, however, Yun prefers to emphasize the character and beauty of Jesus.

This astonishing book will form a watershed in your spiritual life.

Brother Yun travels widely and speaks around the world from his current base in Germany. Paul Hattaway has written several books on the Chinese church and is the director of Asia Harvest.